CIVIL WAR SHARPS CARBINES & RIFLES

EARL J. COATES & JOHN D. MCAULAY

THOMAS PUBLICATIONS
Gettysburg PA 17325

Copyright © 1996 Earl J. Coates and John D. McAulay

Printed and bound in the United States of America

Published by THOMAS PUBLICATIONS
P.O. Box 3031
Gettysburg, Pa. 17325

All rights reserved. No part of this book may be used or reproduced without written permission of the authors and the publisher, except in the case of brief quotations embodied in critical essays and reviews.

ISBN-0-939631-93-8

Cover design by Ryan C. Stouch

Front cover illustration, "42nd Pennsylvania Volunteers—Bucktails" by Don Troiani. Photo courtesy Historical Art Prints, Ltd., Southbury, CT.

CONTENTS

Introduction

1

The Pre-War Years 1851-1860

2

The War Years 1861-1865

13

Sharps & Hankins

28

Sharps in the Sea Service

38

The Serial Numbers of Sharps Rifles & Carbines

46

Notes

103

Bibliography

106

Index to Regiments

108

ACKNOWLEDGEMENTS

The authors wish to express their sincere thanks and appreciation to the following individuals and institutions who helped make this book possible:

Don Bloomer ❖ Jean Jackson ❖ Steve Selenfriend ❖ William Kennedy
Paul Johnson ❖ Roy Marcot ❖ Dave Carter ❖ Ronn Palm ❖ Norm Flayderman
Herb Peck, Jr. ❖ Dean Thomas ❖ Paul Davies ❖ Richard Carlile
Hubert Lum ❖ Brice Harbert ❖ Donald Bates ❖ Ted Myers
Roger Hunt ❖ Western Reserve Historical Society
U.S. Army Military History Institute ❖ Randy Hackenburg ❖ Michael Winey
West Point Museum, USMA ❖ Robert Fisch ❖ Michael McAfee
National Archives and Records Administration ❖ Michael Musick

Introduction

The single shot breech-loading Sharps remained in active military service for a twenty year period from the early 1850s to about 1874. It was then replaced in the Army by the centerfire cartridge 45/70 Springfields. The Navy had turned to the Remington rolling-block design in 1869. During most of its U.S. military service, the Sharps was rated as the best overall single-shot breech-loader.

The first part of the book covers the military history of the Sharps in both U.S. and Confederate service. The Navy first placed the Sharps carbines in sea service in September 1853 when sixty Sharps were on board several ships on an expedition to the northern Pacific Ocean. In 1856 the 2nd Dragoons received 250 Model 1855 Sharps carbines. During the first year and a half of the Civil War, the state of Connecticut purchased nearly 1,500 NM 1859 Sharps rifles directly from the Sharps factory. The first 600 of these rifles were the 36-inch barrel rifles originally slated for sale to the government of Egypt. These rifles were issued to the 1st and 2nd Connecticut Volunteer Infantry who used them at the First Battle of Manassas in July 1861.

Several charts are shown in the chapter on the war years illustrating the distribution of Sharps carbines. Also included is a listing of all Union cavalry regiments reporting Sharps carbines in December 1862 and for the 1865 spring campaign, plus infantry regiments reporting Sharps rifles from 1863 to 1864. For students of the Confederacy, the 1864 portion of the war years contains a May 1864 inspection report of the small arms in Maj. Gen. Nathan B. Forrest's cavalry, plus the ordnance stores in Maj. Gen. Wade Hampton's cavalry command station near Petersburg, Virginia, in November 1864.

The wartime partnership of Sharps & Hankins is also covered, with the naval procurement of Sharps & Hankins carbines in both 19-inch and 24-inch barrel carbines, and the cavalry field usage in the 9th and 11th New York Cavalry.

The second part of the book covers over 4,000 Sharps rifles and carbines serial numbers taken from the regimental company order books. These serial numbers are listed by regiment and, where known, the name of the person to whom the arm was issued. A section of particular note is that of the nearly 180 Berdan DST (double set trigger) NM 1859 Sharps rifle serial numbers not previously reported. These numbers are shown in the 42nd Pennsylvania Infantry (Bucktails) who received them from Berdan in August 1862. In addition are over 600 serial numbers of the .56 caliber NM 1859 Sharps rifles delivered to the Navy in November 1859.

THE PRE-WAR YEARS
1851-1860

The most famous single-shot, percussion small arm of the Civil War was undoubtedly the Sharps. Its inventor Christian Sharps (1811-1874) received his original U.S. Patent No. 5763 dated September 12, 1848, for a sliding breech pin and self-capping gun. Sharps' actual patent claim read:

> What I claim as my invention, and desire to secure by Letters Patent is—
>
> 1. The combination of the sliding breech with the barrel, the breech supporter, and the stock in such a manner that when the sliding breech is forced down the breech bore will be so exposed as [to] enable it to receive a cartridge on a line with the bore, and when the sliding breech is forced up it will shear off the rear end of the cartridge, so as to expose the powder to the fire communications, and will firmly and securely close the breech bore, substantially as herein set forth.
>
> 2. The combination of the cap nipple with sliding breech, substantially in the manner and for the purpose herein set forth.[1]

Two years later, in November 1850, a Sharps carbine was first tested by the Ordnance Department. The board's November 27 report said the Sharps was fired several hundred times without cleaning. Its rate of fire with the Maynard tape primers was ten times per minute. The board found that the Sharps was superior to any other breech-loader submitted for trial and that it should be placed in the hands of the troops to determine whether it was suitable for military service.[2]

1851-1854

With this favorable report, a new firm was formed on October 9, 1851: The Sharps Rifle Manufacturing Company of Hartford, Connecticut. Christian Sharps served as technical advisor to the company and was to receive a royalty of one dollar for each gun manufactured.

On December 2, 1851, Col. Henry K. Craig contacted the Sharps company, asking the price at which it could deliver two hundred Sharps carbines. His letter read:

> The report of the trial of Sharps carbines lately held at Washington Arsenal being sufficiently satisfactory to authorize a further practical test of their fitness for the military service by putting them to use in the hands of troops, I am disposed to procure two hundred (200) of these carbines for that purpose. I desire to be informed of the terms on which that number of carbines can be furnished and how soon it can be done. There should be a wiping rod and screwdriver to each arm and a bullet mould to cast a round and a picket ball to every 10.[3]

John Palmer, president of the Sharps Rifle Manufacturing Company, wrote back that the cost would be $35 each. Craig made a counter-offer, saying he felt that $25 per carbine, excluding appendages, was a fair price. After this negotiation, the Ordnance Department ordered 200 Sharps carbines with appendages at $30 each.[4]

A month later Craig made changes on the January 2 order: "If you will make one hundred fifty with Maynard Primers and fifty with Sharps primers without a change in the price, I would prefer to have the order for the two hundred carbines so filled."[5] The order was eventually filled with 150 Model 1851 and fifty Model 1852 carbines.

On January 9, 1852, the Sharps Rifle Manufacturing Company entered into an agreement with Robbins & Lawrence of Windsor, Vermont, to manufacture Sharps-pattern arms. The first of the M1851 carbines was completed by Robbins & Lawrence on October 5, 1852, and delivery was made to the Ordnance Department of all 150 on January 18, 1853.[6] These .52 caliber M1851 Sharps carbines weighed seven pounds and measured 37 3/8 inches overall. The major characteristic of the M1851 is the back action lock which carries the hammer inside the lockplate. The lockplate has a Maynard primer door marked "EDWARD MAYNARD/PATENTEE/1845." The 21 5/8-inch round barrel has a brass blade front sight with either a single-leaf "squirrel-ear" type or a fixed "v" notch rear sight. The black walnut stock is made in two pieces. All furniture is brass. The military carbines are equipped without a patchbox. On the left side of the frame is fixed a 9-inch sling rod. The breech tang is stamped "C.SHARPS/PATENT/1848" with the serial number to the rear. The serial numbers on the January 1853 delivery were between 100 and 250. They are marked on the barrel "U.S./S.K./P." The ordnance inspector was Samuel Knous. "U.S. 1852" is stamped on the upper tang of the buttplate.[7]

By June 30, 1853, 140 of the 150 M1851 Sharps carbines delivered to the government had been issued to the 1st and 2nd Dragoons.[8] In February sixty carbines were sent to the Fort Union Ordnance Depot and eighty to San Antonio Arsenal in Texas.[9] From Las Lunas, New Mexico, on March 18, 1854, Capt. Richard Ewell of Company G 1st Dragoons wrote that he had had five M1851 Sharps carbines in his company for six months and found them superior to any other firearms furnished to the dragoons.

Capt. Granger of the Mounted Rifles wrote on July 18, 1853, that the Sharps carbine had double the range of the Mississippi rifle (M1841) and with practice could be loaded and fired in fifteen seconds at full speed on horseback with sufficient accuracy to strike a man at 20 to 30 paces. He went on to say that on foot it could be loaded and fired ten times per minute and had a range of one fourth to one half mile.[10]

After the 150 M1851 carbines were delivered in January 1853, Robbins & Lawrence started to work on the fifty carbines to be manufactured with Sharps primers. These carbines, known as the M1852, included the device covered by Sharps' U.S. Patent No. 9,308 of October 5, 1852, for his pellet primer system. To operate this primer system, a brass tube containing twenty-five copper pellet discs was inserted into the lockplate forward of the hammer. This system did away with the need to use the standard percussion cap. The hammer action threw the pellet forward where it was caught in midair by the falling cock and crushed on the nipple. It was not until June 30, 1853, that the first of the M1852 carbines were manufactured with delivery of the 50 carbines being made on September 23, 1853.[11] The Model 1852 Sharps carbine differed from the M1851 in that it was the first side-hammer percussion, slant breech model. The lockplate is marked either "C. SHARP'S/PATENT/1852" or "SHARP'S/PATENT/1852." The Sharps pellet feeding system is located in the upper forward section of the lockplate, as indicated by Sharps' October 5, 1852, patent. The barrel is stamped with "SHARP'S RIFLE/MANUFG CO/HARTFORD CONN" or "ROBBINS & LAWRENCE." While only a few of the M1851 carbines had brass patchboxes, all of the M1852 carbines were so equipped. On these arms the breech lever pin is held in place by a flat spring.

Craig was highly pleased with the Sharps because of its ease of loading, lightness, and its great range. On July 18, 1854, he requested authority from Secretary of War Jefferson Davis to purchase an additional 200 Sharps carbines for service use. Davis gave his approval on July 26.[12] Two days earlier Craig had sent a request to Palmer for 200 Sharps carbines at $30.48 each. In December the Army conducted tests on a number of breech-loading designs. On December 23 a 7 1/2-pound Model 1852 Sharps carbine with a 21-inch barrel was tested. To test for rapidity of fire, the Sharps was loaded and discharged twenty times in one minute and twenty seconds. During this test the gun was not brought to the shoulder but fired from the position of loading. For accuracy, the Sharps was fired at an 8-foot by 8-foot target at various distances with these results:[13]

Distance	No. of Shots	No. of Hits
100 yards	10	10
200 yards	10	10
400 yards	10	3
500 yards	10	2

1855-1857

In January 1855 the Ordnance Board made its recommendations on the various arms. On the Sharps, they wrote, "Inasmuch as this carbine has been frequently examined by previous boards, and a considerable number of them are in the hands of the troops for trial, the Board, from these considerations, as well as, from the favorable results of their own trials, recommend this arm for trials, in the hands of the troops."[14]

In a letter dated January 22, 1855, Craig requested that 25 of the 200 carbines contracted for in July 1854 be equipped for the Maynard primers (M1851). When the 200 carbines were received on February 2, twenty-five were of the Model 1851 and the balance of the Model 1852.[15] Many of these carbines were sent to the St. Louis Arsenal and from there issued to the 2nd Dragoons. Some members of the two companies of dragoons that took part in the battle with the Sioux on September 3, 1855, were armed with Model 1852 Sharps carbines. In this skirmish, Col. William Harney's force of about 600 men from the 2nd Dragoons, 6th and

Colonel Henry K. Craig
Chief of Ordnance from July 1851-April 1861
National Archives photo.

The commanding officer of the 2nd U. S. Dragoons in 1856 was Lieutenant Colonel Phillip St. George Cooke. Shown here as a brigadier general during the Civil War. National Archives photo.

10th Infantry, and 4th Artillery attacked a Sioux village. During the attack and retreat the Indian casualties were eighty-five killed, five wounded, and seventy women and children captured. The soldiers sustained losses of four killed, seven wounded, and one missing.[16] During this action many of the swivel rings on the 1852 Sharps carbines broke, causing the arms to be lost in the high prairie grass. This later became a major factor in shortening the saddle bar.

On April 13, 1855, Craig wrote to Palmer and told him that he wished "to obtain for issue to U.S. troops provided I can have them delivered in due season 400 Sharps carbines with Maynard locks and the same appendages as the last 200 carbines had, for which will be allowed the price last paid, $30 each."[17]

Palmer, believing that the M1851 Sharps—equipped with a Maynard priming system—could be delivered in response to this request, wrote back the next day and stated that he could make delivery in three to four months.[18] Replying to this letter on April 20, Craig wrote, "If 400 carbines can be manufactured within 90 days as stated in your letter of 14th you may proceed to work on them."[19] He continued by saying that the swivel bar was to be reduced to 2 1/2 inches and was to be attached to the breech frame, and that the Maynard priming devices were to be attached to the lockplate of the slant breech type M1852 previously ordered. The model lock to be used was at that time in the possession of Alonzo Perry. Palmer was advised on May 14 that this lock would be sent to him by Perry and that he should hold off production until he received it. Palmer did not receive the model lock from Perry until the end of September. On November 5 he was instructed to brown the barrel, which was to be manufactured on this order. In February 1856 Palmer told Craig that the first 200 M1855 Sharps carbines would not be delivered until the middle of March. This prompted Craig, on February 20, to state that if the weapons were not soon delivered, the Ordnance Department would have to look to other sources. Finally, in April 1856, the first of the M1855 Sharps carbines were completed with all 400 being delivered to Craig by May 15.[20]

The .52 caliber Model 1855 Sharps carbines delivered to the U.S. Ordnance Department in 1856 were brass mounted with brass buttplate, patchbox, and barrel band, and were equipped with a 2 1/2-inch saddle bar swivel. The overall length of these carbines was 37 5/8 inches and the weight was 7 pounds, 10 ounces. The 21 5/8-inch barrel had a brass blade front sight and the rear sight was long friction with a sliding "v" notch bar. The Ordnance Department's proof marks may be found on the barrel with "U.S. JH." The casehardened lockplate is fitted with the Maynard tape primer magazine. The door is marked: "EDWARD MAYNARD/ PATENTEE 1845."

Many of the M1855 Sharps carbines delivered in May 1856 were quickly issued to the regulars. Lt. Col. Phillip St. George Cooke, commanding the 2nd Dragoons at Fort Riley, Kansas, received 250 Sharps carbines for four companies on the Missouri and one company at Fort Riley, while his remaining four companies were armed with Hall carbines and one with Musketoons.[21] The breakdown by companies is shown on the following chart:

M1855 Sharps Carbines
Issued to 2nd Dragoons in 1856[22]

Date of Issue	Co.	Carbines Issued	No. of Ball Cartridges
May 28, 1856	D	51	10,000
May 28, 1856	H	48	10,000
May 28, 1856	K	52	4,000
July 11, 1856	I	49	5,000
August 16, 1856	F	50	4,000

On May 19, 1856, sixty M1855 Sharps carbines were shipped from the New York Arsenal around Cape Horn to the Benicia Arsenal for trial by companies C, E, H, and I, 1st Dragoons then serving in California.[23] In the fall of 1856 sixty-four Sharps carbines were in storage at Fort Union, New Mexico. They were issued sixteen per company to the four companies of 1st Dragoons then in field service in the Department of New Mexico.[24]

By early 1857 the Sharps factory had completed its British contract for 6,000 carbines. The surplus arms from this contract were offered to the Ordnance Department. In March a .577 caliber, 19-inch-barrel British carbine was sent to Craig's office for inspection. On March 16 Col. R.L. Baker, president of the Sharps Rifle Manufacturing Company, told

Craig that the company would furnish the British-style carbine but would make modifications in the length of the barrel and stock. The price would be the same as was charged the British government of $25 per arm with appendages extra.[25] A month later, on April 28, the Ordnance Department requested that the Sharps factory immediately send 200 carbines from inventory, 31,250 cartridges, plus the necessary appendages. From the New York Arsenal, Capt. Robert H.K. Whiteley was notified to inspect the arms when they were ready for shipment.[26] The next day the Sharps factory stated that the carbines would be ready for inspection on Friday, May 1, and that all carbines would have the new improved gas checks.[27] This was the first government delivery in which the early Conant gas seal was used. The May 8 payment for these arms was itemized as follows:

200 Sharps carbines	$5,000.00
200 Space cones	16.00
200 Wiping rods	100.00
200 Cone wrenches	74.00
40 Bullet moulds	40.00
20 Sets spare parts	172.40
1 Bench clamp	3.50
32,000 Ball cartridges	489.60
Packing boxes	78.00
Total	$5,973.50[28]

The 200 British-style carbines delivered on May 1st are found in the low 20,000 serial number range. The .577 caliber, 21 5/8-inch barrel is unmarked except for the British proof marks: a crown over the number 2 under the brass, U.S.-style, barrel band. The front sight is an iron blade atop a stud; the rear sight is a British-style, four-leaf, folding type. The breech block has the British proofs marks on the side of the block. The rest of the markings are similar to those found on the 1856 delivery.

When Whiteley was notified to inspect the Sharps carbines on April 28, he was directed to send them to the St. Louis Arsenal for immediate issue to parties engaged in making wagon roads in the West. Repayment was to be collected from the Department of the Interior.[29] The needs of the mounted service, however, outweighed the need of the Department of the Interior and therefore the arms were issued to the cavalry instead. In November Capt. Edward Fitzgerald's Company D, 1st Dragoons stationed at Tucson, New Mexico Territory, was issued sixteen M1855 Sharps. In a letter dated February 24, 1858, he stated that whenever a small detachment was sent on a dangerous service, it was invariably armed with Sharps carbines. The fire was rapid and accurate and was greatly superior to any other arm furnished his command.[30]

The Sharps carbines in production at the factory in the fall of 1857 were the Model 1853 which had been first introduced in November 1854. Those carbines manufactured before the summer of 1856 were equipped with a 9-inch saddle ring bar and a friction-type sliding "v" notch bar rear sight. In 1857 the Conant patented gas seal and an R. S. Lawrence-type rear sight (which was marked "R.S. Lawrence" in script) were first introduced. In addition the saddle ring bar was reduced in length to 2 1/2 inches. In total about 10,500 Model 1853 carbines were manufactured between November 1854 and December 1857.

On October 30, 1857, Baker wrote the Ordnance Department requesting an order for carbines. His letter reads in part:

> We have on hand nearly 6,000 Cavalry Carbines, about one half of which we have just improved with new slides, rendering them very complete, and, in my opinion, perfect for Cavalry service—They are made with lock for Sharps, and the ordinary primers or cap, are browned, and in every respect serviceable—An order for any part of the whole of these arms, would greatly relieve this company, now suffering, like every other manufactor under the embarrassment of these terrible times.[31]

Three weeks later, on November 21, Secretary of War John Floyd authorized the purchase of 1,400 M1853 Sharps at $30 each.[32] All of the carbines were delivered by the end of the year.

1858-1860

During 1858 five more orders were issued: 340 carbines on January 13; 200 on March 10; 500 on May 17; and 1,000 each on July 4 and 30. All 3,040 contracted for during the year were delivered by January 18, 1859.[33] When Whiteley inspected the 340 carbines of the February 13 delivery he found that the rear sights were insufficient for military use and felt that the improved Lawrence-type rear sight was the answer. He had ordered 200 of the improved Lawrence sights at 75 cents each to repair the Sharps carbines. Later, in October, he said he had 500 of the improved sights for Sharps carbines on hand.[34]

On January 12, 1858, Col. Edwin V. Sumner, commanding officer of the 1st U.S. Cavalry at Fort Leavenworth, requisitioned 680 Sharps carbines—enough to arm eight companies—along with 170 Burnside carbines—arms for an additional two companies. Sumner's request was sent to Army headquarters which accepted it and directed, by Order for Supplies No. 24 dated January 15, 1858, that they be sent.[35] By that spring the 1st Cavalry had taken delivery of their Sharps and Burnside carbines. In July 1858, 600 Sharps carbines and 300 cartridges per carbine were shipped from the New York Arsenal to Vancouver Depot on the steamer St. Louis. On September 1, Capt. Franklin D. Callender at Benicia Arsenal was informed that the arsenal was to receive 300 Sharps, 2,500 rifle muskets, and 500 Colt belt pistols. Fort Union Depot was notified on October 12 that 250 Sharps carbines and 25,000 cartridges were being sent by the first train from the St. Louis Arsenal.[36] By June 30, 1858, 1,622 Model 1853 Sharps carbines had been sent to the regulars.[37] The 300 Sharps Model 1853 carbines and 500 Colt revolvers sent to Benicia Arsenal were shipped on board the Fanny S. Perley. The ship sank en route with the loss of all hands. The rifle muskets were sent on another ship which made it through to California.[38] In July Calleder received 170 Sharps carbines from an earlier shipment at Benicia. These arms were sent to the 1st Dragoons at Fort Walla Walla, Washington, and issued to companies C, E, H, and I. They were previously armed with ten Model 1855 Sharps carbines per company. By the end of the year Vancouver had 332 Sharps carbines on hand but were still in need of 500 more.[39] In November Capt. Carlston of Company K, 1st Dragoons, stationed at Fort Tajan, California, was issued Sharps.

The first of the Sharps carbines to be issued to the 2nd U.S. Cavalry in Texas was a shipment of thirty, which were received by Capt. James Oakes, Company C, at Fort Mason, Texas, on October 30, 1858. Capt. Innis N. Palmer of Company D was issued forty Sharps carbines with Sharps locks on December 8. Two weeks later, on December 22, twenty-five carbines were received by Lt. J.B. Witherall, Company C, at Camp Radziniski, Texas.[40]

In May Gov. Thomas Bragg of North Carolina had a congressman from his state contact the Ordnance Department and request that forty-five Sharps carbines be sent to the state of North Carolina as part of the state's 1858 allotment of arms. The request was honored and the arms were shipped to Salisbury, North Carolina, to the attention of Capt. Thomas Hill of the Rowan Rifle Guard.[41]

At 9 a.m. on July 13 an Ordnance Board had convened at West Point to perform test trials on a large variety of breech-loading systems. The board of officers—Maj. Alfred Mordecai, Capt. Thomas J. Rodman, and Bvt. Maj. T.T.S. Laidley—tested a Sharps carbine with these specifications:

Diameter of Bore	0.52 inches
Length of Barrel	21.7 inches
Number of Grooves	6
Weight of Arm	7 pounds 6 1/2 ounces
Weight of Cartridge	542 grains
Weight of Ball	473 grains
Weight charge of Powder	63 grains
Cartridge—Material	Paper[42]

With 55 grains of powder and a 473-grain ball, the ballistic was 820 feet per second. The Burnside brass cartridge with 45 grains of powder and a 558-grain ball had a velocity of 1,012 feet per second. The results of the various tests are shown below:

	Accuracy at			Rapidity of firing
	100 yds	300 yds	600 yds	40 rounds[43]
Burnside	1	5	3	5 min 5 sec
Gibbs	4	2	6	5 min 31 sec
Sharps	6	3	5	3 min 10 sec
Smith	3	1	1	6 min 5 sec
Maynard	7	4	4	3 min 20 sec
Joslyn	5	9	7	5 min 38 sec
Morse	8	6	8	3 min 48 sec
Colt	9	7	9	7 min 13 sec
Merrill	10	10	10	4 min 20 sec
Symmes	2	8	2	gave out at 27th firing

The board concluded that as in the previous year's trials the Burnside carbines was rated best overall.

In 1858 the Sharps Rifle Manufacturing Company made a number of major changes in the design of its carbines and later in its rifles. Richard S. Lawrence had been working on improving the gas seal at the breech. Lawrence moved the entire breech-lock section forward and placed it at right angles to the axis of the bore. This "straight breech" constitutes the major difference between the previous slant-breech carbines and the New Model 1859 Sharps carbine. Lawrence's patent for this improved gas check method was granted on December 20, 1859, under U.S. Patent No. 22,501.

In addition to the gas check, two other major improvements can be found on the new straight-breech models: First, a change was made to the rear sight. On February 15, 1859, Lawrence was issued U.S. Patent No. 22,959 for improvements in adjustable sights for firearms. These patented rear sights, graduated to 800 yards, have a spring base with a single folding leaf and sliding "v" notch bar. The sight base is stamped "R. S. LAWRENCE/PATENTED/FEB 15th 1859." These rear sights were used on the M1853 since late 1857. Second, an improvement to the cut off for the pellet priming system was made. (The original was invented by Christian Sharps in October 1852.) Lawrence's pellet cut off system allowed the pellet-fed mechanism to be disengaged, the carbine to use the ordinary percussion cap instead of the pellet primers, and the primers to be held in reserve. This patent No. 23,590 was issued on April 12, 1859.

On March 23, 1859, Craig placed an order for 620 of the new pattern carbines. His letter read in part: "Six hundred twenty Sharps carbines of the new pattern with square cut off deliverable at your factory in early part of July next, the cost same as last paid. If the carbine is to be carried on the soldier['s] back, swivels like those on the musket will be required, the lower one near or at the small or round of the stock, the upper one a few inches below the muzzle."[44] The New Model 1859 carbines may, therefore, be identified as having a sling swivel beneath the buttstock and a 2 9/16-inch sling rod on the left side of the frame. On April 8 the contract was increased to a total of 2,500 New Model 1859s to be delivered during the fiscal year ending June 30, 1860.[45] The first 305 carbines on this order were delivered on December 23, 1859, with deliveries continuing to June 19, 1860, when the last 391 carbines were received.[46]

In total about 27,000 New Model 1859 Sharps carbines were manufactured between late 1858 and early 1863. The first of these carbines found in the serial range of 30,000 to 31,332 are stamped on the barrel "MODEL 1859" while those after number 30,786 are marked "NEW MODEL 1859." Those carbines serial numbered between 30,000 and 36,000 have brass barrel bands, buttplate, and patch box, while those over 36,000 are equipped with iron furniture.

While the Sharps factory was busy tooling up for the production of the New Model 1859, the Model 1853 carbine was being issued to the cavalry in large numbers. In October 1859 Company D of the 1st Dragoons at Fort Filmore, New Mexico, under Fitzgerald's command, was issued a full supply of Sharps carbines. The following quantities of M1853 Sharps carbines were issued to the 2nd U.S. Cavalry from the San Antonio Arsenal in 1859:[47]

Date	Officer	Issued
May 30, 1859	Capt. George Stoneman—Co E	50
June 3, 1859	Capt. E.J. Smith—Co B	80
Sept. 29, 1859	Capt. George Stoneman—Co E	20

In an April 1859 report from Fort Crook, California, Capt. John Adams, commanding Companies A and F of the 1st Dragoons, reported on several damaged Sharps in his command. Company A listed nineteen carbines in need of repair, while Company F had fifteen. It is interesting to note that Adams listed the serial numbers of seven of the carbines from Company A which were in need of repairs:[48]

Serial No.	Repairs Needed
13,666 & 16,772	Hammers broke in the act of firing
15,022	Cone broken off, must be drilled out
14,368 & 17,646	Will not stand at full cock
13,215	Barrel bursted at muzzle, caused a flaw
11,537	Flaw in barrel at muzzle

The problem in Company F was that a third of the Sharps carbines were missing the slide to the rear sights. These were lost when soldiers rode at a trot with the carbine hanging, causing enough stress to break the sight slide. The captain also reports that the long sling rod on these carbines (M1853) allowed the muzzle to turn up, when soldiers rode riding at a trot with the carbine slung.

John Brown's seizure of the armory at Harpers Ferry was, of course, big news in October 1859. After Brown's capture by Col. Robert E. Lee, Palmer wrote to Craig saying that if he were given a few of the numbers on the tang of each of the captured carbines, he could trace them back to the parties who bought the Sharps carbines for Brown's raid. Craig's answer was that the carbines were in both the 15,000 and 16,000 serial ranges with no consecutive numbers. If the actual numbers were needed, they could have been obtained from Harpers Ferry. On October 25, Palmer gave the following answer to this puzzle:

Sharps Rifle Mfg Co.
Hartford, Ct. Oct. 25, 1859

Col. H.F. Craig
Chief of Ordnance

Dear Sir:

I have the honor to acknowledge receipt of your favor of the 24th and to say that on the 19th Sept. 1856 we sold the Government of Kansas 200 carbines in case No. 502-531. Omitting several intermediate cases which were marked Springfield, Mass., and that the numbers of the carbines range between 15,000 to 17,000.

Your Obedient Servant
J.C. Palmer, Pres.[49]

An interesting note on the Sharps carbines captured at Harpers Ferry is their apparent subsequent issue to the 1st Dragoons. In some cases the known numbers of the "John Brown" Sharps match the arms issued in 1861 to the 1st California Cavalry. Research which produced the 1st California's numbers also showed that when the 1st Dragoons left California after the outbreak of the Civil War, they left their arms behind—these arms were then issued to the volunteers.

In December 1859 Lt. M. J. White from the Fort Union Depot recorded the following items on hand and the amount requested to be supplied:

	On Hand	Supplies Requested[50]
Percussion Rifle—Cal. 58	120	200
Sharps Carbines	240	200
Colt Revolvers	160	400

By 1860 many of the Sharps carbines had been in field service in California for a couple of years and were in need of repairs. In September from Benicia Arsenal, Callender placed an order to the Ordnance Department for 100 long swivel bars, 200 rear sight leaf screws, and fifty hammers. These parts were needed to repair carbines from Companies A, B, and K of the 1st Dragoons stationed at Fort Tejone, California. Company I, 2nd Dragoons, sent some of their Sharps carbines in for repairs from Fort Bridger.[51]

In early 1860 Companies A, F, and K of the 2nd U.S. Cavalry made requests for Sharps carbines. The 1st U.S. Infantry requested twenty carbines and four Colt Navy revolvers for the non-commissioned staff and band. On June 20 Bvt. Maj. Earl Van Dorn and Capt. Johnson of the 2nd Cavalry were both issued eighty-five of the NM1859 Sharps carbines from the San Antonio Arsenal. The band was also issued its carbines in June.

The first 200 of the NM1859 Sharps carbines arrived at the St. Louis Arsenal on January 16, 1860, and were issued to the 1st U.S. Cavalry. In late January Lt. J.E.B. Stuart, Company G, 1st U.S. Cavalry, was notified that his company was to be armed with the brass-mounted NM1859 Sharps. Also in January Company B was issued twenty-two Sharps carbines. Two months later Company A was told it was to receive forty-six Sharps carbines at Fort Arbuckle, Texas.

It is interesting to note that the NM1859 Sharps carbines took a shorter cartridge than the previous model and therefore on March 12 Captain Whiteley from San Antonio, Texas, had to request 100,000 of the new shorter Sharps cartridges from the St. Louis Arsenal before he could issue any of the new carbines.[52]

In the 1860 ordnance test trials the Sharps cartridge was a major problem. The paper cartridge first used in the trials produced very irregular firing. Each shot struck the target at 100 yards but all missed at 500 yards. It was determined that a portion of the powder which spilled between the working parts of the barrel caused difficulty in working the breech action. When the shorter linen cartridge fitted for the NM1859 carbine was supplied, it produced much better results. At both 100 and 300 yards, all ten shots struck the target. At 500 yards nine out of ten struck the target. In conclusion, however, the board made this surprising decision: "This arm would be serviceable but would require to be kept always in good order, and therefore the board does not recommend it to be adopted into the military service."[53]

With the election of Abraham Lincoln in November 1860 several of the southern states started to purchase arms. The state of Georgia contacted the Sharps Rifle Manufacturing Company in November 1860 to purchase 2,000 of its patented rifled carbines. By December 18, 1860, Gov. Joseph E. Brown was able to report that 1,600 Sharps carbines had been delivered and were in state storage.[54] The remaining 400 carbines were not delivered, but were replaced with the same number of Sharps rifles from W. J. Syms and Brothers of New York City. The New Model 1859 carbines which were delivered were brass mounted and serial numbered between 31,000 and 36,000. During the war, the Sharps carbines were eventually issued to the 1st and 5th Georgia Cavalry, and the 2nd Georgia Infantry State troops and 57th Georgia Volunteer Infantry.[55]

In addition to Georgia, the state of Virginia bought about fifty Sharps rifles in May 1860. The state auditor's office, on May 17, had invoices payable to the Sharps factory for $2,801.25 for rifles, cartridges, and pellet primers. Additional Sharps rifles were also obtained, and by the fall of 1861 over 130 had been issued to the state militia units.[56]

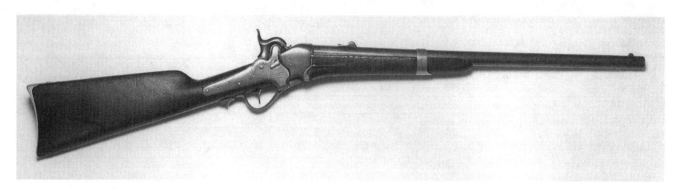

The first order for Sharps carbines placed by the Ordnance Department on January 2, 1852 was partially filled by the delivery of 150 M1851 Sharps carbines. SN 438. John McAuley collection.

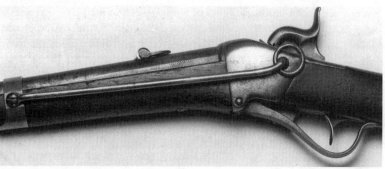

(Above) Note the boxlock door for the Maynard Tape Primer and the single leaf "squirrel ear" rear sight.

(Left) The military version of this carbine also has the 9" sling rod on the left side of the frame.

The Pre-War Years

As part of the first order 50 of these M1852 Sharps carbines were delivered on the January 2, 1852 contract. SN 3601. John McAuley collection.

The M1852 was the first of the side-hammer Sharps or slant breech model Sharps.

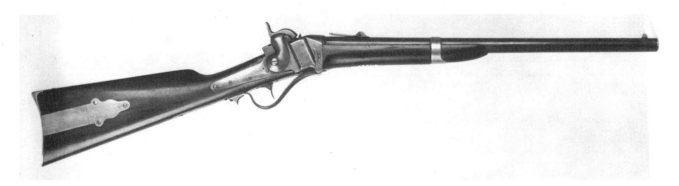

The M1853 Sharps carbine. West Point Museum collection.

Note the spring loaded stud which retains the breech lever pin on the M1853.

The late M1853 Sharps carbines have the Conant patent gas seal; R.S. Lawrence type rear sight and a reduced 2 1/2" saddle bar on the left side of the frame. SN 21,872. Paul Davies collection.

The first order for the brass mounted NM1859 Sharps carbine was placed by the Ordnance Department on March 23, 1859. The first deliveries were issued to the 1st U. S. Cavalry in January 1860. SN 34,527. John McAuley collection.

A close-up view of the NM1859 Sharps. These "straight breech" designed carbines found after 1859 were patented with U.S. Patent No. 22,501 on December 20, 1859 for R. S. Lawrence improved gas check.

The R. S. Lawrence type rear sights which first appeared on the Sharps carbines in late 1857 was patented on February 15, 1859 with U. S. Patent No. 22,959.

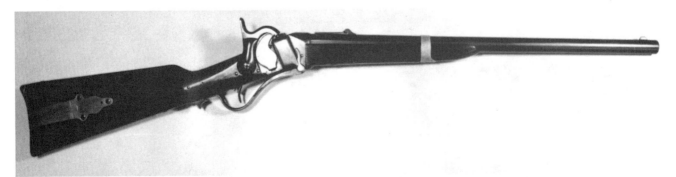

In April 1855 Colonel Craig placed an order for 400 of the M1855 Sharps carbines in .52 caliber. Two hundred fifty of these carbines were issued to the 2nd Dragoons between May 28, 1856 and August 16, 1856. SN 18,310. Hubert Lum collection.

Breech block of the M1855 Sharps with Conant gas seal first delivered to the Army in May 1857.

On May 1, 1857 the Ordnance Department took delivery of 200 Sharps carbines of .577 caliber, 21-5/8" barrel, marked on the barrel only with the British proofs - a crown over the Number 2. These carbines were equipped with the British style rear sight. SN 20,478. John McAuley collection.

THE WAR YEARS
1861-1865

At the outbreak of the war in April 1861 the Sharps Rifle Manufacturing Company was the country's largest manufacturer of breech-loaders. In April company president John Palmer sent a letter to the Ordnance Department, saying:

> I have the honor to inform you that we have on hand some 800 to 1,000 of the very best New Model carbines which we would be glad to sell at $30 each, and also that in as much as the Egyptian Government have not yet provided the funds for paying for the long rifles (600) with sabres we would sell them at $42.50 each. These last have all been inspected by our government inspectors are in first rate order, 36-inch barrels and with sabre attach.[1]

Before the Ordinance Department could acquire the Egyptian Sharps, they were sold to the state of Connecticut on April 20 for $42.50 each.[2] By May 7 the Sharps factory had delivered 740 rifles to Connecticut, along with 50,000 cartridges and 200,000 Elys waterproof caps. The cartridges were purchased at $20 per thousand and the Elys caps at $2.50 per thousand. Connecticut bought an additional 110 Sharps rifles with 30-inch barrels on June 1 and sixty-two more on June 7. Five hundred seventy-six of the Egyptian Sharps rifles were issued to the 2nd Connecticut Infantry. These rifles were later carried by members of the 8th and 11th Connecticut Infantry. Most of the June deliveries, plus a few of the April procurement of Sharps, were issued at the rate of ninety-six per company to Companies A and B of the 4th Connecticut Infantry. This regiment was converted to the 1st Connecticut Heavy Artillery on January 2, 1862. By the summer of 1861 the following infantry regiments were partially armed with Sharps rifles: 1st Connecticut- 144; 2nd Connecticut- 576, and 4th Connecticut—192.[3] On September 16 the state bought 380 more Sharps rifles which were issued to the 6th and 7th Connecticut Infantry. The following charts reflect the state's procurement of Sharps rifles:

State of Connecticut
Procurement of Sharps Rifles[4]

Date of Purchase	Numbers Purchased	Price
April 20, 1861	650 Sharps Rifles	$42.50
April 23, 1861	90 Sharps Rifles	42.50
June 1, 1861	110 Sharps Rifles	42.50
June 6, 1861	62 Sharps Rifles	42.50
September 16, 1861	380 Sharps Rifles	42.50
September 24, 1861	70 Sharps Rifles	42.50
August 19, 1862	80 Sharps Rifles	42.50
Total	1,442 NM 1859 Sharps Rifles	

The 800 New Model Sharps carbines noted in Palmer's letter to the Ordnance Department were sold to the state of Ohio on April 23 and received at Columbus on May 7. The state bought an additional 200 carbines by the end of April, but these arms were not delivered from the factory until September 27.[5] The firm of Schuyler, Hartley, and Graham sold the state of New York 350 Sharps carbines at the price of $32.50. The breakdown of the April 24 sale to New York consisted of fifty .45-caliber Model 1851 Sharps and twenty .52 caliber. The balance of the delivery was .45 caliber Model 1852 and 1853 Sharps carbines.[6] All but three of these carbines were sold by the state to the Ordnance Department on August 30.

At the Battle of Manassas on July 21, 1861, the only units partially armed with Sharps rifles were the 1st and 2nd Connecticut Infantry. Sharps carbines were issued to one company of the 2nd U.S. Dragoons, two companies of the 1st U.S. Cavalry, and four companies of the 2nd U.S. Cavalry. During the battle the 1st and 2nd Connecticut were attached to the 1st Brigade, 1st Division, under the command of Brig. Gen. Daniel Tyler. The 1st Connecticut helped repulse a cavalry and infantry attack early in the battle, while the 2nd held the line with their Sharps rifles. The cavalry commanded by Maj. Innis N. Palmer, 2nd U.S. Cavalry, supported the various batteries and helped cover the retreat. In the battle, the 1st and 2nd Connecticut Infantry suffered thirty-three casualties,[7] while the cavalry listed thirteen wounded and five missing.[8]

A month before the battle, on May 6, Col. Bean of New York City contacted Col. Hiram Duryea of the 5th New York Infantry, saying he was expecting delivery within thirty days of 1,200 Sharps patent breech-loading rifles from the Sharps factory. Bean's price to Duryea was set at $40 per rifle without sabre bayonet and $45 with it.[9] Before Bean received the rifles from the factory, the 5th was ordered to Fort Monroe, Virginia. On June 3 Duryea, in Fort Monroe, wrote to Gen. Winfield Scott in Washington, saying: "There are 500 Sharps rifles here which were intended for the rejected Naval Brigade. Can not they be turned over to me? If we can not have the five hundred, can we not at least have 200 for the flank companies?"[10] Scott gave his approval for 200 for the flanking companies. It appears that Beam owned these rifles because on the next day Maj. Gen. Ben Butler contracted with Bean for 200 Sharps rifles with sabre bayonets at $40.25 for each rifle with its accoutrements and $5 for each sabre bayonet with sheath. On hand were 110 rifles with sabre bayonets. The ninety rifles without bayonets were to be supplied by Bean. All 200 rifles with sabre bayonets were to be delivered by the end of June.[11] Bean was unable to obtain the latest style sabre bayonets called for in the contract, therefore only 110 Sharps rifles with sabre bayonets reached Butler. These rifles were issued to Companies E and I of Duryea's 5th New York Zouaves. In July, the 5th New York Zouaves were ordered to Baltimore where they spent the next eight months in garrison duty.

On June 29 the Ordnance Department placed its first wartime procurement of 3,000 Sharps carbines for the volunteer cavalry regiments being formed. On July 4 it placed an additional request with the factory for 3,000 more carbines.[12] In August Maj. Hubbard from the War Department at New York bought 1,575 Hall rifles, 1,059 Hall carbines, a quantity of muzzle-loading rifles, plus 431 Sharps carbines and 668 Sharps rifles from the Union Defense Committee.[13] On September 16 the Ordnance Department took delivery of one hundred .56 caliber Sharps rifles which had been previously offered to the Navy. These .56 caliber rifles were issued to Capt. Steele of the Sturgis Rifles, a unit assigned as bodyguard to Maj. Gen. George McClellan.

In October the St. Louis Arsenal received 200,000 of the .54-caliber Sharps rifle cartridges, and in November Palmer was told to send a half million cartridges from the factory to Col. John Symington at the Pittsburgh Arsenal. These cartridges were .56 caliber and marked on the boxes "New Model 56/100" with ten cartridges per package. As late as October 1870 some 213,000 of the .56 caliber cartridges were still in storage at the Allegheny Arsenal. Starting on September 3 the first 300 carbines from the June order were received. By the end of the year 5,800 Sharps carbines had been received and paid for at a cost of $30 each on the two contracts.

A Berdan Sharpshooter infantry style cartridge box believed to have been fabricated by Emerson Gaylord of Chicopee, Massachusetts. The Berdan Sharps cartridge boxes were made to be worn on the waistbelt. Paul Johnson photo and collection.

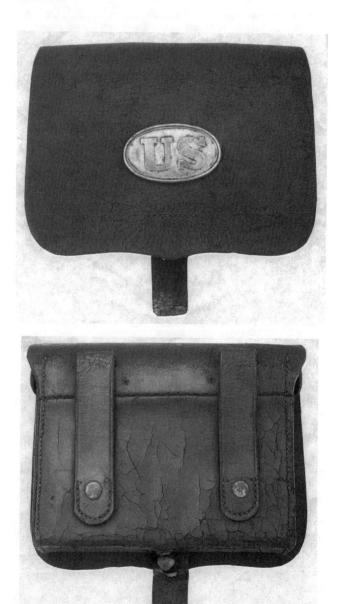

The War Years

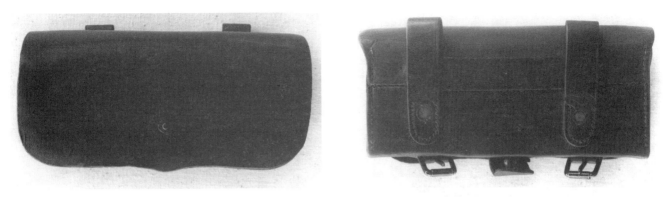

A Sharps carbine cartridge box manufactured by Hoover Calhoun & Co. Ordnance Memo # 1 lists the Sharps carbine cartridge box to be worn on a shoulder belt. Note the Sharps screwdriver and nipple wrench. Paul Johnson collection.

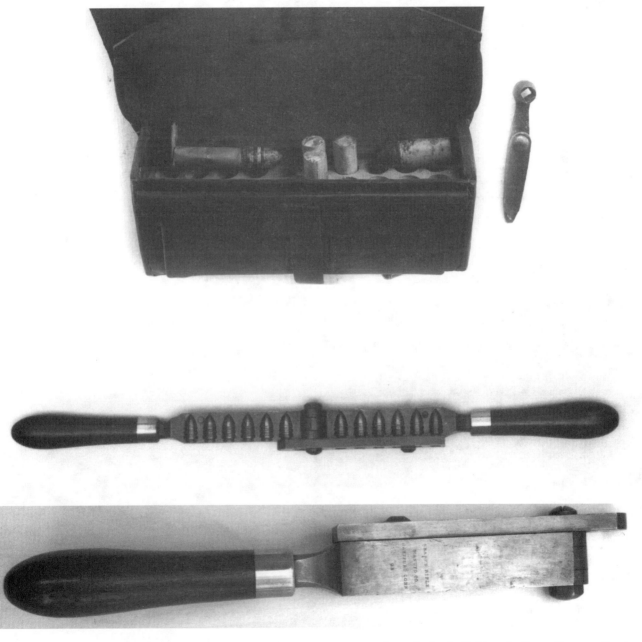

A six cavity mold for the NM1859 Sharps carbines and rifles. These cost the U. S. Gov't 12.50 each. Dave Carter collection.

15

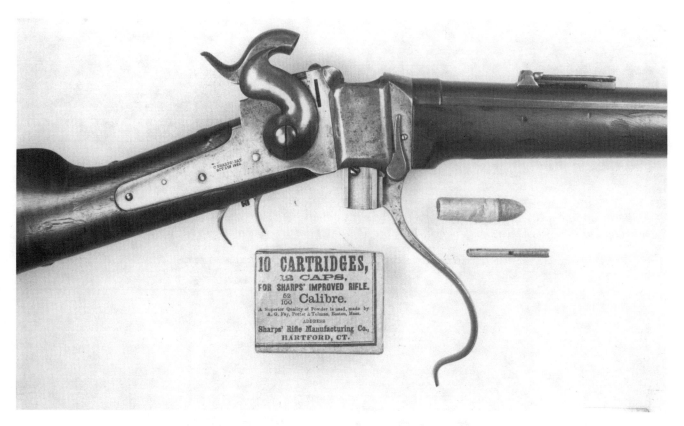

A close-up of the receiver of the Berdan Sharps rifle showing the "double set trigger." Also shown is a packet of ten .52 caliber linen Sharps cartridges, a single cartridge, and a tube of pellet primers. Photo courtesy of Roy Marcot.

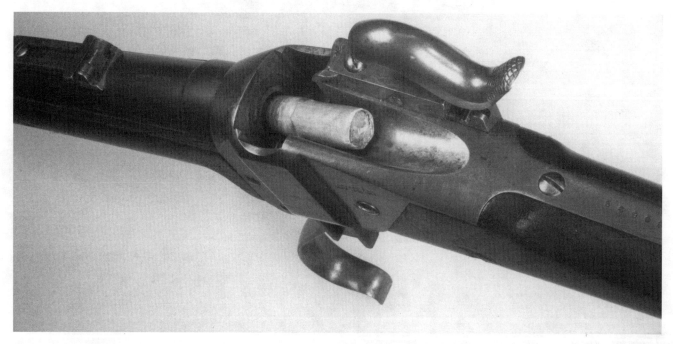

A close-up of the same rifle showing how the cartridge was loaded into the gun. Courtesy of Roy Marcot.

The DST Berdan Sharps NM1859 rifle with angular bayonet. Photo courtesy of Roy Marcot.

The 36 inch barrel NM1859 Sharps rifle with saber bayonet purchased by the State of Connecticut in April 1861.

The last of the percussion Sharps carbine, the NM1865 of which about 5,000 were manufactured. SN 44,139.

COL. BERDAN'S REGIMENT OF SHARP-SHOOTERS!

20 MORE RESPECTABLE MEN WANTED TO COMPLETE
CAPTAIN G. S. TUCKERMAN'S COMPANY!
Now stationed at NORTHERN HOTEL, Utica, N.Y.

'Many are called but few chosen.'

This Company consists of gentlemanly men--none other need apply--as it is the "Crack Regiment" in the Service.

OUR WAGES ARE HIGHER THAN ANY OTHER COMPANY'S!

As many furnish their own Rifles, but the Government supplies each man with one of Berdan's Improved Sharp's Rifle, which will fire 1 1-4 mile, at the rate of 18 times per minute. We have no drill but Skirmish Drill, no Picket duty; our manner of warfare is like the "Guerillas" or Indian. Our uniform is "Green" for summer, color of the grass and foliage, and "Miller's Grey" for fall and winter. You are privileged to lay upon the ground while shooting, picking your position; no commanders while fighting. I will pay board and traveling expenses as soon as enlisted.

H. L. HURLBUT!

Is the regular United States authorized recruiting officer for this Company, and will remain here for enlistments, at the

HOTEL,

GENTLEMEN--This is a beautiful chance for those wishing to see something of this life away from home. The $100 BOUNTY, LAND WARRANT, &c., same as in all other Regiments.

APPLY IN UTICA TO CAPT. TUCKERMAN, BAGG'S HOTEL.
Here to

H. L. HURLBUT.

Nov. 30, 1861.

A recruiting poster for Colonel Berdan's Regiment of Sharpshooters. Norm Flayderman collection.

1862

The year started with the December 21 carbines contract in effect, which said in part: "You will continue to supply this department with Sharp's carbines, to the utmost capacity of your factory, until further orders."[14] In the first three months of 1862 the Sharps factory delivered 4,633 carbines under this contract.

The most famous units to be issued the Sharps rifles were Col. Hiram Berdan's 1st and 2nd U.S. Sharpshooters. To be accepted as a member of Berdan's Sharpshooters, an individual had to place ten consecutive shots in the target, no farther than an average of five inches from the center of the bull's eye, at a distance of 200 yards. The majority of both units of sharpshooters were organized by October 1861. Berdan wrote directly to Secretary of War Simon Cameron on October 22, 1861, requesting Sharps rifles. His letter reads in part: "We are exceeding anxious to have these improved breech-loaders with long bayonets. The price is $43 but this includes fly lock, double triggers and the long bayonet with sheath. The additional charge of 50 cts over the ordinary gun is certainly very reasonable for the extra work."[15]

Berdan eventually got his way. Gen. James Wolfe Ripley placed the order for 1,000 rifles by telegram on January 27, 1862. This order was for the 1st U.S. Sharpshooters; the 2nd U.S. Sharpshooters order was placed for 1,000 Sharps rifles on February 6. The second order reads: "Sir: Be pleased to furnish this department with 1,000 Sharps rifles as soon as possible. These rifles should be made in the manner and supplied with the same appendages and accoutrements as those lately ordered by this department for the use of a regiment of Berdan's Sharpshooters. I desire that you will supply 100,000 cartridges suitable for these arms."[16]

Since it was already in full production manufacturing carbines, the factory couldn't change over to make the Berdan Sharps rifles with double-set triggers until the first week in March. On March 4 Palmer wrote Ripley saying he would try to send the first 1,000 rifles by March 20 and the remaining 1,000 by April 10. Six days later Palmer wrote to Ripley pointing out that the delay was caused by Berdan's changes. The letter reads: "Col. Berdan has no cause of complaint against you on this account or any other that I know of, but the real occasion for delay has been in consequence of his insisting on having different sights and bayonet, and double triggers put on to the rifles, which he was well informed would cause the delay by me." By April 9 only about 150 to 200 were ready to be shipped. From the factory, Palmer stated in his April 9 letter that sub-inspectors Hartwell and Chapman had proved nearly all the barrels and had inspected several hundred finished barrels. The day before, Palmer had been notified by Capt. George T. Balch that John Taylor would take over the inspection of the Berdan contract and was authorized to inspect 200 arms per day. As soon as 100 rifles had been inspected they were to be sent forward. Five days later Palmer wrote to Ripley saying: "two hundred fifty of the rifles are sent forward to Fort Monroe and we shall send 140 to 150 every other day until 1,000 have gone there. All of the 2,000 sets of accoutrements and all of the 200,000 cartridges and primers went to Washington Arsenal on or before the 1st of April as directed."[17] On April 28 Ripley notified Palmer to send the Sharps rifles for the 2nd U.S. Sharpshooters to the Washington Arsenal, and not to Fort Monroe where the 1st U.S. Sharpshooters was receiving its shipment. The boxes were to be marked "FOR BERDAN SHARPSHOOTERS." Shipments continued until May 24 when the last of the 2,000 Berdan rifles were received. Company F, 1st U.S. Sharpshooters, was the first to receive its Sharps rifles at Yorktown, Virginia, on May 8. The remainder of the regiment received theirs by the end of May. The 2nd U.S. Sharpshooters was issued its Sharps while at Fredericksburg on June 1st. With the completion of the Berdan contract, the factory returned to manufacturing of carbines; a week later, on May 31, 500 carbines were delivered to the Ordnance Department.

To date the lowest known serial number on a Berdan Sharps rifle is 54,374; the highest is 57,574.[18] The major characteristics of the Berdan Sharps are a 30-inch barrel equipped to take a Collins and Co. angular bayonet, double set triggers; and a "J T" inspector cartouche on the left side of the stock.[19] A little-known fact on the Berdan rifles is that the pin punch mark found in the inside cover of the patchbox is the final inspection and approval mark made by John Taylor.

The Berdan Sharpshooters used these NM1859 Sharps rifles with deadly effectiveness. At the Battle of Antietam on September 17 the 2nd U.S. Sharpshooters saw severe action, incurring six killed, fifty-eight wounded, and two missing—25 percent of those present for duty. While lying on the open ground the sharpshooters did more damage to the Confederates than any brigade in their front or to their right. Opposite the 2nd U.S. Sharpshooters was Col. Aiken's 7th South Carolina Infantry. The 7th South Carolina suffered losses of 140 out of 268 men. Later a Union burial detail placed 192 Confederate dead into a single grave opposite where the 2nd U.S. Sharpshooters had been engaged.[20]

A month after the Battle of Antietam the 1st U.S. Sharpshooters showed 508 Sharps rifles on hand as of October 24. The breakdown by company was:

Company A	34
Company B	73
Company C	65
Company D	16
Company E	36
Company F	73
Company G	57
Company H	38
Company I	43
Company K	34

There were thirty-nine more rifles in the hands of the regimental armorer.[21] Several hundred Berdan rifles were also in storage and were eventually issued to other units. On August 10 the 42nd Pennsylvania Bucktails drew a

By the time of Ripley's Annual Ordnance Report of June 30, 1862, he was able to report from the beginning of the war to June 20, 1862, that the Ordnance Department had purchased 13,005 Sharps carbines. For the remainder of 1862 two additional three-month contracts were given for all the carbines which could be delivered during the three-month period. In the last six months of 1862 the Sharps factory delivered 11,001 carbines on these contracts. In all the Sharps Rifle Manufacturing Company supplied 2,000 Berdan Sharps rifles and 17,134 carbines for the year.

By December 1862 more than 60 percent of all breech-loading carbines in field service were Sharps. The December 31, 1862, list of ordnance stores in the hands of the cavalry shows 13,600 Sharps carbines; 1,900 Smiths; 500 Gwyn and Campbells; 900 Gallagers; 1,040 Merrills; 1,900 Halls; and 900 Burnsides carbines.[23] The following cavalry regiments were listed with Sharps carbines:

1st U.S.—332	2nd U.S.—469
3rd U.S.—83	4th U.S.—180
5th U.S.—321	6th U.S.—621
1st California—355	2nd California—601
1st Colorado—63	2nd Illinois—338
4th Illinois—463	6th Illinois—248
7th Illinois—399	8th Illinois—440
11th Illinois—19	3rd Indiana—54
1st Iowa—9	2nd Iowa—226
3rd Iowa—70	5th Iowa—131
5th Kansas—106	6th Kansas—56
7th Kansas—88	3rd Kentucky—92
1st Lousiana—294	1st Maine—12
1st Massachusetts—102	2nd Massachusetts—168
1st Maryland—75	1st Michigan—385
2nd Michigan—8	3rd Michigan—37
1st Minnesota—115	1st New York—22
2nd New York—402	3rd New York—192
5th New York—39	6th New York—410
7th New York—301	8th New York—334
9th New York—373	1st New Mexico—8
3rd Ohio—184	3rd Ohio—53
4th Ohio—288	5th Ohio—131
1st Pennsylvania—481	2nd Pennsylvania—92
3rd Pennsylvania—307	4th Pennsylvania—200
6th Pennsylvania—43	8th Pennsylvania—295
9th Pennsylvania—35	11th Pennsylvania—93
16th Pennsylvania—200	1st Rhode Island—70
1st Tennessee—146	1st Vermont—152
1st West Virginia—36	2nd Wisconsin—6

As of December 1862 the following infantry units were listing Sharps rifles:[24]

42nd Pennsylvania—140	12th Kentucky—101
6th Connecticut—178	15th Massachusetts—22
7th Connecticut—168	1st Minnesota—30
8th Connecticut—92	26th Missouri—70
11th Connecticut—78	5th New York—22
13th Connecticut—192	2nd New Hampshire—60
14th Connecticut—36	

Union cavalryman armed with the NM1859 or 1863 Sharps carbine. Richard Carlile collection.

number of Berdan Sharps; the 16th Michigan Infantry was issued about 300 during this same period. Most of these extra rifles were turned back in for issue to Berdan's men. It appears that about 180 Berdan Sharps rifles were maintained by the 42nd Pennsylvania Bucktails during its military service. (The serial numbers of the 42nd Pennsylvania Berdan's Sharps Rifles can be found in the serial number section of this book.)

Duryea's 5th New York would get a chance to use its Sharps rifles at the Battle of Gaines Mill, Virginia, on Friday, June 27. At about 12:30 in the afternoon Lt. Col. Hiram Duryea sent forward flank companies E and I as advance skirmishers to meet the advancing Confederate infantry. Within a few minutes they returned to the main command. Leading the Confederate advance was the 1st South Carolina—Orr's Rifles. When the Confederates came into the open they were attacked by the 5th New York. In the melee that followed the 5th New York suffered 162 casualties out of 450 engaged, while Orr's Rifles incurred eighty-one killed and 234 wounded out of 537. Although the battle of Gaines Mill was a Confederate victory, the 5th performed its duty well.[22]

It is interesting to note that neither of the Berdan Sharpshooters regiments reported their December inventory of ordnance stores.

1863

The year 1863 was the turning point in the war, with Gen. George Gordon Meade repulsing Gen. Robert E. Lee at Gettysburg and Gen. Ulysses S. Grant's capture of Vicksburg. The year saw the Sharps factory deliver 22,205 carbines and twenty rifles to the Ordnance Department. The twenty rifles with sabre bayonets received in April were issued to Col. Gilmore Marston's 2nd New Hampshire Infantry.[25]

The year started with a contract for all the carbines that Sharps could manufacture for the first three months of the year. In this period the Ordnance Department received 5,100 carbines. During this time the company began converting the NM 1859 to the "New Model 1863" carbines. The basic difference found between the NM1859 and 1863 was the barrel marking—"NEW MODEL 1863" and the improved cleanout screw in the breech-block.

The correspondences from Ripley to Palmer on April 1 were to have a major effect on both the price that the government would pay for the Sharps carbines and the pattern of the arm. Ripley's first letter said: "this department will receive from you, at the current price of thirty dollars for each carbine and appendages, all such carbines of the present pattern as you may now have completed, or in process of construction."[26] His second letter called for the carbines to be manufactured without a patch box, to be paid for at the reduced rate of $28.25, including appendages of one cone wrench, screwdriver, and brush and leather thong. On the contract of April 1 Sharps delivered 5,514 at the old rate of $30 each and 1,000 without the patch box at the reduced rate of $28. For the balance of the year the factory would deliver only carbines without patch boxes at the stated rate of $28.25.

At Snicker's Gap on November 3, 1862, a Union force of forty-six men from the 1st Massachusetts Cavalry commanded by Lt. Col. Horace B. Sargent, plus parts of the 6th, 7th, and 14th U.S. Infantry, skirmished with Confederate cavalry and infantry. In this action the 1st Massachusetts suffered the death of one officer and three men wounded. They were armed with Smith carbines which were found to be worthless because it took several caps to set off the cartridges. In January Sargent wrote to brigade headquarters asking permission to discard his 508 Smith carbines and trust his future with the eighty-four Sharps carbines presently on hand, plus the Colt revolver. After inspection of the Smiths, the brigade had them recalled and a full compliment of Sharps carbines were issued to the 1st Massachusetts.[27]

The major battle fought in the East in 1863 was the three-day Battle of Gettysburg from July 1-3. Over 60 percent of the breech-loaders in Union cavalry at Gettysburg were Sharps carbines. The first shots of the battle were by Union pickets located on the Chambersburg Pike at about 7:30 a.m. This post was manned by Company E, 8th Illinois Cavalry, with Lt. Marcellus Jones firing the first shot from Sgt. Levi Shafer's Sharps carbine.[28] The following chart reflects the armament of the Union cavalry at the time of the battle:

Small Arms in the Union Cavalry at Gettysburg[29]

Sharps Carbine	4,724

(67 of this # were Sharps & Hankins in 9th New York)

Burnsides Carbine	1,387
Smith Carbine	309
Gallager Carbine	271
Merrill Carbine	208
Spencer Rifles	572

(issued to 5th Michigan and Companies E and H of the 6th Michigan)

.44 caliber Colt Revolvers	8,608
.36 caliber Colt Revolvers	569
.44 caliber Remington Revolvers	555
.36 caliber Remington Revolvers	503
.44 caliber Allen Revolvers	33
.44 caliber LeFaucheux Revolvers	111
Sabres	10,120

The Union cavalry with Sharps carbines at Gettysburg were:[30]

Brigade	Units	# of Carbines
Gamble	8th Ill.	311
	3rd Ind.	12
	8th NY	210
Devin	6th NY	232
	9th NY	314
Huey	2nd NY	166
	4th NY	245
	6th Ohio	208
	8th Pa.	50
Merritt	6th Pa.	231
	1st U.S.	361
	2nd U.S.	245
	5th U.S.	373
	6th U.S.	367
McIntosh	1st Md.	93
	3rd Pa.	264
Gregg	1st Maine	101
	4th Pa.	165
	16th Pa.	317
Custer	1st Mich.	213
Farnsworth	5th NY	39
	1st Vt.	140

On the second day at Gettysburg Berdan took one hundred of his sharpshooters (Companies D, E, F, and I) of the 1st U.S. Sharpshooters and 200 men from the 3rd Maine Infantry and made a reconnaissance of the extreme left of the Union line. In a hotly contested twenty-minute action against Brig. Gen. Cadmus Wilcox's Brigade of Alabama Infantry, the Berdan Sharpshooters averaged ninety-five rounds of ammunition per man. In his official report on the battle Berdan said that his 450 men expended 14,400 rounds of Sharps ammunition during the battle.[31] In a letter dated a year after the battle Col. Theodore G. Ellis of the 14th Connecticut Infantry said that during Pickett's Charge his two companies with Sharps rifles ran out of .52 caliber ammunition. They then turned to the men next to them, who were armed with .58 caliber Springfield rifle muskets, and used their Springfield ammunition without any apparent damage to the Sharps.[32] Other infantry units at Gettysburg partially armed with Sharps rifles were the 1st Minnesota, the 1st Company of Massachusetts Sharpshooters, the 2nd New Hampshire, and the 42nd Pennsylvania Bucktails.

Later in the year the following infantry regiments were reporting Sharps rifles as part of their stores:[33]

Regiments	Date	No.	Date	No.
42nd Pennsylvania	Sept.	153	Dec.	176
6th Connecticut		147		148
7th Connecticut		118		118
8th Connecticut		80		40
11th Connecticut		65		65
13rd Connecticut		140		134
14th Connecticut		36		113
11th Kentucky		58		0
1st Minnesota		27		0
26th Missouri		47		46
2nd New Hampshire		41		41
146th New York		14		0
New York Sharpshooters		65		68
66th Illinois		381		339
2nd Indian Infantry		13		13
Massachusetts Sharpshooters		56		56
8th Minnesota		55		0
1st U.S. Sharpshooters		0		289
2nd U.S. Sharpshooters		0		138
3rd Michigan		0		21

In the western theater of operations Grant would call Grierson's raid "one of the most brilliant cavalry exploits of the war." On April 17 Col. Benjamin Grierson left LaGrange, Tennessee, with a force of 1,700 cavalry consisting of the 6th, 7th Illinois, and 2nd Iowa. In sixteen days his raiders rode over 600 miles through Mississippi and reentered the Union lines at Baton Rouge, Louisiana, on May 2. In this operation Grierson tied up most of the Confederate cavalry, a third of the infantry, and at least two regiments of artillery. This allowed Grant to cross the Mississippi River unopposed south of Vicksburg and led to its capture on July 4. In the raid Grierson suffered thirty-six casualties while killing and wounding about a hundred and capturing 500. They also captured a thousand horses and mules and destroyed large quantities of Army supplies and government property.

(Right) Union Infantryman armed with the NM1859 Sharps rifle with angular bayonet. Richard Carlile collection.

In June, shortly after the raid, Grierson's cavalry listed the following small arms in its inventory:

Sixth Illinois:	Cosmopolitan Carbines	346
	Sharps Carbines	147
Seventh Illinois:	Sharps Carbines	474
	Smith Carbines	94
Second Iowa:	M1855 Colt Revolving Rifles	313
	Sharps Carbines	238

1864

If 1863 was the turning point of the war, 1864 was the year of attrition for both armies. By the end of the year, Grant had Lee under siege at Petersburg while Sherman had captured Atlanta and marched to the sea. It is interesting to note that in Sherman's March to the Sea, his cavalry had expended 56,000 Burnside, 500 Henry, 62,000 Sharps, 21,000 Smith, and 141,396 Spencer rifle cartridges.[34]

The year 1864 saw the largest deliveries of Sharps carbines during the war. In total, 25,039 carbines reached the Ordnance Department. These carbines were delivered under two contracts of January 26 and September 20 at the reduced rate of $24 each. In March the serial numbers reached 100,000; at this point the factory converted to using the prefix "C" for 100,000.

On February 23 Palmer wrote to Dyer, saying that the factory had on hand nearly one and a half million cartridges and if the Ordnance Department was not in need of them, they would reduce this quantity of ammunition. He went on to say that 750,000 of the one million cartridges ordered by the government had been sent forward. The balance of the order was sent on March 12.[35] Six days after Palmer's letter of February 23 he was told that in the future the government arsenals would manufacture the Sharps cartridges. By the end of the fiscal year, June 30, the St. Louis Arsenal had fabricated over 4.7 million Sharps cartridges.[36]

Throughout the war field cavalry sent many reports on the effectiveness of the Sharps carbines. The following 1864 reports were typical of this period. Maj. Caspar Crowninshield of the 2nd Massachusetts Cavalry wrote, "The Sharps carbine is in my opinion far superior to any of the other carbines which I have seen used in the Army." Maj. William Thompson of the 1st Iowa wrote, "Sharps carbine have no superior. In range is fully equal to a minie rifle and the facility and accuracy with which it is loaded and discharged renders our dismounted cavalry more than equal the enemy's infantry and far superior to their cavalry." Col. Thomas Hovick of the 7th Kansas wrote: "Sharps carbines [are] undoubtably the best arm for cavalry service in the South West." Interestingly, not all reports of the Sharps carbines were favorable. For example, Maj. Patton of the 3rd Indiana found the following problem with the Sharps carbine: "The small springs in the locks are more easily broken or damaged than any other part of the gun. An armorer could easily repair most guns condemned as unfit for service if extra articles of this kind were provided."[37]

The cavalry in the Army of the Potomac was constantly skirmishing with the Confederate cavalry in Grant's 1864 campaign. By late June they had been in action at Todd's Tavern, Yellow Tavern, Haw's Shop, Cold Harbor, and Sheridan's Trevillian raid. As of June 30 the following arms were listed in the cavalry of the Army of the Potomac:[38]

Sharps Carbines	4,881
Spencer Carbines	1,045
Burnside Carbines	1,942
Smith Carbines	257
Starr Carbines	13
Gallager Carbines	25
Joslyn Carbines	22
Sharps & Hankins Carbines	184
Spencer Rifles	175
Springfield Rifle Muskets	2

The cavalry units in the Army of the Potomac armed with Sharps carbines as of June 30 were:[39]

Unit	Count	Unit	Count
1st Connecticut	25	1st U.S.	129
3rd Indiana	133	2nd U.S.	204
8th Illinois	98	5th U.S.	89
1st Maine	172	6th U.S.	317
1st Massachusetts	353	2nd Ohio	39
1st Michigan	40	6th Ohio	108
5th Michigan	13	1st Pennsylvania	217
3rd New Jersey	175	2nd Pennsylvania	392
2nd New York	137	4th Pennsylvania	203
4th New York	182	6th Pennsylvania	195
5th New York	7	8th Pennsylvania	129
6th New York	238	13th Pennsylvania	178
8th New York	140	16th Pennsylvania	380
9th New York	46 Sharps	17th Pennsylvania	235
	184 Sharps & Hankins	10th New York	118
1st Vermont	165		

In addition to cavalry units in the Army of the Potomac, over a hundred other regiments during this period were armed with nearly 24,000 Sharps carbines.

As of June 30 the Union infantry had thirteen regiments listing Sharps rifles. They were:[40]

Unit	Count	Unit	Count
8th Connecticut	603	Mass Sharpshooters	15
13th Connecticut	130	1st U.S. Sharpshooters	147
14th Connecticut	52	2nd U.S. Sharpshooters	118
1st Minnesota	26	190th Pennsylvania	98
2nd New Hampshire	20	16th Michigan	27
NY Ind. Sharpshooters	81	66th Illinois	180
3rd New Hampshire	14		

(Left) Union Infantryman armed with the NM1859 Sharps rifle with saber bayonet. Richard Carlile collection.

The following tables show the quantities of carbines in storage at the various northern arsenals as of November 5:

Ballards	501	Maynard	1,191
Burnside	296	Sharps	1,006
Cosmopolitan	12	Sharps & Hankins	37
Joslyn	335	Smith	1,058
Gallager	169	Starr	701
Gibbs	218	Spencer	647
Greene	11	Warner	549
Hall	320	Pistol Carbine	178
Linder	344	Rifled Musketoon	45
Merrills	619	Smooth-bore Musketoon	125

While the Union cavalry was starting to be fairly well standardized with ordnance stores in each regiment, the Confederate cavalry was armed with an incredible assortment of ordnance. This fact is shown in the following three field inspection reports conducted during 1864.[41]

Maj. Gen. Nathan B. Forrest Cavalry
Ross' Brigade of Jackson's Division
November 1864

	3rd Texas	6th Texas	9th Texas	27th Texas
.577 caliber Enfield Rifles	98	83	65	87
.54 caliber Austrian Rifles	12	35	7	10
.52 caliber Sharps Carbines	49	48	32	46
.56 caliber Spencers	28	21	11	13
.54 caliber Ballard Carbines	4	—	1	4
.52 caliber Union Carbines	3	2	15	5
.56 caliber Burnside Carbines	—	2	5	5
.50 caliber Gallager Carbines	—	2	—	—
.50 caliber Smith Carbines	—	1	4	4
.54 caliber Merrill Carbines	—	—	—	1

Earlier in the year, on May 25, in Meridian, Mississippi, Forrest's cavalry command was inspected and the following equipment was reported:

	1st Div.	3rd Div.	Holston Brigade	Escort Company
.69 cal. Musket	24	18	—	—
.58 cal. Ashville Rifle	482	870	33	—
.54 cal. Miss. Rifle	1,475	854	265	—
Shotgun	—	2	—	—
.54 cal. Hall Carbine	4	—	—	—
.52 cal. Sharps Carbine	725	400	—	63
.50 cal. Colt Carbine	11	—	—	—
.56 cal. Burnside Carbine	52	—	—	5
.70 cal. Belgian Rifle	3	47	—	—
.51 cal. Maynard Carbine	67	—	—	5
.52 cal. Hall Rifle	—	18	—	—
French Pistol	190	163	—	—
.44 cal. Revolver	291	150	14	31
.36 cal. Revolver	701	337	24	32
.54 cal. Holster Pistol	24	—	—	—
Sabres	188	7	13	—

Reports of inspection made in Petersburg, Virginia, November 29-30, 1864, lists a number of small arms with The Cavalry Corps of the Army of Northern Virginia. The report shows:

Major General Wade Hampton—Commanding
Hampton's (Old) Division

Butler's Brigade
4th, 5th & 6th South Carolina — Springfield muskets and Enfield rifles; Spencer and Burnside carbines.

Young's Brigade
10th Georgia, Cobb's Legion, Phillip's Legion, and Jeff Davis Legion — Austrian, Springfield, Enfield rifles and muskets; Richmond, Spencer, Henry, Maynard, and Sharps carbines.

Maj. Gen. H.F. "Rooney" Lee Division

Chambliss' Brigade
9th Virginia — Sharps, Burnside and Spencer carbines; Enfield rifles.
10th Virginia — Sharps, Burnside, Spencer and Merrill carbines; Enfield rifles.
13th Virginia — Sharps carbines and Enfield rifles.

Barringer's Brigade
1st North Carolina — Spencer, Austrian and Enfield rifles; Burnside, Smith and Sharps carbines - Robinson Sharps.
2nd North Carolina — Spencer and Enfield rifles; Burnside, Smith and Robinson Sharps carbines.
3rd North Carolina — Burnside, Sharps and Richmond carbines; Spencer and Enfield rifles.
5th North Carolina — Smith, Burnside and Sharps carbines; Richmond, Austrian and Enfield rifles.

Dearling's Brigade
8th Georgia — Burnside, Sharps and Richmond carbines; Springfield muskets and Enfield rifles.
4th North Carolina — Enfield rifles and Sharps carbines.
16th North Carolina Battalion — Richmond and Sharps carbines; Enfield rifles.

The following is a partial list of Confederate cavalry regiments in 1864 who list Sharps Carbines as part of their ordnance stores:

	Regiments
Regulars—C.S.	1, 3, 7, 8
Georgia	4, 7, 8, 11, 59
Louisiana	3
Mississippi	2, 11, 18, 19, 26, 42
North Carolina	1, 2, 3, 4, 5, 16
South Carolina	2
Tennessee	9
Texas	3, 6, 9, 27
Virginia	1, 5, 6, 7, 9, 10, 13, 24, 30

Dyer contacted Palmer from the Ordnance Department on November 25 and requested the price and quantity of all the Sharps rifles that could be delivered. A week later, on December 1, an order was given for 150 .52 caliber rifles at a price of $38 each. These New Model 1863 rifles were not delivered until February 6 of the following year. Later in December Dyer inquired about the price for 1,000 rifles. Palmer offered them for $36 each, and on December 31, Dyer wrote back and offered $33.50.[42]

1865

On Jan. 2, 1865, Palmer refused Dyer's price of $33.50 because the company could not turn a profit from that price. Five days later Dyer accepted Palmer's original offer of $36 each with deliveries to be made in fifty days. These rifles were intended to be used by Maj. Gen. Winfield S. Hancock's Army Corps. Dyer also stated that the Springfield Joslyn rifle muskets that were being manufactured at the Springfield Armory would have been used but they would not be ready in time.[43]

Up to this time the rifles being sent to the Ordnance Department were in the 57,000 serial range, using leftover parts from the Berdan order of 1862 with both barrels marked NM1859 and 1863. This was the status of the 150 Sharps rifles delivered in February. However, when they went to manufacture the order of January 7 for 1,000 rifles they found that the barrel bands were forged by hand and after the Berdan order was completed, all the hand tools had been disarranged. Therefore, the company had to make new tools to forge the barrel bands, delaying delivery until March 21.

At the time of the January order for 1,000 Sharps rifles Hancock was in Washington, D.C., engaged in organizing the first Veteran Army Corps. One inducement to enlisting in this corps was the promise that upon discharge, the soldier could retain his rifle. (Serial numbers and the names of those receiving these arms are found in the serial numbers section of this book.)

On February 26 Hancock was ordered to Winchester, Virginia, to take command of the Middle Military Department. The 1st and 2nd U.S. Veteran Volunteer Infantry Regiments were sent to Harpers Ferry, Virginia, as part of Hancock's force. The 1st U.S. Veteran Volunteer Infantry left Washington, D.C., under the command of Lt. Col. Charles Bird on March 1 for Harpers Ferry. Bird's two flanking companies were armed with the 150 Sharps NM1863 rifles sent on February 6. Lt. Col. Charles von Kusserow's 2nd U.S. Veteran Volunteer Infantry left for Harpers Ferry late in March armed with 500 of the NM1863 Sharp rifles delivered on March 21.[44] The balance of the March 21 delivery was sent forward for Bird's command on March 30 when 210 were sent and the rest (290) on April 8.[45] Bird's 1st U.S. Veteran Volunteers used their Sharps rifles in an engagement with Col. John Singleton Mosby's Partisan Rangers near Hamilton, Virginia, on March 21. In this skirmish the Union cavalry was attacked by Mosby's men and forced to retreat. Mosby's attack was easily driven off by volleys from the 1st U.S. Veteran Volunteers. In this action both sides suffered about thirteen casualties each.[46]

Needing additional breech-loading rifles to arm the Veteran Volunteer Infantry regiments being formed at Washington, Dyer wrote Palmer on February 27, asking if the Sharps factory could deliver 5,000 Sharps rifles adapted for the metallic cartridge and if so at what price. Since the factory was not geared to produce arms for the rimfire cartridge, Palmer replied they could deliver their current percussion rifle at $33 which was agreed to on March 7. Deliveries were to start on April 15 but were not sent forward until May when 2,028 were received, with the balance delivered in June. In May the Middle Military Division was listing 1,047 NM1863 rifles in its department; 1,121 NM1863 Sharps rifles in Department of Washington as of June 1 and the Army of the Potomac with 466 NM1859 Sharps rifles at the time of the fall of Petersburg in April.[47]

On the carbine order of September 20, 1864, some 7,000 carbines were received in 1865 with the last 1,000 received on April 7. Even after the war the Sharps factory was trying to deliver 2,000 Sharp rifles as late as December 18 but was turned down since the arms were no longer needed by the Ordnance Department.

Wartime Procurement of Sharps by Ordnance Department

	Carbines	Rifles
Sharps Rifle Mfg. Co.	77,180	8,270
Col. Bean	100	398
Union Defense Committee	431	668
Schuyler, Hartley & Graham	300	2
Joseph C. Grubb and Company	132	0
State of New York	347	0
Other Firms	59	13
Total	78,549	9,351

16,306,500 cartridges were also procured at a cost of $347,410.57

In late 1864 the Ordnance Department tried to have the less-effective carbines turned in and replaced with Sharps, Spencers, or Burnsides for the upcoming 1865 spring offensive. The following chart lists cavalry regiments armed in 1865 with Sharps carbines:

Union Cavalry Regiments Armed with Sharps Carbines in 1865[48]

Regiment	Count	Regiment	Count
2nd Arkansas	666	2nd California	131
3rd Illinois	35	4th Illinois	394
5th Illinois	509	7th Illinois	603
9th Illinois	88	10th Illinois	907
17th Illinois	649	1st Indiana	139
3rd Indiana	40	4th Indiana	272
5th Indiana	254	8th Indiana	34
1st Iowa	672	9th Iowa	721
2nd Kentucky	14	7th Kentucky	154
5th Kansas	94	9th Kansas	73
11th Kansas	81	15th Kansas	821
1st Louisiana	532	1st Maryland	408
2nd Maryland	580	3rd Maryland	59
1st Massachusetts	217	2nd Massachusetts	24
3rd Massachusetts	507	4th Massachusetts	30
2nd Minnesota	179	1st Mississippi	259
1st Missouri	598	1st Missouri State	21
3rd Missouri State	75	8th Missouri State	12
8th Michigan	400	1st New Hampshire	122
2nd New Jersey	412	4th New York	135
6th New York	488	8th New York	217
9th New York	512	10th New York	160
1st New York Lincoln	179	1st NY Mounted Rifle	633
2nd NY Mtd. Rifle	366	2nd NY Vet. Vols.	716

15th Missouri	32		16th Missouri	16
Bracketts Battalion	168		Adams Independence	126
13th New York	425		Upper Potomac Force	494
1st Battalion Nevada	159		15th New York	601
16th New York	530		22nd New York	352
24th New York	105		3rd Ohio	142
4th Ohio	140		6th Ohio	155
10th Ohio	250		1st Pennsylvania	209
2nd Pennsylvania	491		3rd Pennsylvania	408
5th Pennsylvania	348		6th Pennsylvania	650
8th Pennsylvania	316		13th Pennsylvania	267
15th Pennsylvania	381		17th Pennsylvania	467
19th Pennsylvania	317		21st Pennsylvania	480
1st Rhode Island	143		1st Tennessee	286
6th Tennessee	675		10th Tennessee	176
12th Tennessee	20		1st Texas	255
2nd U.S.	234		3rd U.S.	209
5th U.S.	233		6th U.S.	215
3rd U.S. Colored	746		4th U.S. Colored	59
5th U.S. Colored	152		1st Vermont	397
1st West Virginia	34		3rd West Virginia	10
2nd Wisconsin	23			

In the 1865 spring campaign about a hundred regiments were listed with Sharps carbines with over 30,000 in field use. About eighty regiments were armed with over 25,000 Spencer carbines.[49] For the spring campaign the New York Ordnance Agency sent to the field 800,000 Sharps pellet primers for the Sharps carbines, with a half million being sent to the Virginia area of operation. In addition, one million Sharps ball ammunition were purchased from the Sharps factory.[50]

From a May 30, 1864, directive by the Ordnance Department each separate Army or Military Department on the first of each month had to report the quantity of ordnance stores in its possession. The following list shows the quantity of Sharps carbines in the various departments as of March 1, 1865:[51]

Department of Potomac	3,237
Department of Missouri	812
Department of Mississippi	3,930
Department of North West	471
Middle Military Division	3,913
Department of Virginia & North Carolina	1,588
Department of Washington	1,673
Department of Cumberland	5,328 (April totals)
Department of Arkansas	2,266

With the close of the war in the spring of 1865 the Army quickly reduced its force by mustering out the volunteer infantry and cavalry regiments. Under General Order No. 101, enlisted men were allowed to retain their small arms after having the value deducted from their mustering-out pay. In this manner 3,454 Sharps rifles and 2,549 Sharps carbines were taken home.[52] Several soldiers wrote to the Ordnance Department requesting their small arms. 16-year-old Pvt. Alexander Hyland of Company B, 6th New York Cavalry, writing from his hospital bed in Washington, D.C., asked that he be allowed to purchase a Sharps carbine, sabre, and Remington or Starr revolver. Young Hyland stated that he enlisted in December 1863 at the age of 15 and had been in all the cavalry action of 1864 until being wounded in the left forearm at Smithfield, Virginia, on August 29, 1864. His request was granted by the Ordnance Department.[53] Also on this date, from Vermont, came a letter to Gen. Lewis A. Grant requesting that members of Companies G and H, 4th Vermont Infantry and formerly of Berdan U.S. Sharpshooters be allowed to retain their Sharps rifles which they had carried since 1862. The price of $8 per rifle was then deducted from the members' mustering-out pay when the request was honored by Grant.

Regiments Armed with Sharps Carbines During the War

Cavalry

Adams Ind Btn.	2nd Arkansas	3rd Arkansas
4th Arkansas	1st California	2nd California
Brackett and Hatch Battalions		1st Btn. Calif
1st Colorado	3rd Colorado	1st Dakota
1st Illinois	2nd Illinois	3rd Illinois
4th Illinois	5th Illinois	6th Illinois
7th Illinois	8th Illinois	9th Illinois
10th Illinois	11th Illinois	14th Illinois
15th Illinois	16th Illinois	17th Illinois
1st Indiana	3rd Indiana	4th Indiana
5th Indiana	6th Indiana	8th Indiana
1st Iowa	2nd Iowa	3rd Iowa
4th Iowa	5th Iowa	6th Iowa
9th Iowa	2nd Kansas	5th Kansas
6th Kansas	7th Kansas	9th Kansas
11th Kansas	14th Kansas	15th Kansas
1st Kentucky	2nd Kentucky	3rd Kentucky
4th Kentucky	6th Kentucky	7th Kentucky
11th Kentucky	12th Kentucky	1st Louisiana
1st Maryland	2nd Maryland	3rd Maryland
1st Massachusetts	2nd Massachusetts	3rd Massachusetts
4th Massachusetts	40th Mass. Mtd Inf	1st Michigan
2nd Michigan	3rd Michigan	4th Michigan
5th Michigan	8th Michigan	1st Maine
1st Minnesota	2nd Minnesota	1st Mississippi
1st Missouri	2nd Missouri	3rd Missouri
4th Missouri	6th Missouri	7th Missouri
10th Missouri	11th Missouri	15th Missouri
16th Missouri	1st Mo. State Mil	3rd Mo. State Mil
7th Mo. State Mil	8th Mo. State Mil	32nd Mo. Mtd Inf
1st Nebraska	1st Nevada	1st Nevada BN
1st New Hampshire	1st New Jersey	2nd New Jersey
3rd New Jersey	1st New Mexico	1st New York
1st N.Y. Lincoln	1st New York Vet.	1st NY Mtd
2nd New York	2nd New York Mtd	2nd NY Vet
3rd New York	4th New York	5th New York
6th New York	7th New York	8th New York
9th New York	10th New York	13th New York
14th New York	15th New York	16th New York
19th New York	20th New York	22nd New York

24th New York	1st Ohio	2nd Ohio
3rd Ohio	4th Ohio	5th Ohio
6th Ohio	10th Ohio	13th Ohio
1st Oregon	1st Pennsylvania	2nd Pennsylvania
3rd Pennsylvania	4th Pennsylvania	5th Pennsylvania
6th Pennsylvania	8th Pennsylvania	9th Pennsylvania
11th Pennsylvania	12th Pennsylvania	13th Pennsylvania
15th Pennsylvania	16th Pennsylvania	17th Pennsylvania
19th Pennsylvania	21st Pennsylvania	22nd Penna.
Rimggold Btn.	1st Rhode Island	1st Tennessee
2nd Tennessee	3rd Tennessee	3rd Tn. Mtd. Inf
6th Tennessee	10th Tennessee	11th Tennessee
12th Tennessee	1st Texas	2nd Texas
1st Vermont	1st West Virginia	2nd West Virginia
3rd West Virginia	1st Wisconsin	2nd Wisconsin
4th Wisconsin	1st U.S.	2nd U.S.
3rd U.S.	4th U.S.	5th U.S.
6th U.S.	3rd U.S.C.T.	4th U.S.C.T.
5th U.S.C.T.	Upper Potomac Force	

Regiments Armed with Sharps Rifles During the War
Infantry

1st Connecticut (became 1st Ct. H. Artillery)	
2nd Connecticut	4th Connecticut
6th Connecticut	7th Connecticut
8th Connecticut	11th Connecticut
13th Connecticut	14th Connecticut
20th Connecticut	66th Illinois
113th Illinois	20th Indiana
11th Kentucky	11th Kentucky Mounted Inf.
12th Kentucky	Massachusetts S.S.
15th Massachusetts	3rd Michigan
5th Michigan	16th Michigan
17th Maine	1st Minnesota
8th Minnesota	26th Missouri
27th Missouri	2nd New Hampshire
3rd New Hampshire	5th New Hampshire
3rd New Jersey	30th New Jersey
2nd New York	5th New York
41st New York	76th New York
146th New York	151st New York
New York Ind. S.S.	38th Pennsylvania
42nd Pennsylvania	105th Pennsylvania
149th Pennsylvania	150th Pennsylvania
190th Pennsylvania	2nd Rhode Island
4th Vermont	4th Wisconsin
1st U.S. Sharpshooters	2nd U.S. Sharpshooters
1st U.S. Vet. Vols.	2nd U.S. Vet. Vols.
4th U.S. Vet. Vols.	5th U.S. Vet. Vols.
6th U.S. Vet. Vols.	2nd Indian Home Guard
37th U.S. Colored Troops	

Cavalry

1st Colorado	1st Illinois
13th Illinois	15th Illinois
1st Indiana	1st Iowa
3rd Iowa	5th Kansas
6th Kansas	7th Kansas

9th Kansas	11th Kansas
1st Louisiana	1st Maine
2nd Michigan	3rd Michigan
1st Minnesota	3rd Missouri
4th Missouri	7th Missouri
7th New York	14th New York
3rd Pennsylvania	11th Pennsylvania
2nd U.S.	

The last Sharps carbine delivered to the Ordnance Department in 1865 occurred on July 10 and cost $50. This carbine had been ordered to be given to the government of Denmark. On May 15 a Col. Racaloff from the Danish Legation in New York had requested one Sharps carbine with extractor and 1,000 metallic cartridges, which was granted by the Assistant Secretary of War Charles A. Dana.[54] With peace returning the future for the arms companies would be the metal cartridge arms which had been so successful in the war.

John M. Snively, Co. C, 7th Kansas Cavalry with Sharps carbine. Richard Carlile collection.

Sharps & Hankins

At about 8 a.m. on July 1, 1863, the advance element of Maj. Gen. A. P. Hill's Confederate infantry attacked Brig. Gen. John Buford's dismounted union cavalry located near Gettysburg. For over two hours the Union cavalry held back the Confederate assault until it was relieved by Union infantry. During this action part of one of Buford's cavalry regiments—the 9th New York Companies C, D, and H—were armed with Sharps & Hankins carbines. These three companies were the only members of Buford's cavalry division armed with the advanced metallic rimfire cartridges carbines. These weapons had been in the 9th New York inventory since late in 1862.[1]

The Sharps & Hankins story has its origin with Christian Sharps' departure from the Sharps Rifle Manufacturing Company in June 1854 after he had reached a final agreement with the company. This agreement of April 10 called for the company to pay Sharps a royalty of one dollar for every gun manufactured plus twenty-five cents for each lock made by the company. It also called for a cash payment of $4,000 and 400 Model 1852 Sharps carbines.[2] After receiving the last 200 carbines from the company on June 13 he departed for Philadelphia where he took up residence at 486 Green Street and established a small shop at 336 Franklin.

By the time of the outbreak of the war in April 1861 Sharps was in partnership with Ira B. Eddy and Nathan H. Bolles in the firm of C. Sharps and Company. From 1856 to 1864 the Sharps operations were located at the west side of 30th Street in West Philadelphia at the Wire Bridge. The four-story brick building measured 140 feet by 40 feet. On the factory's first floor were the heavy forging operations; the second floor was used for barrel making, third floor for tool making, and the fourth floor for the making of small parts as well as assembly.

In 1860 William C. Hankins, a woodworker by trade, joined the firm as superintendent of the rifle works. He brought much-needed additional capital to the business. In 1861 both Eddy and Bolles left the firm. The following year Hankins became a full partner, but it was not until 1863 that the firm's name was changed to Sharps & Hankins.[3]

The Sharps & Hankins models are covered by three of Christian Sharps' patents. In U.S. Patent No. 32,790 of July 9, 1861, Sharps asserts: "My invention relates to an improvement in breech-loading firearms in which a barrel or barrels arranged to slide to and fro on the stock are used; and my improvement consists in a device, described hereinafter, for locking and releasing the lever which operates the barrel."[4]

The portion of this patent covering the sliding of the barrel was rejected by the Patent Office as having been anticipated by his own patent No. 22,752 of January 25, 1859. This claim was allowed, however, on Sharps patent No. 2,482 reissued on February 24, 1867; U.S. Patent No. 32,899 dated July 23, 1861, covered the rear sight used on the Sharps & Hankins while the safety mechanism was patented on October 22, 1861, with U.S. Patent No. 33,546.

The Sharps & Hankins firearms feature a number of firsts for military arms, including:
* Separate firing pin within the receiver.
* A hammer safety mechanism to keep the hammer face from contacting the firing pin.
* An extractor system—a spring loaded catch in the frame to extract the cartridge and prohibit the forward movement of the cartridge case when the breech is open.

Sharps wasted little time after the outbreak of the war to have his rifle tested by the Navy Department. On July 20, 1861, Lt. Wainwright test fired a Sharps & Hankins rifle 500 times. The fifteen failures were caused by faulty rimfire ammunition. The defective ammunition was made of brass and the head of the cartridge burst in firing. The features of the rifle tested were:

Diameter of the Bore	.5635 inches
Length of Rifle	47.28 inches
Length of Barrel	32.80 inches
Diameter of Ball	.56 inches
Length of Ball	.91 inches[5]

Nine days later, on July 29, 1861, the Navy contracted with Christian Sharps for five hundred of these rifles with sabre bayonets at $36 each. The contract reads:

> Bureau of Ord & Nydro[6]
>
> Washington
> 29th July 1861
>
> Sir:
>
> You will please make and deliver with all practicable dispatch, at such places as the Bureau may hereafter designate, subject to the usual inspection before reception, the following quantities of Sharp's Breech loading Rifles patented in 1859:—
>
> (500) Five Hundred Rifles with sabre bayonets. Length of barrel thirty three (33) inches & caliber 52. Fifty Two Hundredths. It being understood that the price is to be ($36) thirty-six dollars per rifle complete; & likewise that the first lot of one hundred (100) are to be delivered in one week after six months from this

date, & the reminder at the same ratio each succeeding weeks.

You will at the same time deliver fifty-thousand (50,000) metal cased cartridges of the kind adapted to the rifles, at the rate of nineteen ($19) dollars per thousand.

>Very Respectfully
>Your Obt Sert
>Andrew A. Harwood
>Chief of Bureau

To Christian Sharps, Esq.
Washington

The first of these rifles did not arrive at the Philadelphia Navy Yard until about March 19, 1862, when 100 rifles were delivered. On April 16 Sharps was notified that the next delivery of 150 rifles was to be sent to New York, where they were received on April 28. Seven days later William Temple, assistant inspector of ordnance at the New York Navy Yard, was directed by Andrew Harwood, chief of naval ordnance, to notify Sharps & Hankins that it had to replace one rifle with a broken stock and some defective ammunition. The company was also to send the spare parts needed for these rifles.[7] The next delivery of 150 rifles was sent to the Boston Navy Yard on May 27 and paid for on July 5 at a cost to the Navy of $4,892.14.[8]

The last installment on this contract was made on June 28, 1862, when 100 rifles were delivered, this time at the Washington Navy Yard. The invoices for this lot show that the prices were set at:

100 rifles at $36 each	$3,600.00
10M cartridges @ $19	$190.00
Extra parts for rifles	$26.77
Total cost of Inventory Goods	$3,816.77[9]

Upon receipt of these last hundred rifles Lt. Comdr. W. W. Green at the Washington Navy Yard had them tested beginning August 30, 1862. The Sharps & Hankins rifles used during these rates were serial numbered 565, 554, 547 and 568. After the tests were completed Green submitted this conclusion, "I respectfully report the rifles as fit for service."[10]

On March 29 Sharps was notified that in addition to his previous order of July 29, he should send an additional 100 Sharps rifles patent 1859, together with the necessary spare parts and ammunition, to the Washington Navy Yard.[11] They were delivered in September 1862 along with 10,000 rimfire

Six hundred Sharps & Hankins M1861 rifles were delivered to the Navy in 1862. John McAuley collection.

The Sharps & Hankins rifle shown with the action open. Note that the entire barrel and forend slides forward on the grooved frame.

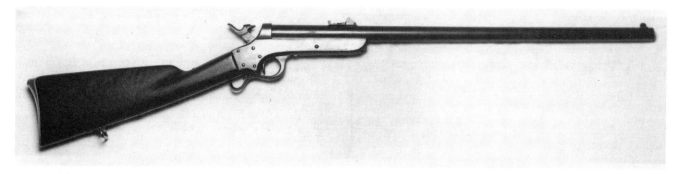

In September 1862 two hundred fifty M1861 Sharps & Hankins carbines were delivered to the Ordnance Department. Many of these carbines were issued to the 9th New York Cavalry and saw service at Gettysburg on the first day of the battle. SN 824. John McAuley collection.

cartridges. Payment was made on September 22 for $3,225.00. An error had been made in this payment, so Sharps was notified on October 29 to return the payment and a correct draft in the amount of $3,416.97 would be sent to him.[12] In December 7,000 Sharps & Hankins cartridges were directed to be sent to New York and 20,000 to Washington. The Washington order of December 24 states:

> Sir: In addition to previous orders the Bureau wishes you to send to the Ordnance Yard here, Twenty thousand (20,000) ball cartridges for the Sharps & Hankins rifles.[13]

The 600 Sharps & Hankins rifles received by September 1862 consisted of the "Old Model" (1861) with the firing pin in the hammer. The description of these .52 caliber rimfire (52 56) Sharps & Hankins cartridges rifles have an overall length of 47 5/8 inches and weigh 8 pounds, 8 ounces, with a two-piece black walnut stock. The 32 3/4-inch barrel is either blued or browned. It has an iron front sight and rear sight of the Sharps base tangent type, graduated to 800 yards with the base notched at one-hundred-yard intervals. A bayonet lug is found under the barrel. The barrel is held to the forestock by three solid oval barrel bands.

The receiver is marked on the right side: "SHARPS/HANKINS/PHILADA" and on the left side: "SHARPS/PATENT/1859." The serial number is found on the upper tang and all major parts. The receiver, hammer, lever, and tang are case-hardened. The butt plate is made of brass.

The sabre bayonet used with this rifle is twenty-five inches long and has a 20 1/4-inch blade marked "COLLINS & CO." and dated 1861. The bayonets were serial numbered with rifles.

On July 22, 1863, the Navy requested that Sharps & Hankins deliver to the New York Navy Yard 500 improved rifles plus 50,000 cartridges.[14] Interestingly, the company's response is that it had no rifles but could supply 500 carbines with short leather covers and equipped with side swivels. These are the 19-inch-barrel carbines.[15] The Navy accepted Sharps & Hankins' proposal and by early 1864 these 19-inch-barrel carbines were delivered at New York.

The Sharps & Hankins rifles were used by the Navy to arm the Marine guards aboard ship. They were also put to use on the gun boats operating on the Mississippi River. In 1863 sixty of these rifles were sent to St. Louis to be used on these boats.[16] These rifles remained in naval service throughout the war. As late as October 12, 1864, the Navy ordered 30,000 Sharps & Hankins rifle cartridges to be sent to the Philadelphia Navy Yard. Earlier, in April 1864, it had ordered 1,000 metallic cartridges for the Sharps & Hankins rifles plus spare parts to be sent to the *U.S.S. Wabash* located off of Charleston, South Carolina.

U.S. Navy Procurement of Sharps & Hankins Rifles[17]

Purchase Date	Kinds of Stores	Price
March 1862	100 S&H Rifles w/bayonets	$36
April 1862	150 S&H Rifles w/bayonets	$36
May 1862	150 S&H Rifles w/bayonets	$36
June 1862	100 S&H Rifles w/bayonets	$36
Sept. 1862	100 S&H Rifles w/bayonets	$36

Navy Carbines

In March 1862 Christian Sharps sent a carbine to the Washington Navy Yard for inspection. The inspectors were so impressed with the carbine that the Navy placed an order for 1,000 with leather-covered barrels. The price for the carbines was set at $30 and the ammunition at $22.50 per thousand. The March 26 contract reads in part:

> You will please manufacture for the Dept, one thousand (1,000) of Sharps carbines, Patent 1859, to conform in all respect to the model submitted, in leather cased barrel, caliber & spare parts at the price stated of thirty dollars ($30) per carbine, to be submitted to such inspection & proof as the Bureau may choose to direct prior to reception.
>
> You will likewise hold to the order of the Bureau (100) one hundred round of copper cased ammunition per carbines, at the stipulated price of twenty two dollars & fifty cent $22 50/100 per thousand.[18]

The first 250 carbines were delivered at the Philadelphia Navy Yard in September. In October Sharps was told to send half of the next 500 carbines to Boston and the balance to New York. These arms failed inspection and were returned to the company in December, although why the arms failed is not known. To complete the March 26 contract the company delivered 250 carbines to Philadelphia in March 1863 and additional 250 there in June plus 250 to the New York Navy Yard in June 1863.[19]

The company's second contract for carbines was issued on June 29, 1863. This order called for 1,000 Sharps & Hankins carbines and 100,000 ball cartridges to be sent to Boston consigned to Commodore J. B. Montgomery. The boxes were to be marked "Naval Ordnance." By the end of 1863 the Navy had placed eight more orders, totaling 1,898 carbines. The sizes of the orders ranged from fifty carbines for the Portsmouth Navy Yard to 500 for New York. Deliveries amounted to 2,543 carbines in 1863.[20]

The Navy had placed such a large number of orders for carbines that it appears to have lost track of the numbers ordered and the balance due. On January 15, 1864, the Navy wrote the Sharps & Hankins company requesting to know the balance of carbines still to be delivered. The company answered that 619 carbines were still due on the New York orders. As of February 19, 1864, the company listed outstanding orders of 300 carbines for New York; 370 for Boston; and 170 for Philadelphia.

To make the inspections more effective, the company was notified on October 29, 1863, that all future inspections would take place at the factory before delivery. When the company had carbines ready for inspection, it was to contact the Philadelphia Navy Yard and an inspector would be sent to the factory. During the balance of the year 775 carbines were inspected at the factory. The inspection reports of 1864 indicate the 3,655 carbines were accepted after being inspected. The following report of December 26, 1863, is typical of the reports submitted by the ordnance inspector:

Officers of the U.S.S. Mendota on the James River in 1864. On the large Parrott gun is a cartridge box and cutlass. The Sharps & Hankins carbines can be seen stored on the side of the ship between the two officers nearest the cannon. National Archives collection.

Phil. Navy Yard
Ordn. Dept., Dec. 26th, 1863
Sir:

I have to report that, in obedience to your order of the 22 inst., I have inspected two hundred and fifty-five (255) breech-loading Carbines at the manufactory of Messrs. Sharps & Hankins, at Fairmount, Philadelphia.

Each Carbine was fired eight times. Of the two thousand and forty (2040) cartridges used, only two (2) failed at the first fire, and they ignited on the second fire. I passed the two hundred and fifty five carbines as fit for service.

            Very respectfully
            Your Obedt servant
            H. S. Adams
            Ass't. Inspector of Ordnance
Lieut Cmdr. Irwin
Inspection of Ordnance
            Approved
            John Irwin
            Inspector of Ordnance[21]

In 1864 the Navy gave Sharps & Hankins eleven more orders for 2,550 carbines, all at the stated price of $30 each. The last wartime procurement was in answer to a Sharps & Hankins letter of January 23, 1865, saying the company had 1,000 carbines on hand for ready delivery. The Navy's response says, "The Bureau desires you to send to the Navy Yard, Philadelphia 200—two hundred—Sharps & Hankins Carbines—cal .52, with 20,000—twenty Thousand—Ball Cartridge for as subject to the usual inspection."[22] Payment was made a week later.

The final delivery of Sharps & Hankins carbines did not occur until two years after the war, when on July 7, 1867, six carbines were ordered by Capt. Wise. The order reads, in part:

> You will please furnish this Bureau with (6) six navy carbines of the most improved pattern with five thousand (5,000) cartridges.
>
> These arms are intended as a present for a foreign government, and you will therefore please have them packed in a neat black walnut box properly lined. The arms are to be such as heretofore furnished to the Navy.[23]

These carbines, along with six Spencer rifles, were presented to the Prime Minister of Siam in August. In accounting for payment of the last six carbines, they were itemized as follows:

  August 9, 1867
    6 Sharps & Hankins carbines $120.00
    5,000 metallic cartridges $26 per M   130.00
    Walnut case for guns   12.00
        Total Cost $262.00[24]

The following charts shows the contracts and deliveries by year for the Sharps & Hankins arms.

U.S. Navy's Contracts and Deliveries for Sharps & Hankins[25]

Year	Rifles Contracts	Rifles Deliveries	Carbines Contracts	Carbines Deliveries
1861	500	—	—	—
1862	100	600	1,000	250
1863	—	—	2,898	1,550
1864	—	—	2,550	4,680
1865	—	—	200	200
1867	—	—	6	6
Totals	600	600	6,654	6,686

U.S. Navy Orders for Sharp & Hankins Carbines

Date	Qty	Destination	Price
3-29-62	1,000	—	$30
6-23-63	1,000	Boston Navy Yard	30
7-27-63	500	New York Navy Yard	30
8-4-63	50	Philadelphia Navy Yard	30
8-27-63	50	Portsmouth Navy Yard	30
9-14-63	300	New York Navy Yard	30
9-15-63	50	Washington Navy Yard	30
10-29-63	98	Naval Academy	30
11-13-63	350	New York Navy Yard	30
11-21-63	500	New York Navy Yard	30
2-1-64	300	Philadelphia Navy Yard	30
2-9-64	200	New York Navy Yard	30
5-10-64	250	New York Navy Yard	30
6-23-64	100	Philadelphia Navy Yard	30
6-28-64	500	New York Navy Yard	30
9-2-64	200	Portsmouth Navy Yard	30
9-5-64	100	Philadelphia Navy Yard	30
10-20-64	300	Philadelphia Navy Yard	30
10-24-64	100	Philadelphia Navy Yard	30
11-21-64	300	New York Navy Yard	30
12-19-64	200	Philadelphia Navy Yard	30
1-23-65	200	Philadelphia Navy Yard	30
7-7-67	6	Portsmouth Navy Yard	20

The carbines delivered to the Navy were of the improved New Model (1862). The basic difference between this model and the previous model (1861) was the design of the hammer and firing pin. The Old Model had the firing pin in the hammer while the New Model had a floating firing pin in the rear of the receiver. It also had a stringer mainspring and added an oil hole to the extractor well. The marking on the carbines are the same as the rifles. The barrel length on most of the Navy carbines was 23 5/8 inches and covered with leather cover. At the muzzle is an iron ring to which the front sights are mounted.

In addition to these carbines, the Navy also bought carbines with 19-inch barrels, short leather covers, and added side swivels. As the letter of July 23, 1863, said, Sharps & Hankins was willing to supply 500 of these carbines on the New York contract of the day before. As of September 1865 the New York Navy Yard had on hand about 100 of these 19-inch carbines in need of repairs while the Washington Navy Yard had 200 of the 19-inch barrel carbines, also in need of repairs.[26]

In early 1864 five hundred of the 19-inch cavalry style carbines were delivered to the New York Navy Yard. This navy carbine is SN 6002. Steve Selenfriend collection.

A close-up of carbine SN 6002. Note the post war naval anchor and U. S. on frame.

The Sharps & Hankins carbines saw extensive sea service during the war. In September 1863 the factory was notified that the 300 carbines to be sent to New York were scheduled for the West Gulf Blockading Squadron. Two months later they were notified that 350 carbines and 35,000 cartridges were being sent to California. In January 1864 ninety-eight carbines and 8,000 cartridges were sent to the Naval Academy at Newport, Rhode Island. June 1864 saw 100 Sharps & Hankins carbines being issued to the Navy ships *Suwanee, Shamokin, Nina, Pinta* and *Yazoo*. Later in the year, 40 carbines were sent to Erie, Pennsylvania, for the U.S. Steamer *Michigan* and four were to be issued to the *U.S.S. Shamrock* by Comdr. Lynch from Norfolk, Virginia. Many of the carbines were sent to Lynch, who was inspector of ordnance in Norfolk, Virginia. In November 1864 three hundred fifty barrels of powder and 300 Sharps & Hankins carbines plus 30,000 cartridges were sent from the Philadelphia Navy Yard to Lynch in Norfolk. The last 200 carbines received by the Navy in January 1865 were also directed to be sent to Lynch in Norfolk in February 1865.[27]

Army Procurement and Field Service

In May 1862 Sharps contacted the Ordnance Department, hoping to get a contract for his carbine. On May 31 he was notified that while the Ordnance Department needed good carbines for immediate issue, his price was too high and the department was therefore declining the offer. Sharps reduced the price from $30 to $25, an offer that was accepted in July. On July 22 Maj. T. T. S. Laidley at the Frankford Arsenal was told to buy 250 Sharps & Hankins carbines. Laidely's instructions read:

> Ordnance Office, War Department,
> Washington, July 22, 1862
>
> SIR: The Secretary of War having accepted the offer of Messrs. Sharp & Hankins, of Philadelphia, for 250 of their improved carbines, you will please inspect and receive each of them as you may deem suitable for the service. You will also procure from these gentlemen two hundred cartridges for each arm, a peculiar kind being required. The price named by these gentlemen in their offer is $25 per arm; $20 per thousand for the cartridges. It is understood that suitable appendages and packing boxes will be supplied by the makers without additional cost to this department.
> Respectfully, your obedient servant,
> J. W. RIPLEY
> Brigadier General, Chief of Ordnance.
> Major T. T. S. LAIDLEY,
> United States Arsenal, Bridesburg.
> A true copy:
> S. V. BENET
> Brevet Lieutenant Colonel U.S.A., Commanding[28]

Laidley placed the order with Sharps & Hankins six days later. Delivery was made on September 9 and payment sent to the company on the 22nd. Most of the carbines delivered were probably the old model (1861) with firing pin located in the hammer. These carbines have a 23 3/8-inch barrel without the leather covering and also manufactured without a saddle bar and ring. The 600 Navy rifles plus these 250 carbines brings the serial numbers on the Old Model (1861) to about 900.

It would be a year before the next Army order was placed for the Sharps & Hankins carbine. The order of September 12, 1863, called for 1,200 carbines—Sharp's new pattern at $25 each plus 480,000 metallic primed cartridges at $22.50 per thousand. Deliveries were to be made within six weeks.[29] All 1,200 carbines were received by November 5, 1863. As of the date of this delivery only thirty-seven Sharps & Hankins carbines were listed in storage at the Washington Arsenal.[30] These improved pattern carbines delivered to the Army were similar to the Navy carbine but without the leather covering on the barrel and the iron ring at the muzzle.

As of June 1863 three companies of the 9th New York Cavalry were listed as having about seventy Sharps & Hankins carbines while Company C of the 11th New York Cavalry was shown to have thirty-five Sharps & Hankins carbines. The balance of the 11th New York was armed with only Colt revolvers and sabres.

At about 8:30 a.m. on June 27, 1863, Maj. Remington with about 100 men of Companies B and C of the 11th New York Cavalry encountered the advance pickets of the 6th Virginia Cavalry near Fairfax Courthouse, Virginia. These Confederate pickets were the advance elements of Wade Hampton's cavalry. Remington charged the pickets and captured nearly half of them before being forced to cut his way through the major part of Hampton's cavalry, which quickly came to the rescue. In this "spirited encounter" as Gen. J.E.B. Stuart wrote in his report, the 11th New York casualties amounted to four killed, fourteen wounded and fifty-five missing. Remington returned to camp with only eighteen men. Stuart's report also noted that in addition to the capture of several prisoners, they also took several horses, arms and equipment. It is likely that a few of Company C's Sharps & Hankins carbines were also captured by Hampton's cavalry.[31] Within the next couple of months the 11th New York was fully armed with Burnside carbines.

As of September 30, 1863, the 9th New York Cavalry was listing 123 Sharps & Hankins carbines on hand. Col. William Sackett of the 9th had the following comments on the effectiveness of the Sharps & Hankins: "Could the spring that holds the guard on Sharps & Hankins carbines and the catch that draws back the copper after firing be strengthened that arm would certainly be better than Sharps, Burnsides or Starrs, as the ammunition never dampens or breaks and no capping being required. The rapidity of fire makes it a very fine skirmishing weapon." A week after this report Sackett wrote the Chief of Ordnance requesting addition Sharps & Hankins for his command:

> Headquarters 9th N.Y. Cav.
> Oct. 6, 1863
>
> Colonel:
> I have the honor to state that this regiment is partially armed with Sharps & Hankins carbines and am informed that there were some at the arsenal. I would respectfully ask if such is the case and if I can obtain them by making the proper requisitions.
>
> Very Respectfully
> Your obedient servant
> Wm. Sackett
> Col Comdg 9th N.Y. Cav.[32]

The response from the Ordnance Department was at the present time there were no carbines on hand.

The September 12 contract for 1,200 carbines was to fill Orders For Supply No. 7,160 directed for Capt. Francis J. Shunk, chief of ordnance, Department of the Gulf. When Sackett requested Sharps & Hankins carbines, a second inquiring was made to the company for 1,200 more carbines. This Order For Supplies No. 8,322 was to be sent to Capt. James G. Benton at the Washington Arsenal. The manufacturer was unable to supply the arms until January 1864, therefore the Ordnance Department did not place the second order for 1,200 carbines. It does appear that some of the 1,200 carbines scheduled for the Gulf were directed to the Washington Arsenal and issued to the 9th New York in late 1863 or early 1864. During the 1864 Virginia campaign, Companies, B, C, D, E, F, G, K, and L of the 9th were armed with Sharps & Hankins carbines while the rest of the regiment had Sharps carbines.

In the 1864 campaign eight Medals of Honor were awarded to the 9th New York Cavalry, five of which were presented to individuals whose companies were armed with Sharps & Hankins. Two of the medals were received by Capt. John F. Rutherford of Company L. The first was given for the charge he led at Yellow Tavern on May 11 in which ninety prisoners were taken. The second medal was award for action at Hanovertown, Virginia, two weeks later on May 27.[33] It was at Yellow Tavern where J.E.B. Stuart was mortally wounded. In the cavalry fight near Trevilian Station, Virginia, on June 11, 1864, the 25-year-old commander of the 9th, William Sackett, was mortally wounded while leading his regiment into action. He died three days later. For his wartime action Sackett was given the brevet of Brigadier General, U.S. Volunteers, dated March 13, 1865.[34]

In March 1864 the 11th New York Cavalry was transferred to the Department of the Gulf. The regiment was armed only with Burnside carbines until September 21, 1864, when Companies C and M were issued Sharps & Hankins carbines.[35] As of September 30 they were listing ninety-one Sharps & Hankins and 351 Burnsides.[36] By April 1865 the 11th was listed as having 257 Sharps & Hankins and 190 Burnside.[37] See the serial numbers section.)

Two other regiments are known to have received a few Sharps & Hankins carbines. One of these units was the 10th New York Cavalry. During 1864's first-quarter reports from the field Capt. Benjamin F. Sceva, Company F, 10th New York Cavalry, said he found the Sharps & Hankins a most durable arm for cavalry use.[38] Sceva became a lieutenant colonel of the 10th in March 1865 and was wounded at Dinwiddie Courthouse on the 31st and died of those wounds. How many Sharps & Hankins carbines were in this regiment is not known. The other regiment was the 3rd New York Cavalry. In March 1863 while in the Kinston, North Carolina, area of operation Company A was listing Sharp & Hankins carbines in its regimental company property books. (See the serial number section of this book.) In August 1863 the state adjutant general for New York, Gen. Perrine, was interested in obtaining the new Sharps carbine for metallic primed cartridges for the 2nd New York Veteran Volunteer Cavalry, then in the process of being formed. In February 1864 the 2nd New York Veteran Volunteer Cavalry was sent to the Department of the Gulf and may have received some of the Sharps & Hankins carbines sent to Capt. Shunk for the Army of the Gulf.

On November 23, 1863, Secretary of War Edwin Stanton ordered that a caliber of .50 be adopted as the standard rimfire cartridge for all future contracts. Maj. Alexander B. Dyer at the Springfield Armory was directed to conduct experiments to determine the best powder charge for this cartridge. The next day the chief of ordnance sent the following letter to Merwin & Bray for the Ballard, to A.P. Bruff for the Joslyn, and to Sharps & Hankins:

This Department having adopted a general plan for Cavalry Carbines has decided that all such carbines as may be ordered in the future shall conform to that plan, the principle features of which are that the barrel shall be twenty-two inches long, with a caliber of half an inch (.50) and that the weight of the arms shall be not over eight nor under six pounds. With a view of making experiments to determine the best charge for these arms you will be pleased to make for this Department with least possible delay, six of your Patent Carbines, on the foregoing principles: The chamber of each one to be counter bored to fifty-two hundredths of an inch (.52) and of the proper length to receive cartridges as follows:

    1 for a 35 grain Copper Cartridge
    1 for a 40 grain Copper Cartridge
    1 for a 45 grain Copper Cartridge
    1 for a 50 grain Copper Cartridge
    1 for a 55 grain Copper Cartridge
    1 for a 60 grain Copper Cartridge

Be pleased to signify your acceptance or non-acceptance of this order, and if you accept please state the time when the six carbines will be furnished and the cost of each."[39]

Sharps & Hankins' response to this letter read:

This order we accept and will make the carbines in two weeks from time of receiving notice, at thirty five dollars each, providing you approve of our suggested modification. We will take .52 as the standard for counterbore, in consequence of which the case of the cartridge must necessarily be .51 in order to give it the proper amount of forcing. The calibre including depth of rifling will be .50, the ball of course will be same.[40]

These six carbines were sent to the master storekeeper at Springfield Armory in late December.

Later Stanton directed that .44 caliber rimfire cartridge should also be tested against the .50 caliber cartridge. To this end the Ordnance Department sent Sharps & Hankins a request that in addition to the carbines previously contracted for, the company was to send to Major Dyer:

Six carbines of .44 barrel, .52 chamber, .46 ball, with 1,000 rounds of cartridges of your own make for each gun, or such as you can prepare with space allotted by the lever. Please prepare, with as much despatch as possible, four (or six if you can get the cartridge into the bore in these of 55 or 60 grains) prepared for a ball of 4375 diameter, and in which the diameter of the chamber will be .44, for a ball arranged thus the bore will be .42. No cartridges will be required. Please advise this office when you can forward each lot. The last one is wanted at as early a day as possible, and will be sent to Major Dyer, who will advise you of the depth of counter boring for each of the changes required.[41]

On these two requests a total of seventeen carbines was delivered by January 1864. (Note that the ledger books do not reflect these deliveries until January 1865). Payment of $595 was sent to the company for the carbines plus $384 for the 12,800 cartridges which they had provided. Dyer performed tests on both the .44 and .50 caliber cartridge but by November had settled on the .50 caliber as the standard caliber for all future carbine contracts.

During the war the Ordnance Department purchased 1,001,000 Sharps & Hankins rimfire cartridges at a cost of $27,402.00. These cartridges were 1.67 inches overall, with the length of the case being 1.15 inches. The bullet diameter was .54 and weighed 450 grains. The powder charge was 45 grains.

Sharps & Hankins made one last proposal to sell carbines to the Army. On February 6, 1864, the company contacted Stanton offering to sell 2,000 carbines at $27 each. The Ordnance Department countered with an offer of $24 for 1,000 carbines, an offer the company rejected, citing the increased costs of materials and labor. It is likely that they were sold instead to the Navy since the Navy was currently buying arms from the company at $30 each.

In September 1864 the Sharps & Hankins, Spencer, Sharps, and Joslyn carbines were tested for rapidity of fire at the Washington Arsenal. The results show that the Sharps & Hankins carbine was fired 14 times in 1 minute and 37 seconds while a Spencer was fired 14 times in 1 minute and 7 seconds. The Sharps carbine was the slowest in that it was fired 14 times with percussion caps in 2 minutes and 15 seconds. The Joslyn results were 14 shots in 1 minute 53 seconds.[42]

At the close of war in the spring of 1865 the Sharps & Hankins carbines were turned in by the cavalry units as the men were mustered out of service. In the Navy both the carbine and rifle remained in sea service until early 1870 when they were replaced by the Remington rolling-block carbines and rifles. As of December 1, 1866, the various navy yards inventoried these quantities of Sharps & Hankins carbines and rifles:

Location	*Carbines*	*Rifles*
Portsmouth, New Hampshire	321	
Boston	537	214
New York	1,066	
Philadelphia	495	
Washington	241	
Norfolk	539	
Mare Island, Calif	237	
TOTAL	3,436	214

Earlier in the year the Ordnance Department was listing nearly 500 Sharps & Hankins carbines at the following locations:[43]

Date	*Location*	*Serviceable*	*Unserviceable*
5-10-66	Springfield Armory	12	6
5-14-66	St. Louis Arsenal	—	190
5-22-66	Baton Rouge Arsenal	40	14
7-1-66	New York Ord. Agcy	1	71
7-10-66	Washington Arsenal	53	104
	Total	104	385

Most of the 6,654 Sharps & Hankins improved M1862 carbines delivered to the Navy were of this type with the 24 inch leather covered barrels. SN 11,199. Steven Selenfriend collection.

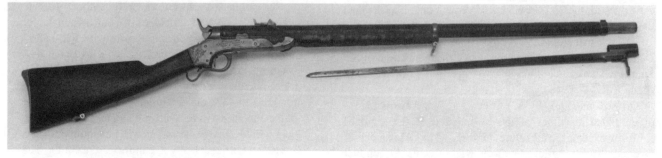

An unusual Sharps & Hankins old M1861 rifle with leather cover and with bayonet. Steven Selenfriend collection.

In the summer of 1868 the Navy received numerous reports of small arms performance aboard ship. The reports came from as far away as South America and the Far East. In a report dated June 20 Lt. Comdr. Stuyvesant of the *U.S.S. Wateree* gave the results of a test by the Marine guard while off the coast of Peru. The Sharps & Hankins rifles used in the trials were fired at a distance of 100 yards with these results:

Number of shots fired	339
Number of hits	85
Number of hits within six inches of bull's eye	13

Stuyvesant concluded his report with, "The Sharps & Hankins rifle is easily comprehended by the men and seems well adapted to the wants of the service."[44] In August the *U.S.S. Piscataqua* located near Japan recorded out of 380 shots fired with a Sharps & Hankins carbine at a distance of 100 yards, 122 hit the target.[45]

By the fall of 1869 the Navy had adopted the Remington rolling-block design as the standard Navy arm. These new 50/70 centerfire cartridge arms made the rest of the Navy's inventory of small arms obsolete, so the rest were quickly sold off. On October 18, 1869, the New York firm of Schuyler, Hartley & Graham was notified that the Washington Navy Yard had for sale fifty-three Sharps & Hankins rifles with bayonets and fifty-seven Sharps .56 caliber rifles at $15 each. A year later, on October 7, 1870, the New York Navy Yard listed the following items for sale:

4,000	Sharps & Hankins carbines	$12 each
560	Spencer Rifles	20 each
5,369	cal. .69 Plymouth Rifles	6 each
1,164	cal. .58 Rifle Muskets	6 each

A month later the price had dropped to $9 for the Sharps & Hankins carbines and $5 for the Plymouth rifles. The cartridges for the Sharps & Hankins were listed at $18 per thousand and the Plymouth rifle cartridges at $14 per thousand.[46]

Most of the Army's extra Sharps & Hankins carbines were sold from the Washington Arsenal and New York Agency between May 1875 and June 2, 1879. During this period 767 carbines were sold at prices ranging from 75 cents to $4.55 each.[47] As late as August 1902 seven carbines were sold to W. Stokes Kirk of Philadelphia for $1.10 each; one was sold to Nathan Spering for 62 cents by the New York Arsenal.[48]

The operations at the Sharps & Hankins factory ended in 1867 and all stock was sold by early 1868. In late 1867 William Hankins left the firm and the name was changed to C. Sharps & Co. After 1870 Christian Sharps left Philadelphia and moved in 1871 to Vernon, Connecticut, where he remained until his death from tuberculosis on March 12, 1874. He left his wife Sarah, daughter Satella, and son Leon Stewart Sharps. Sharps' estate was valued at $341.25.

Sergeant Frank A. Fletcher
Company G, 2nd New Hampshire Volunteer Infantry
Collection of Michael J. McAfee.

Unidentified, Co. A, 151st New York Volunteer Infantry
(Bowen's Independent Rifles)
Collection of Michael J. McAfee.

Sharps In The Sea Service

A Sharps was first introduced to the sea service in October 1850 when a Sharps carbine was tested at the Marine Barracks in Washington, D.C. The test trials were conducted by Bvt. Capt. Ansill. Ansill concluded that the Sharps was the best breech-loader that he had ever used but did not feel there was a need at the present time to issue them for sea service. It would be three years before the Navy bought its first Sharps. Despite this inauspicious beginning the Sharps would be part of the sea service arsenal of small arms for the next twenty years.

During the summer of 1853 the New York Navy Yard was busy outfitting a number of ships for expedition to the north Pacific Ocean. Capt. Ringgold and Lt. Rogers led the expedition. They first traveled to Hong Kong and Japan, then continued to the Bering Strait and the Aleutian Islands before returning in 1855. A letter written aboard the *U.S.S. Vincennes* at the start of the expedition is of interest to the Sharps story. It reads:

> U.S. Ship *Vincennes*
> Simons Bay, Sept. 23, 1853
> Sir:
> The following is a list of small arms on board of this ship, and delivered by me to this squadron:
>
> 88 Jenks Carbines
> 4 Flint Muskets
> 94 Pistols
> 135 Cutlasses
> 50 Revolving Pistols
> 49 Sharps Rifles
> Deliveries to the *John P. Kennedy*
> 10 Sharps Rifles
> Deliveries to the *Brig. Perry*
> 1 Sharps Rifle
>
> I am Sir Very Respectfully
> Your Obt. Servt.
> James C. Davies
> Gunner[1]

Com. C. Ringgold
Comdg. Ex. Expedition to
North Pacific Ocean

The sixty Sharps rifles identified in this letter were actually M1851 Sharps carbines. These carbines can be readily identified with the "USN" stamped on the buttplate. The record is unclear when the Navy obtained these carbines but it was probably in August or September 1853.

On September 7, 1853, the Navy asked the Sharps Rifle Manufacturing Company to send three carbines for inspection. The letter states, "You are requested to send to this Bureau three of Sharps carbines and appendages with a bill of their cost and also a statement of the price for which 250, 500, 750 or 1,000 could be delivered at one of our navy yards subject to such inspection as may be ordered by the Bureau, in case any should be wanted for the Navy."[2]

Five days later Sharps company president Palmer wrote that 250 Sharps rifle carbines with Sharps primers (M1852) would sell for $30 each and that 1,000 were priced at $27.75 each. In both cases the appendages were extra. Palmer also writes that the Sharps carbine equipped with Maynard tape primers (M1851) was being discontinued.[3] The three Sharps carbines were quickly sent to the Washington Navy Yard for trials. During the tests one of the carbines was fired 51 times, then became so clogged at the breech that it was impossible to move. Even with this problem the board's opinion was that a few carbines should be purchased for actual service. Due to budget constraints the Navy didn't contact the Sharps factory until 1856. Early that year Lt. John A. Dahlgren wrote the company asking for a rifle and a carbine for inspection and was sent one M1853 rifle and a carbine. In February Dahlgren asked permission from Capt. Henry W. Morris, chief of the Bureau of Ordnance and Hydrography, to buy a small number of breech-loaders. Permission was granted and a fund of $10,000 was set aside for their procurement.

On March 14, 1856, Dahlgren wrote Palmer that the Navy would place an order for 150 Sharps rifles at $36 each. Dahlgren's letter to Palmer said in part:

> Please furnish for the use of the Navy, 150 of the Sharps rifles according to sample sent by you to this office, including rod, brush, cone wrench, screwdriver, extra cone, cartridge stick, ball mould and with the following exceptions, viz.
> The U.S. Navy nipple is to be substituted for your own.
> The Maynard Primer is to be substituted for the Sharp Primer.
> Please send 100 rounds of ammunition and 300 primers for rifles.

One hundred of these rifles are to be delivered within 20 days—50 at New York and 50 at Norfolk.[4]

In addition to the payment of $36 for the rifle and appendages, the price for ammunition was set at $15 per thousand rounds and primers at $1 per thousand. On March 19 he again wrote Palmer saying that the Navy would give fifty days for delivery of the rifles, and that he did not wish to place an order for any carbines at this time. Dahlgren goes on to say that a "ship leaving within 30 days for station infested with pirates and your arm might be called on to exhibit its capacity."[5] Palmer made his official acceptance on March 29. At the time of this order, Dahlgren had also placed an order for 150 Perry carbines at $25 each. Only fifty carbines were delivered on Perry's contract.

In an April 24, 1856, letter from Dahlgren to Palmer, the Navy asked that fifty of the 150 Sharps rifles ordered on March 14 be furnished with the Rollin White's self-cocking device. This invention of Whites'—U.S. Patent No. 12,529, March 15, 1855—was an attempt to automatically cock the hammer through the operation of the lever. Dahlgren's letter continues by saying, "The Merrimac leaves in a week for sea and it is highly desirable that some of the Sharps rifles should go with her.[6]

During this period of time, April 1856, the Sharps factory had completed 300 of the Army's order for 400 carbines; the complete order was ready by May 15.

As of June 18 the Navy still had not received its Sharps and it was not until June 23 that Palmer was able to write Dahlgren at the Washington Naval Yards that the 150 rifles contracted for were nearly ready to be shipped.

Finally, on August 28, 1856, Palmer was able to tell Dahlgren that 100 of these rifles had been sent to Washington and the remaining fifty with the White device would be sent in the course of a week. In addition, Sharps was willing to sell the Naval Department an additional fifty rifles. On September 3 Dahlgren passed this offer of an additional fifty Sharps rifles to the chief of ordnance, Capt. Ingraham. Getting the approval for the additional fifty rifles, Dahlgren wrote Palmer on September 9 that he had the authority to accept them. He gave this order even though the March 14 order had still not arrived.

Shortly after the September 9 correspondence between the Navy and Palmer, the 150 rifles arrived at the Washington Navy Yard. On September 24 Dahlgren was able to write to Palmer and state that the first 100 rifles had been inspected, were accepted, and that payment would be sent. The fifty with the White self-cocking arrangement were then under examination. In addition, the last fifty rifles ordered on September 9 still had not been received as of the 24th. In accounting for payment on the 100 rifles, they are itemized as follows:

100 Sharps Rifles with appendage	$3600.00
15 Packing boxes	37.50
50 Maynard Primer boxes	50.50
15 Cartridges boxes	232.50
Total Cost for 100 rifles	$3920.50[7]

Up to this point the Sharps factory had been late on its orders but had received payment on all rifles that had been inspected. This trend was to change with Dahlgren's letter of October 17, when he had to report that only thirty-one of the fifty rifles ordered on September 9 had passed inspection and would be paid for. Eighteen of the nineteen that had not been approved had breech-plate screws broken off just at the triggerplate; the remaining one had a crack across the sliding breech-plate. Palmer asked for clarification for the reasons they were rejected and received this answer, "it is the front vertical screw which cuts the stock immediately in rear of breech clean through to the trigger plate and right angle to the hammer screw."[8]

As if this letter wasn't bad enough, Palmer received further bad news on October 24 when he was notified that only twelve of the fifty rifles with the White device had passed inspection and would be paid for at $36 each. Of the thirty-eight that did not pass inspection, twenty-six did not allow the chamber to open enough to receive the charge and in many others the springs for the self-cocking arrangement were too weak. Therefore, in a span of a week, Palmer had learned that only forty-three of the last 100 Sharps rifles would be paid for. Delays on the delivery of the British order and fifty-seven out of a hundred rifles rejected by the U.S. Navy created a real problem for John Palmer. The Navy did, however, sympathize with his dilemma and allowed the Sharps to be returned to the company for corrections so they would meet the inspection requirements. On March 15, 1857, the nineteen rifles rejected on October 19 were returned and accepted. And finally, on June 5, 1857, the thirty-eight Sharps rifles made with the White device were accepted and paid for at $36 each after the device was removed.[9]

Dimensions of the .52 calibre rifle are an overall length of 44 1/4 inches and weigh nine pounds. The case-hardened lockplate is fitted with the Maynard tape-primer. The primer door is marked "EDWARD MAYNARD/PATENTEE/ 1845." The lockplate is unmarked except for the fifty made with the Rollin White device which are marked "ROLLIN WHITE'S/PATENT/1855." The forestock and buttstock are black walnut. The buttplate, patchbox and barrel band are made of brass.

The 28 1/4-inch round barrel is fitted for the bayonet. The long-range rear sight is graduated to 800 yards. The barrel is marked "SHARP'S RIFLE/MANUFG. CO/ HARTFORD CONN." The tang is marked "SHARPS'/ PATENT/1848" with the serial number directly to the rear of this marking.

By June 1857 the Sharps factory had completed its British contract for the Model 1855. Because he had carbines left over, on June 17 Palmer wrote to Ingraham to see if the Navy would be interested in buying the Sharps carbine. Ingraham's reply of June 30 states:

> With the sanction of the Secretary of Navy, the Bureau will purchase from you, to be delivered at the Navy Yard Brooklyn, New York, subject to inspection and approval 100 of Sharps Rifle carbines, with

spare parts and appendages complete, to be paid for at the price named in your letter of the 17th instant to the Navy Department, viz $25 each. If accepted how soon for deliveries.[10]

Three days later the Sharps factory answered that 100 carbines would be ready for delivery on July 8 and recommended that the inspection be made at the Sharps factory in Hartford. The letter continues, saying that the appendages are in addition to the $25 price quoted in their June 17 letter and that they could supply ammunition packed in boxes containing 1,000 cartridges each.[11] Since the Navy Department already had Comdr. Steven C. Rowan in Hartford to inspect Colt revolvers then on order, it sent him across town to the Sharps factory to inspect the Sharps carbines as well.[12]

The U.S. Navy Model 1855 Sharps carbines Rowan inspected were stamped with the letters "U.S.N." on the brass buttplate. Stamped on the patchbox is "I/SCR/1857" which stands for "Inspection/S.C. Rowan/1857." They are .577 caliber with 18-inch barrels and a British-type rear sight. The barrel band is brass and there is no marking on the barrel. The Maynard primer door on the lockplate had the Maynard patent of 1845 and the breech tang is stamped "SHARPS/PATENT/1848" with a serial number to the rear. The 100 Navy M1855 Sharps carbines are found in the serial number range of 20,000 to 26,000. They are also equipped with a 2 1/2-inch sling swivel bar.

When the *U.S.S. Plymouth* sailed from Norfolk, Virginia, in June 1858, the M1855 rifles were aboard. During the period 1857-1860, many of the Sharps carbines were being used by the Marines. In June 1860 the Navy ordered 20,000 ball cartridges for the M1855 Sharps rifle be sent to the Norfolk Navy Yard, and six months later an additional 3,000 cartridges were delivered to the Portsmouth Navy Yard.[13] The reason they were delivered to Portsmouth was because the *U.S.S. Macedonian* was being outfitted for sea service. Eighty Sharps rifles (M1855) had been sent from Boston for the *Macedonian*. However, when they arrived it was found that 32 of them were actually carbines (M1855)—"short barrels without bayonets."[14]

Over two years passed before more Sharps rifles were ordered. In early September 1859 the Navy asked Palmer at what price would the Sharps factory furnish the Navy with rifles. In response Palmer wrote on September 6 that the price would be $37.50 each. Finding this price acceptable on September 9, 1859, the Navy contracted with John Palmer for 900 Sharps .56-caliber rifles with sword bayonet and scabbard at that price. The sword bayonets were to be manufactured by Ames Manufacturing Company of Chicopee, Massachusetts. On this same date the Navy also ordered 500 Joslyn percussion rifles and 100 Colt revolving rifles. The Sharps contract states:

> The Bureau will receive from you to be delivered at the Navy Yard Washington within four months from this date, nine hundred of Sharps rifles, with sword bayonet and scabbard, cone wrench and screwdriver, brush, and throng, rod cartridge stick, extra cone and primer spring for each arm, and one ball mould for every five arms—The caliber to be 0.58 and the length of barrel 30 inches as stated in the letter to you from the Bureau of the 9th ultimo. The whole to be subject to a rigid inspection in the Ordnance Department of said yard, all that pass a satisfactory inspection will be paid for at a rate of $37.50 each. A pattern or dimension of the sword bayonet will soon be furnished you.[15]

It would be over a year before the first delivery was made. On November 5, 1860, the Navy wrote Palmer that the Washington Navy Yard had taken delivery of 300 Sharps Navy rifles. These and all later deliveries were packed ten rifles per arms chest. Eleven days later the Navy received an additional 210 rifles. The Philadelphia Navy Yard was to receive 120 Sharps rifles on November 20. (The serial numbers of these 630 Sharps Navy rifles are found in the serial number section of this book.) These rifles were not listed in the Navy accounts payable ledgers until the following month. On December 13 Dahlgren wrote Capt. Franklin Buchanan, chief of Naval Ordnance at the Washington Navy Yard, that he had inspected the first 300 Sharps rifles. These rifles were .56 caliber with a 30-inch barrel and fitted for the sabre bayonet. In his report Dahlgren says that the bullet used with these .56 caliber rifles weighed 550 grains and used seventy grains of powder.[16] While Dahlgren found the recoil strong it was not excessive. Two more deliveries were received in 1861 with the last lot of 120 rifles being received on April 13, 1861. In all, 900 rifles were delivered on the September 9 contract.[17] Most of these .56-caliber Navy Sharps rifles were manufactured in the 33,000 to 34,000 serial number range.

In early 1860 one of the improved NM 1859 Sharps rifles was sent to the Marine Barracks, Washington, D.C. From the Marine Barracks on February 6, 1st Lt. John Green, U.S.M.C., sent a report to Col. John Harris, commandant of the Marine Corps. The report outlined the test results of the Sharps rifle and the M1855 rifle musket in use by the Marine Corps. In the trials Green selected a recruit who had never loaded or fired either arm. In two minutes the recruit loaded and fired the rifle musket four times and only hit the target once. In the same amount of time the recruit fired the Sharps nine times and hit the target eight times. At distances ranging from 100 to 450 yards, the recruit hit the target 20 out of 60 rounds with the rifle musket while with the Sharps he hit the target 53 out of 67 times. Green concludes his report by recommending its adoption by the Marine Corps. The .56-caliber Sharps rifles were quickly placed on board two ships being outfitted for naval service. Eighty Sharps rifles were delivered to the *Mississippi* and 70 for the *Vincennes*.[18] Even with these deliveries the ships still needed 390 revolvers, 330 muskets and 550 Sharps rifles plus 30,000 cartridges. Sharps were also used to replace the damaged Jenks carbines on the *St. Lawrence*. In early May 1861, 200 Sharps rifles were sent from New York to Boston while the Boston Navy Yard also received an additional eighty Sharps and 50,000 .56-caliber cartridges from the Washington Navy

Sharps in the Sea Service

In July 1857 one hundred .577 cal. M1855 carbines were purchased by the Navy. SN 21,220. John McAuley collection.

U.S.N. stamped on the buttplate of the July 1857 carbine procurement.

The patchbox stamped I/SCR/1857 were inspected by Commander Steven C. Rowan.

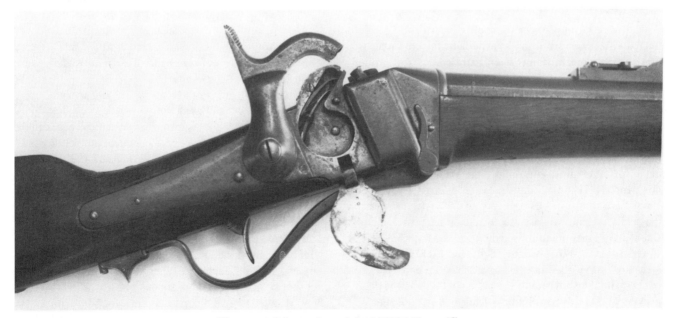

Close-up of the action of the M1855 Navy rifle.

Yard. During this period seventy rifles were sent to Philadelphia from Washington. Even with these transfers of Sharps to the various yards, the Navy could not keep up with the demands for them. On May 20 Capt. Harwood wrote to New York saying he had no extra Sharps on hand. The only small arms available were smoothbore percussion muskets which the Navy Department had accepted from the Army. These arms would have to do until further breechloaders could be obtained.

During the first months of the war the Union Defense Committee of New York City bought a large amount of small arms for naval use. The small arms procurement consisted of single-shot pistols, Hall carbines, musketoons, Savage revolvers, and 100 Sharps rifles. The committee bought the 100 Sharps rifles at $45 each, plus 5,000 cartridges at $25 per 1,000 from the New York firm of W. J. Syms & Co. on April 27, 1861. These small arms were sent to the Brooklyn Navy Yard in June by the order of W. A. Aspinwall.[19]

In May the Philadelphia Navy Yard wrote to Captain Harwood in Washington that there were no Sharps rifles to be had in town. Officials at the yard wrote that maybe in two or three weeks they would be able to obtain about 250 for $47 each, which they felt was too high a price to pay.[20] To help supply this critical need, the Navy turned to John T. Mitchell, acting agent for the Sharps Rifle Manufacturing Company to supply them with 1,500 rifles. On June 4, 1861, Andrew A. Harwood, chief of Naval Ordnance, contracted with John Mitchell that said, in part:

> That the said John T. Mitchell hereby agrees to deliver at the Navy Yards at Boston, New York and Philadelphia 450 Sharps rifles on or before the 10th day of June present being 150 at each said yards, and Ten Hundred and Fifty of said Sharps rifles at said Navy Yards of Boston, Philadelphia and New York, that is to say 350 at each of said yards on or before the 25th day of June (present).[21]

The price to be paid for Mitchell's order of .52 caliber Sharps rifles was set at $43 each including appendages: brush, cone wrench, screwdriver, extra cone, extra primer springs and one bullet mold for every five rifles.[22] The sabre bayonets were ordered from the Ames Sword Company of Chicopee, Massachusetts, on June 5.

When the first 150 rifles were not delivered at the New York Navy Yard by June 10, Harwood wrote to Mitchell on June 13 saying, "since this is an urgent and imperative demand for those arms, your immediate attention is called to this matter."[23] The next day Harwood directed the Boston Navy Yard to use its first delivery of 150 rifles to replace the Jenks carbines as fast as possible in all vessels being fitted out of Portsmouth for sea duty.

On August 9, 1861, Mitchell delivered 1,000 rifles to the New York Navy Yard in two lots of 500 rifles each, packed in chests holding ten rifles. The price paid for each of these packing chests was $3. Six days later the last 500 rifles on the June 4 contract were received at the Boston Navy Yard.

The total cost on this contract came to $64,950 which included the 1,500 Sharps rifles and 150 arms chests.[24]

Having the Sharps rifles in both .52 and .56 caliber caused the Navy many headaches in supplying ammunition for them. A September 1861 letter written from the Philadelphia Navy Yard to Washington complained that the 100 Sharps rifles received at Philadelphia were .52 caliber instead of the .56 caliber in storage there.

On August 28 Palmer wrote the Navy saying, "we have 80-100 Navy rifles with sabre bayonets all complete of 56 bore as same as previous 900 ordered price with appendages was $42.50. Will wait until Saturday for reply." Palmer went on to say that the War Dept. wanted them all but he would keep his offer to the Navy open.[25] Since the Navy did not reply in time the rifles were delivered to the Army in September.

The .52 caliber rifles delivered by Mitchell were soon placed in service. Three hundred rifles with ammunition were sent to William Nelson in Cincinnati for use on the Mississippi River. These rifles had been requested in July.[26] Forty of the rifles, along with eighty muskets, forty revolvers, eighty pistols, and 130 swords were requested and approved for the U.S. Sloop of War *Pensacola*.[27] By May 1862 all Sharps rifles had been placed aboard ships, so when Lt. Sanford from Cairo, Illinois, requested Sharps he had to be told there were none available for issue.

Two ships in Flag Officer David G. Farragut's fleet that captured New Orleans on May 1, 1862, were the *Mississippi* of seven guns and the *Pensacola* of 23 guns. In operation against the batteries at Port Hudson on March 14, 1863, the *Mississippi* was destroyed by the Confederate shore batteries after she ran aground. The executive officer of the *Mississippi* during this engagement was 26-year-old Lt. Comdr. George Dewey. Thirty-five years later on May 1, 1898, Dewey led the attack against the Spanish fleet in Manila Bay. During the years that the Sharps were in active sea service, they were found on the following vessels:

Plymouth	*Maumee*	*Aroostook*
Merrimac	*Ticonderoga*	*Franklin*
Sequoia	*Dacotah*	*Roanoke*
Susquehanna	*Huron*	*John P. Kennedy*
St. Lawrence	*Oneida*	*Perry*
Seminole	*Resaca*	*Vincennes*
Mississippi	*Pensacola*	*Macedonian*

For the next three years the only transactions between the Navy and Sharps were for spare parts and ammunition. As late as August 13, 1864, the Navy ordered 10,000 Sharps rifle .56 caliber cartridges to be shipped to the L.A.B. Squadron. In October 10,000 .52 caliber Sharps rifle linen cartridges were ordered for California.

Needing additional small arms the Navy on October 21, 1864, wired Palmer asking if Sharps could supply 150 rifles with bayonets immediately. Palmer responded that the factory was only producing carbines at the time, so they could not supply the rifles. It appears that in early March 1865 the Navy decided to give Sharps a contract for 5,000 rifles if the arms could be delivered by April 15. Palmer accepted this order on March 18 but due to the Army's order for a like number of rifles, no deliveries were made on this contract. With the Army contract nearly completed in June Palmer again asked the Navy to give him an order for 5,000 to 10,000 rifles—but with the war at an end, no contract was forthcoming.[28]

In the early months of the war it appears that the Navy had purchased a small quantity of Sharps carbines. A major characteristic of these NM1859 Sharps carbines is that they were not equipped with a saddle bar and ring on the left frame of the receiver. The receivers found on these carbines are serial numbered between 40,000 and 44,000. The amount and where they were from is not known. A post-war correspondence between Capt. William R. Shoemaker, commanding officer at Fort Union Arsenal, and the Army Ordnance Department gives a clue to how many there were. On January 17, 1871, Shoemaker said he had on hand 190 of the 50/70 converted Sharps carbines equipped without saddle ring and bar which made them unsuited for cavalry use. Instructions to Maj. James G. Benton at the Springfield Armory asked how the 190 carbines had been obtained and directed him to replace them with 200 carbines which did have the side swivel bar and ring. On January 30 Benton wrote the Ordnance Department that the arms had arrived at the Sharps factory for conversion to centerfire. These arms arrived without the side swivel bar and since Benton did not have the authority to modify the receivers, they were not changed. It was his intention to issue them last but they were sent off before Benton was aware that the carbines had been issued. Benton closes the letter by saying that these arms had been originally made for the Navy and he had no idea of how they came into the possession of the Army.[29] The answer to this question can be found in a letter written by Secretary of the Navy Gideon Welles dated June 19, 1865, to Secretary of War Edwin Stanton. In the letter Welles requests permission to allow the storage of naval guns, ammunition, and stores at Jefferson Barracks near St. Louis. This naval ordnance was being turned in from vessels of the Mississippi Squadron. The request was being made because the Navy did not have any convenient place for storing these items. Permission was granted by Assistant Secretary of War Charles A. Dana that the Ordnance Department give the order for the storage.[30] Three years later when the St. Louis Arsenal was directed to send the Sharps carbines and rifles to the Sharps factory for alteration, the Navy Sharps were also sent for conversion.

In the post-war period the Navy was holding in inventory as of December 1, 1866, the following:

Sharps Rifles (12/1/66)[31]

Location	.52 Cal.	.56 Cal.
Portsmouth, N.H.	73	72
Boston	112	
New York	653	77
Philadelphia	65	595*
Washington	4+	10
Norfolk	129	3
Jefferson Barracks	145	
Pensacola, Florida	341	44
Mare Island, Calif.	8	20
Total	1,530	821

* Twenty-eight were Model 1855 Sharps carbines
+ M1855 Sharps Rifles

The 1868 quarterly reports of target practice with small arms aboard naval vessels reveals the Sharps rifles were in use by the Marine guards aboard the *U.S.S. Ticonderoga*, *U.S.S. Dacotah* and the Steamer *Huron* while Sharps carbines were listed as aboard the U.S. Steamer *Oneida*.[32]

Shortly after the close of the war the Navy was starting to sell off its excess small arms. As of April 15, 1867, William Reed & Co. of Boston was notified that the Boston Navy Yard had 112 Sharps rifles for sale at $10 each but only forty of the rifles were equipped with sabre bayonets. On December 29, 1868, Charles Pond of New York City was told that the Navy had in storage 404 Sharps rifles with sabre bayonets but the price for the arms had not been established. A year later, on October 18, 1869, the Washington Navy Yard had fifty-three Sharps & Hankins rifles and fifty-seven Sharps rifles, all .56 caliber, for sale at $15 each.[33]

U.S. Navy Procurement of Sharps

Seller	Date of Purchase	Quantities	Price
Sharps Rifle Mfg Co.	Sept 1853	63 Carbines M1851	$30.00
	Sept 1856	131 Rifles M1855	36.00
	Oct 1856	12 Rifles M1855 w/ whites device	36.00
	March 1857	19 Rifles M1855	36.00
	June 1857	38 Rifles M1855	36.00
	July 1857	100 Carbines M1855	30.00
	Dec 1860	630 NM1859 Rifles .56 cal. w/ appendages & sword bayonets	37.50
	Feb 1861	150 NM1859 Rifles .56 cal. w/ appendages & sword bayonets	37.50
	April 1861	120 NM1859 Rifles .56 cal. w/ appendages & sword bayonets	37.50
Union Defense Committee	June 1861	100 NM1859 Rifles .52 cal w/ appendages	45.00
John T. Mitchell	August 1861	1,500 NM1859 Rifles .52 cal w/ appendages	43.00

By the late 1860s the centerfire cartridge was starting to be accepted as the standard military ammunition, replacing the percussion system and rimfire cartridges. A naval board was established on March 29, 1869, to determine the best breech-loading design for the centerfire cartridges used in naval service. The board was headed by Capt. William Reynolds, with Capt. Nicholson, and Comdr. Breese, all of the U.S. Navy and Capt. Tilton of the Marine Corps. The breech-loaders tested were the Springfield 50/70 trapdoors, Remington rolling-block design and the Sharps rifles. The features of the Sharps rifles tested were:

Length of Rifle	47.7 inches
Length of Barrel	30.2 inches
Diameter of Bore	0.50 inches
Total Weight	8.94 pounds
Weight of Barrel	3.84 pounds[34]

A series of tests was performed with each of the rifles. The Sharps rifle cartridges were loaded with 70 grains of powder and a 450-grain bullet. One hundred rounds were fired with the Sharps from a fixed rest in eight minutes. Firing from the shoulder at a distance of 100 yards, thirteen rounds were fired in one minute and sixteen rounds in a minute without aiming. It was fired 1,000 times to test the durability of its parts. To test the effect of moisture on the action the rifle was placed in salt water for three and a half hours and then exposed to the atmosphere until the next day. It was found to be fairly coated with rust around the breech-loading parts. The first cartridge would not enter the chamber readily and had to be pushed in with a stick. The cartridge did ignite when fired, but the cartridge then would not eject without using the ramrod. By the fifth cartridge, the action worked fine. After the firing the rifle was cleaned and oiled. It was found to be uninjured and in good serviceable order. Even with its overall good showing, the board on August 2 recommended the Remington rifle for the naval service.[35]

Palmer, writing for the company on August 19, said that Sharps was prepared to give the most liberal terms if the Navy were to find in favor of the Sharps.[36] The Navy had, however, made up its mind on the Remington, so nothing came of Palmer's actions.

Although in service for less than twenty years, the Sharps rifles and carbines helped establish the Navy as a future sea power.

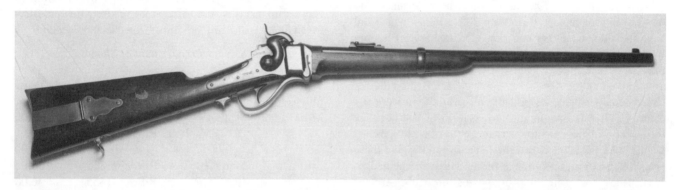

A Navy NM1859 Sharps percussion carbine. SN 43,279. John McAuley collection.

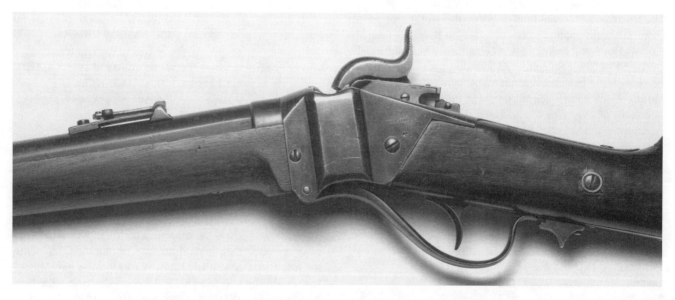

The left side view of the NM1859 Navy carbine without the saddle-bar and ring.

This .56 caliber Sharps NM1859 rifle. SN 33,623 was delivered to Washington Navy Yard on November 5, 1860 in packing box #21. Steven Selenfriend collection.

A naval shore party armed with Sharps rifles. National Archives collection.

The NM1859 Navy Sharps converted to centerfire 50-70. One hundred ninety of these arms were at Fort Union Arsenal in January 1871. SN 43,804. John McAulay collection.

THE SERIAL NUMBERS OF SHARPS RIFLES AND CARBINES

The names and serial numbers listed here were taken entirely from the regimental books of the various units cited. They were initially copied for my own use, consequently, every effort was made to assure their accuracy. When illegibility cast any doubt on a number, it was omitted. Despite this, errors are possible and no guarantee of total accuracy can be made. It is my sincere belief, however, that the numbers are highly reliable. It would perhaps be sufficient to say that the authors would not, and have not, hesitated to purchase Sharps based on the information presented here.

Regimental books were kept by every regiment serving in the Civil War. Separate volumes served as a permanent record of regimental correspondence, orders, issues of clothing, and ordnance as well as individual service of enlisted men. When the war ended, Union regiments turned their books over to the War Department. Those of Confederate regiments probably went home with regimental officers and the location of all but a very few is unknown. Excerpts from existing books containing orders and correspondence were later to become part of the published *Official Records of the War of the Rebellion*. Those volumes with records of individual enlistment and service proved invaluable in determining pension eligibility for Union veterans. Unfortunately for today's student of Civil War arms and uniforms, the vast majority of the books that recorded issuances of clothing and ordnance were destroyed. Why is anybody's guess, but probably no one in the late 19th century envisioned that the information would be of any value. This should not be surprising when it is considered that such data from all of our 20th century wars is not known to exist to any real extent.

How do we then account for the information contained in this volume? The answer is simple. Nearly all soldiers, both officers and enlisted men serving in the Civil War, were volunteers. Although they often fought like professionals, military procedure frequently gave way to practicality. If it were more convenient or made more sense to keep such information as the serial number of an arm issued in the same book as a company's orders or service records, they did. By this breech of military formality, these "nonprofessionals" left behind a record which adds a new dimension to gun collecting.

The fact is that there is no set pattern for where these numbers exist. This made it necessary to go through every existing regimental book belonging to every regiment known to have carried serial numbered small arms. Over the past several years, as work on this project advanced, the authors and several friends have proven that these arms do exist on today's collector market. Diligent searching at gun shows and auction catalogs has been fruitful. My own "find" was a Sharps carbine serial number 92480 which was issued to Sergeant David Darragh, Company G, 13th New York Cavalry. Here is a carbine that saw action in northern Virginia chasing the elusive "Gray Ghost," John S. Mosby. Interestingly enough, the arm was first purchased by a dealer friend in upstate New York near where Sergeant Darragh lived. As with nearly all these arms, number 92480 shows wear and use. Clearly visible is the area where the carbine sling hook

Major General Phil Sheridan. By the summer of 1864, over half of his Army of the Potomac Cavalry Corps was armed with Sharps carbines. (National Archives)

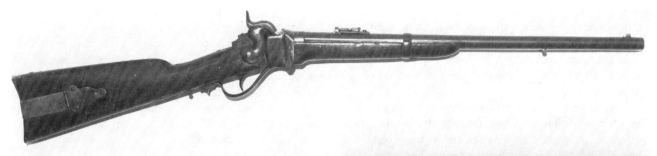

Sharps carbine SN 92480 carried by Sgt. David Darragh of the 13th New York Cavalry.

rubbed as its owner rode with Company G over the roads of Fauquier and Loudon Counties, Virginia. Far from "mint" condition, this is an arm that saw service and has a story to tell.

Other such treasures await some fortunate collector. One of the most interesting results of this research was the realization that the arms of the 1st California Cavalry were those left in California by the 1st U.S. Dragoons when they departed for the seat of war in Virginia in November 1861. But even more exciting is the discovery that some numbers issued to this regiment match those captured from John Brown in 1859 at Harpers Ferry. These had apparently been issued to the Dragoons after capture. Considering the interesting history of the 1st California, the potential of finding such an arm would excite anyone with an interest in Civil War or Western history.

Another group of historic Sharps, listed here for the first time, are the rifles of the 42nd Pennsylvania Infantry, the famous "Bucktails." These rifles were among those originally intended for the 1st and 2nd U.S. Sharpshooters. They were being held in reserve at the Washington Arsenal and by mistake were issued to the 42nd. As might be expected, the lucky Pennsylvanians who received them refused to give them up. Within these numbers are some that reside in collections today as Berdan Sharps.[2] They can now take their place in history with a regiment whose record is second to none.

Those who use this listing should keep several important points in mind. One detail that is often overlooked is the prefix letter "C" on Sharps serial numbers. When the Sharps Rifle Company reached the number 99,999 in the summer of 1863, it simply incorporated the Roman numeral "C" for 100,000 and started to renumber with 1. Thus C.1 = 100,001. Often in writing "C" numbers in regimental books, the person recording the number would omit the letter. In most cases, the date of issue, and extreme unlikelihood of very early Sharps being reissued, make determination of deleted "Cs" obvious. When this was certain, the letter has been reinserted.

The most noticeable "C" series arms are the rifles issued to several regiments of Hancock's Veteran Corps in 1865. The men comprising the regiments of this unique corps were all discharged veterans who had seen service in combat regiments and whose original enlistment had ended. Part of the inducement to reenlist in this corps was the promise of a breechloading rifle that the soldier could retain upon discharge. All Sharps military rifles numbered in the "C" range were made especially to be issued to Hancock's Corps. That these regiments saw almost no hard service because of the war's end certainly accounts for the superior condition of many of these arms.

Another point will be immediately noticed by those using this list. Serial numbers will in some cases be listed more than once. In nearly every case, this indicated multiple issuances of the same arm. There are two primary reasons for this. First, if the initial recipient was killed, wounded, or discharged, the arm was turned in to the regiment and given to another soldier. Or, as often happened, the regiment turned in its arms and were issued different weapons. This then would result in the original arms being reissued to another regiment. In nearly every case where an arm changed hands, there is an interesting story to be gleaned.

The decision to include the names of the men to whom these Sharps were issued added a great deal of work to the project. It was felt, however, that the effort would add materially to the usefulness of this book. Those preparing to research one of the men listed must keep several things in mind. First and foremost, is that all this information was copied from handwritten lists. Although every effort was made to decipher what might be termed imaginative spelling, at times this was also accompanied by all but illegible handwriting. In some cases the researcher will simply have to use a process of elimination combined with some detective work to arrive at the true name of the original owner of the arm concerned. In most cases, the result should yield a positive identification. In some few instances, the use of a professional researcher working at the National Archives may be required. The citation of the books where the numbers are to be found should allow ready access to the original list. In most cases, the pages can be photocopied if special arrangement is made. This will require additional time and expense but will provide irrefutable proof of an arms provenance.

When collecting historical arms, it is important to know when the arm was in use. The knowledge that the owner of a particular carbine or rifle was in a major battle is certainly of interest, but it relates only to the person not necessarily to the firearm itself. For this reason, whenever possible, a determination has been made on when the particular Sharps involved was actually issued. In most instances, this was done by a careful study of names on the issue list with subsequent lists of deaths, desertions, or discharges. In some cases, this was verified by checking the approximate date of manufacture of the arm itself. Altogether, this proved to be a reasonably accurate determination. This information is provided in the regimental biographies preceding each list.

Subsequent volumes documenting other Civil War arms are being planned. Comments and suggestions are welcome and may be directed to the publisher.

Earl J. Coates
Columbia, Maryland

Union cavalryman with Sharps carbine and Colt revolvers
(Richard Carlile)

Union cavalryman with Sharps carbine and Colt revolver
(Richard Carlile)

2ND ARKANSAS CAVALRY (COMPANY L)

History: The 2nd Arkansas was one of four regiments of Federal cavalry raised among the pro-Union white men of that state. They were organized at Helena, Arkansas, and Pilot Knob, Missouri, and mustered in July 1862. Most of their duty consisted of scouts and skirmishes with guerrillas in both Arkansas and Missouri. They were mustered out August 20, 1865.

Arms: The Sharps carbines listed below were probably issued in late 1864. The number range was determined by the authors to be in the "C" series. Production at this time would establish these carbines as Model 1863.

Source: The names as serial numbers listed were found in the *Regimental Letter, Order, and Guard Report Book*.

Carbines

Serial #		Name	Company
C	2484	Briscoe, Martin	L
C	22705	Maynor, Cpl. William	L
C	22836	Pope, David	L
C	23006	McIntyre, John	L
C	23349	Arrington, Levi	L
C	23722	Dean, John W.	L
C	23725	Hawell, John W.	L
C	23744	Ford, Cpl. James M.	L
C	24167	Boyce, Joseph	L
C	24202	Miller, Sr. John W.	L
C	24337	Carny, Wm.	L
C	24373	Kendall, James	L
C	24523	Hendricks, Thos.	L
C	24550	Dyer, George H.	L
C	24640	Pollard, Cpl. Isaac G.	L
C	24685	" "	L
C	24694	Stephenson, John A.	L
C	24770	Meadows, Archabald	L
C	24906	Bushong, Sgt. William M.	L
C	24909	Killingworth, James	L
C	24937	Holman, James	L
C	24959	Covington, Richard	L
C	24962	Penter, George	L
C	24993	Sagely, John	L
C	25039	Spoon, John	L
C	25047	Gregory, Hyram	L
C	25060	Bryson, Wm. B.	L
C	25061	Miller, Daniel	L
C	25080	Penter, William	L
C	25099	Meadows, Cpl. John F.	L
C	25118	Forbus, Willilam	L
C	25189	Brown, Cpl Jasper	L
C	25201	Arrington, Joel	L
C	25286	Miller, Jr. John W.	L
C	25327	Rankins, Cpl Henderson	L
C	25369	Duvall, William C.	L
C	25375	Davis, Cpl Enoch	L
C	25423	Haward, William	L
C	25597	Pope, John	L
C	25623	Wilburne, Curtis	L
C	25666	Kirkpatrick, Wm.	L
C	25732	Dean, D. H.	L

1ST CALIFORNIA CAVALRY

History: The 1st California was initially organized as a battalion of five companies at Camp Merdiant near Oakland, California, and mustered in between August and October 1861. By May 1863 they had been raised by increments to full regimental strength. They saw action against Confederate forces in Arizona, New Mexico, and Texas. Later, they also participated in skirmishes with both Apache and Navajo Indians. The regiment was mustered out March 6 to October 19, 1866.

Arms: The regiment was first armed with Colt navy revolvers and Sharps carbines. The Colts were issued in November 1861 and the Model 1853 Sharps approximately the same time. The serial number list of the initial Sharps issue dates from February 1862. There were subsequent issues of Sharps carbines of later models which date from early 1863. An interesting and important sidelight of this study is the matching of several serial numbers of Sharps carbines in the first issue with those taken from John Brown at Harpers Ferry in 1859. The reason for this match was solved when the authors found similar matches of Colt navy numbers with those issued to the 1st U.S. Dragoons. The 1st Dragoons were stationed in California until November 1861 when they left by ocean steamer to join the Federal forces concentrating near Washington, D.C. It is obvious that the Dragoons had been issued the confiscated carbines and left them in California upon their departure.

Source: The serial numbers for the 1st California were found in the *Individual Roster Book* and the *Hospital Roster* of the regiment. Issues were confirmed by reference to the quarterly returns of ordnance issued.

Carbines

Serial #	Name	Company
8623	Sawtelle, John E.	C
8735	Wells, Sgt. Richard	E
9003	Weltz, Sgt.	C
9165	Jennison, Albert	E
9675	Plunnett	C

Sharps Carbines & Rifles

9675	Annan, Private Wm.	C	13707	Williams, Charles	E
9702	Berry, Samuel	E	13758	O'Brien, John	E
9762	Leaton, Robert	C	13759	Brier, Christopher	E
9784	Lewis, Henry	C	13816	Taylor	C
9882	Morely, George	E	13905	Seily, Warren	C
9977	Rzason, Christopher	C	13908	Davidson, Solomon	E
9977	Ryson	C	13916	Donnell, Cpl. John C.	E
10065	Risdon, Josiah A.	C	13934	Miller	C
10142	Wood, Cpl.	C	13950	Casi, James H.	E
10333	Corders, Malachi	C	13952	Leroy, Sgt. Phillip K.	E
10333	Weltz, Sgt.	C	13976	Worrell, Charles H.	E
10360	Lee, John H.	C	13991	Goggin, Edward D.	E
10410	Pooel, Wm. R.	E	14005	Chamberlin, William	C
10661	Lee, Cpl. John H.	C	14010	Creath, Carrol A.	C
10661	Neal, Cpl.	C	14054	Brick 2nd, Charles G.	C
10661	Brown	C	14054	Buck, C. G.	C
10747	Canterbury, Rufus T.	C	14056	Yager, Corp George	E
11464	Longet, Williams	E	14083	Phieffle, John G.	E
11777	Keams	C	14105	Andrews, Pvt. David P.	E
11778	McNamara, John	C	14209	Lange, August F. C.	E
11798	Fairchild, Cpl. Elliott	E	14230	Hoyt	C
11923	Monroe, Oscar	C	14230	Hay, Hiram	C
11934	Hall, Robert K.	E	14348	Benedict	C
11935	Beman, Charles D.	C	14358	Wynkoop	C
11942	Labbring, Antoine Sgt.	C	14358	Taylor, Silas M.	C
12073	Kennedy, Richard	E	14506	Lucas, Thos. J.	E
12106	Wilson, James	C	14552	Martin 2nd, George W.	C
12574	Snyder, George	E	14564	Mattingham, Jerome	E
12642	Brown, Cpl.	C	14650	Blanc, Louis	E
12656	Searles, Hiram	E	14659	Pearce, Sgt.	C
12678	Parrish, Albert G.	E	14659	Felmer, Sgt.	C
12781	Turner, Addison A.	E	14659	Knapsen	C
12784	Lang, Ferdinand	E	14698	Randall, Philip	E
12790	Pritchard, David	E	14701	Bell, Joseph E.	C
12794	Parquett, John	C	14713	Hawes, Charles A.	C
12794	Werrner	C	14718	Eichoff, Edward Cpl.	C
12796	Haulser	C	14757	Hatheway, Daniel S.	C
12816	Wznkoop, John	C	14797	Ellis	C
12831	Pcarce, Henry S.	C	14798	Priest, Eli B.	C
12860	Bullen, Wm.	C	14798	Peist, Cpl.	C
12891	Wenner, John	C	14814	Carpenter, George M.	E
12897	Martin, Henry G.	E	14816	Harrington, George L.	E
12897	Logan, Farrier William	E	14846	Mallory, Auerill	C
12922	Walker, Thomas	C	14855	Parker, James W.	C
12935	McGinnis (Co. D)	E	14857	O'Connor, Wm.	C
12935	Conner, Enoch S.	E	14907	Arnold, Granville S.	E
12976	Tallman, William D.	E	14915	Chappius, Edward	E
12976	Haulser, Charles	C	14952	Martin 2nd	C
12993	Wangh, John	E	14952	Harthan, Lucins	C
13114	Hart, John	C	14959	Garvey, Frank	C
13115	McDonald, John	E	15034	Morrison, Howard	E
13131	Travis, Clovis M.	E	15034	Martin, Henry G.	E
13138	Timmons, Corpl.	C	15050	Barry, Luther M. Corp.	C
13197	Hoyt, John B.	C	15062	Cook, Ceylon A.	E
13197	Bruman	C	15081	Reynolds, Joseph A.	C
13601	Bunch, Lambert	E	15110	Christophel, Charles	E
13669	Ruggles, S.	C	15119	Jones, William	E

15124	DeHague, Joseph A.	E		17221	Baker, Nelson G.	E
15127	Argo	C		17226	Ryer, Henry	E
15131	Scott, John H.	C		17247	Careden, Patrick	E
15138	Timmons	C		17326	Reed 1st, Abraham S.	C
15151	Scott	C		17326	Fay	C
15174	Reed, John S.	E		17373	Smith	C
15179	Dierston, Wm.	C		17606	Smith, Allen E.	C
15181	Hooper, Thomas	C		17651	Branch	C
15186	Bryden, James W.	E		17744	Horner, Farrier	C
15219	O'Connor	C		17856	Bartlett, Cpl.	C
15219	Starkweather, Eugene	C		18164	Burman, Aaron	C
15305	Foster, George P.	E		18164	Garvey	C
15364	Hibbets, John	E		18202	Knox, Sgt.	C
15392	Brown	C		18274	Pearce, Sgt.	C
15523	Barnes, Augustus	E		18415	Allyne, Saml. H.	E
15524	Plannett, Charles A.	C		18615	Corders	C
15547	Magill, James	C		18615	Weber, Henry H.	C
15574	Beatty, Saml. H.	E		18801	Kuhl, Sgt. Chas	E
15641	Dewey, Henry G.	E		18926	Kiel, William	E
15641	Kelly, William	E		19079	Martin, Henry G.	E
15651	Westervelt, James H.	E		19109	Kelly, William	E
15704	Johnson, Wm. S. F.	E		19113	Allyne, Saml. H.	E
15713	Wescott, Elliott	E		33669	Ruggles 1st, Nathaniel	C
15736	Saenger, Edward L. W.	E				
15756	Waters, Nathan E.	E				
15758	Moble, Aaron J.	E				

1st California Cavalry, Veteran
Carbines

15798	Martin, 1st, Wiley	C
15914	Ayer, Cpl. Edward E.	E
15965	Holmes	C
15965	Holmes, James H.	C
15988	Shriver, Aaron P.	C
15999	McGann, James	E
16014	Mitzger	C
16032	Metzger, Elias B.	C
16041	Ruggles 2nd, Silas	C
16041	Reed, Charles W.	C
16130	McCall, Bernard	E
16156	Pursell, Abner L.	E
16167	Trinkle, John	C
16196	Dorland, Robert R.	C
16211	Reed 2nd, Charles W.	C
16211	Daniels, Charles	C
16238	Cate, Daniel	E
16247	Elliott	C
16506	Carroll, Wm. C.	E
16526	Webb, John B.	C
16681	Roberts, Thaddeus	C
16681	Risdon, Josiah	C
16681	Roberts	C
16779	Webb, Sydney M.	E
16788	Monroe, James	E
16801	Webb	C
16801	Knapen, Edgar	C
16877	Blackmer, Burgess	C
16877	Welty, Sgt.	C
17123	Weber	C
17184	Brick 1st, Walter	C

50596	Chapel	B
51264	Weir	B
51264	Wallace	B
59188	Estes	B
70832	Warneilh	B
73696	Andrews	B
73793	Milligan	B
78002	Calhoun	B
78318	Clarke I	B
81996	Clarke II	B
87422	Ayers, Private	B
87720	Barry	B
89406	Zorkowsky	B
89844	King	B
90358	Klegg	B
90383	Metcalf	B
92254	Brandes	B
92491	Warneith	B
93044	Dunlap	B
93829	Horobin	B
94065	Taylor	B
94795	Diemer	B
95359	Mister	B
95444	Carte	B
95602	Gallagher	B
95639	Belknap	B
95662	Rafferty	B
95727	Dougherty	B
95743	Hoey	B
95770	Walker	B

95809	McGuire	B
95921	Shrewsberry	B
95940	White	B
96053	Carpenter	B
96114	Martin	B
96117	Susee	B
96117	Mapes I	B
96147	Fisher	B
96147	Peck	B
96165	Mapes II	B
96172	Brakebill	B
96186	Hurley	B
96186	Hurt	B
96186	Hawes	B
96204	Webb	B
96215	Morris	B
96238	Jamieson	B
96282	Smith	B
96382	Drinan	B
96409	Koyt	B
96409	Soles	B
96447	Lee	B
96549	Hayes, Corp.	B
96610	Burke	B
96636	Harlin	B
96650	Williams	B
96679	Cleveland	B
96679	Bradley	B
96732	Anthony	B
96753	Billian	B
96805	O'Connor	B
96818	Reddy	B
96840	Lawsen	B
96840	Sampson	B
96853	Green	B
96889	Dean	B
96898	Hershman	B
96956	Winters	B
97241	Noble	B
97284	Brownshaw	B

1st Colorado Cavalry (Company D)

History: The 1st Colorado Cavalry was organized from the 1st Colorado Infantry on November 1, 1862. At this time, nearly all the regular army troops had been pulled east to fight in the war, and it fell to the volunteers to fill the void. The regiment served its entire enlistment in the Great Plains. In this theater, the enemy was not Confederates but hostile Indians. The duties assigned to the regiment were primarily protecting stagecoach routes and scouting, but there were numerous skirmishes with the Indians. Most of these took place at obscure places such as Cedar Bluff, Colorado, and Walnut Creek, Kansas. Unfortunately the single fight for which the regiment gained notoriety was the infamous Sand Creek Massacre in November 1864. Under their commander, Colonel John M. Chivington, the troops attacked a peaceful Indian village and indiscriminately killed men, women, and children. The regiment was mustered out at Leavenworth, Kansas, on November 18, 1865.

Arms: The 1st Colorado was armed with a combination of Sharps and Starr carbines as well as both Colt and Remington army revolvers. The serial numbers cited below appear on a list which dates from April 1865 but which probably includes the arms issued when the regiment was formed.

Source: The serial numbers and names listed here can be found in the *Company Order Book of Co. D.*

Carbines

Serial #	*Name*	*Company*
43571	Treakle	D
48252	McDaniels, Robt.	D
50195	Barnes, H	D
54484	Hair, Jesse	D
54940	Hence, J. H.	D
57300	Durmitt, Wm.	D
60936	Pevry, Edgerton	D
69887	Hibner	D
72709	Price, Wm.	D
73345	Day	D
73389	Maynard, Benj. F.	D
74934	Maynard, Benj. F.	D
78323	Parker, Wm.	D
85477	Robberts, Charles	D
85513	Wheeler, Charles	D
86464	Bates, Wm. G.	D
87213	Olson, Benedick	D
87357	Carson, Robert O.	D
91303	Thomas, Charles	D
91767	Gray, W. C.	D
92043	Driscoll	D
92554	Wilson, S.	D
94274	Pyatt, Amos	D
94274	Byrd, A.	D
94956	Dorn	D
95352	Beach, William	D
95537	Grim, G.	D
95625	Ferris, James	D
95779	Griffith, James	D
95854	Caine, James	D
96061	Habick	D
96686	Gaznor, Wm.	D
96717	Benninger, Michael	D
96821	Short, W. H.	D
96845	Cramer, John	D
96940	Prickett, Edward	D

96952	Darnall, Benj.	D
97114	Vance, Conrad	D
97248	Brown, J. L.	D

2ND ILLINOIS CAVALRY (COS. B, C, AND D)

History: The 2nd Illinois Cavalry was organized at Camp Butler, Illinois in August 1861. They participated in the Battle of Belmont, Missouri on November 7, 1861 and continued to operate in the western theater of the war until mustered out January 3, 1866. The regiment had a history of scouts, skirmishes, and battles which took them throughout Kentucky, Tennessee, Mississippi, Louisiana, Alabama, and finally Texas.

Arms: The regiment had a mixture of Sharps and Burnside carbines as well as Colt navy revolvers along with Starr and Remington army revolvers. The Sharps which appear in this listing were issued in May 1863.

Source: The names and serial numbers listed appear in the *Company Order Book* which includes Cos. B to G. The arms of Co. C are on a list entitled "Receipts for Arms Received of Captain Samuel Whitaker, Co. C — Stationed at Memphis, Tennessee May 20, 1863."

Carbines

Serial #	Name	Company
32616	Potter, Sylvester	C
32619	Thompson, George A.	C
33051	Houchens, Geo. C.	D
33056	Houchens, Geo. C.	D
33478	Lyles, Fountain	D
36259	Grey, Thomas	D
40735	Gerber, Abraham	B
44447	Bennet, Ira	C
44504	Ringland, Thomas A.	C
44544	Winchell, Albert	C
44544	Myers, William D.	C
44596	Stolt, Christian	C
44961	Ellsworth, William C.	C
46438	Murphy, Thomas	C
46613	Smith, Hannan	D
46640	McCauly, Eli A.	D
46640	Flannigan, Barney	D
46650	McCauly, Eli A.	D
46676	Thompson, Wm. C.	C
46828	Long, Dennis	C
46828	Reeves, Francis M.	C
46828	Potter, Sylvetus	C
46849	Kee, Marcellus	D
46898	Ewing, Wm. W.	B
46980	Dance, Grant	C
46995	Tippy, John	C
47059	Tinsley, Charles O.	D
47076	Willson, Thomas	C
47100	Conley, James	C
47112	Hill, Wm. H.	C
47150	Tippy, Willis A.	C
47157	Schrader, David	B
47189	Summers, Miles	B
47240	Marshall, Charles	B
47248	Musick, John R.	B
47251	Long, Dennis	C
47280	Tucker, John W.	B
47302	Adams, Sgt. Robert	C
47307	Johnson, Andrew	D
47311	Stewart, Firman	C
47311	Thompson, William	C
47319	Busbee, Stephen J.	C
47355	VanNaken, Mannis	C
47355	Moseley, Robert	C
47372	Morrisey, John	C
47376	Ecker, David C.	C
47482	Taylor, George	B
47506	Ellsworth, Wm. C.	C
47520	Little, William	D
47533	Gallant, Lloyd	B
47535	Westerfield, Francis	C
47591	Shroder, John	C
47615	Hulbert, Frank	D
47618	Westerfield, Barton	C
47618	Parks, Robert C.	C
47666	Wright, William T.	C
47666	Johnson, William	C
47681	Bohlier, Candliss	C
47681	Johnson, William	C
47681	Stover, Henry C.	C
47710	Littell, George W. C.	C
47783	Anderson, Joseph	C
47801	Kilgore, Mathias	C
47820	Beckenhorst, John	C
47820	Conley, James	C
47878	Conwell, John	C
47885	Doldrer, Charles	C
47891	Gilson, Edward	C
47891	Reeves, Francis M.	C
47951	Shroder, John	C
47997	Meyer, George	C
48030	Ryan, Edward	C
48048	Lowe, George M.	D
48119	Arthur, Quintus	B
49098	Zappe, Frank	C
49098	Potter, Sylvetus A.	C
49322	Eaton, Robert	C
49322	Tucker, Rufus J.	C
50913	Shirley, Oliver A.	B
51550	Nobles,	B
51579	Kellon, Clemmons	D

52591	Walker, Marcellus D.	C		54017	Gullet, Jacob	D
52591	Cashiel, John	D		54037	Green, Jones	B
52591	Thompsom, John C.	C		54038	Beer, Percy C.	D
52606	North, Samuel J.	C		54039	Hughes, Wm.	D
52648	Stover, Henry C.	C		54047	Wayland, Albert G.	D
52650	McGraw, Walter	B		54047	Emery, Samuel G.	D
52738	Burnell, Livingston Sgt.	C		54049	Figon, Anton	D
52738	Wall, William	C		54050	Deadman, Wm.	D
52814	North, Michall	C		54077	Houchins, Bruce T.	D
53001	Cole, James M.	C		54116	Snyder, John E.	C
53256	Grimsley, Augustus L.	D		54687	Rolley, William	C
53262	McCumber, Perry T.	D		59779	Henselman, George	B
53270	Jones, Wm.	B		61668	Howell, Chester	C
53414	Shay, Dennis	D		65615	Foskett, Wm. M.	C
53443	Dolbow, George W.	D		66301	Howell, Chester	C
53443	Nott, Charles W.	D		66773	Lippold, Goetleb	D
53444	Dalzell, Howe	B		69236	Jewett, Christopher C.	B
53457	Halcomb, Martin	D		69678	Little, Wm.	B
53472	Dolehouse, George	D		70197	Eby,	B
53489	Golhoffer, Joseph	D		72359	Hayes, A. T.	B
53510	Boyd, Wm.	D		74809	Warberson, S. G.	B
53555	Williams, James C.	D		75475	Martin, Samuel F.	C
53579	Harpole, John Adam	D		75826	Forker, Wm. J.	C
53584	Wood, Charles T.	D		75841	Trott, W. C.	B
53586	Warner, Leopold	D		75895	Arnold, Fred	B
53601	Hounshell, August	D		75994	Lyon, Lewis S.	B
53617	Rhodemeyer, Adam	D		76094	Shaw, Francis	D
53631	Ost, Nicholas	D		76248	Summers, V. H.	B
53651	Blankinship, James P.	D		76266	Westerfield, Barton	C
53651	Teroy, James	D		76372	Hays, John W.	B
53657	Robertson, James H.	D		76425	Dorrell, Francis	C
53684	Block, Charles	D		76545	Ryan, Edward	C
53698	Moore, David	D		76742	Thompson, John C.	C
53722	Commill, Christian	D		76781	Hill, Wm. B.	C
53745	Burke, James	D		76783	Robert J. Mosely	C
53751	Zeaffle, August	D		76800	Blakeley, W. L.	B
53779	Nichols, John L.	B		76836	Prince, John	B
53785	Steile, Andrew	D		76848	Morrison, Hugh A.	B
53788	Dudley, Samuel S.	D		77215	Siderman, August	B
53799	Walker, John	D		77465	Martines, Harvey	B
53821	Bennack, George	D		77577	Kiplinger, James B.	B
53821	Alward, William	D		77602	Stoddard, Allen P.	B
53824	Grimsley, Isom D.	D		77712	Murry, John	B
53835	Glass, John	D		77713	Gans, Henry	C
53862	Hummert, Fred	D		77715	Frank, Amos	B
53883	Ridde, David	D		77959	Wren, John	B
53889	Fraier, Wm. C.	D		85380	Martin, Samuel F.	C
53901	Kurtz, Daniel M.	D		85483	Bennett, Ira	C
53907	McKenzie, James	D		85511	Ryan, John	D
53926	Riley, Wm.	D		85643	Warberson, S. G.	B
53928	Goodwin, James	D		86051	Mosley, Robert J.	C
53929	Baker, Richard P.	D		86093	Jenkins, James	D
53962	Larkin, Francis	D		86100	Myers, William D.	C
53975	Diller, Francis X.	D		86289	Harpole, George	D
53983	Swartsweller, Abner	D		86295	Hill, William H.	C
53996	Davis, Marshal	D		86322	Brennan, Michael	D
54008	Smith, James	D		86325	Tunison, Dewitt C.	D

86339	Quick, Robert	D
86439	Buslry, Stephen	C
86576	Marvel, George	B
86816	Cotterman, Adam	C
86933	Singer, Oliver	D
86977	Shroeder, Francis	D
90896	Lewis, James	D
91638	North, Samuel F.	C
94248	Westerfield, Francis	C
94628	Shroder, John	C

5TH ILLINOIS CAVALRY (COS. C AND I)

History: The 5th Illinois Cavalry was organized at Camp Butler, Illinois from August to December 1861. They moved first to Benton Barracks, Missouri in February 1862. From then until they were mustered out on October 27, 1865, they served in the theater of the war which encompassed generally the line of the Mississippi River from Tennessee to Vicksburg, Mississippi.

Arms: The regiment first received Sharps carbines in late 1863. Prior to this date, they had been armed with Cosmopolitan carbines. They had also received Colt and Remington army revolvers as well as the French pin-fire, Lefaucheaux. The arms listed below appear to be the original Sharps issued to the regiment.

Source: The names and serial numbers of the arms listed appear in the bound volumes of *Company Descriptive Books*. This includes two books, one covering Cos. A to F and another Cos. G to M.

Carbines

Serial #	Name	Company
29122	Kelly, Richard F.	I
30119	Davis, Walter P.	I
30328	Crane, Lysander	I
30328	England, Jefferson	I
34468	Evans, Cpl. Jeremiah	I
34468	Larrie, Samuel A.	I
46885	Pelky, Joseph	I
46885	Mreure, Charles	I
46885	Brooke, Thomas E.	I
52425	Miller, Sylvester	I
52425	Garrison, Manchester	I
54216	Davis, Roswell R.	I
54216	Brown, James F.	I
58658	Jones, James K.	I
61108	Mulraney, James	I
61522	Heritage, John	I
61592	Quick, John	I
61592	Dyson, Romine	I
62071	Richey, J. D.	I
62071	Mixer, Henry	I
62090	Potvine, Charles	I
62090	Lenard, Wm.	I
64278	Buchanan, Joseph F.	I
64681	Derrennes, Louis	I
64878	Buchannan, Jos. R.	I
67031	Rigg, James	I
67238	Weaver, Thomas H.	I
67238	Smith, Wm. F.	I
67792	Martin, W. G.	I
67792	Starbeck, Leroy C.	I
67937	Gorton, Tyler W.	I
68486	Miler, Larkin C.	I
68486	Burnett, Joseph W.	I
69685	Trees, Davis	I
69782	Lyons, John C.	I
71283	Alexander, Joseph	I
71908	Jones, James K.	I
72217	Haga, Gabriel	I
72888	Foster, Adam	I
77237	Larue, Corp. Samuel A.	I
78132	Mefford, Wm.	I
78132	Adams, David	I
78135	Johnson, Matthew S.	I
78152	Baker, Walter	I
79248	Grass, John S.	I
79459	Johnson, Corp Matthew S.	I
79733	Belles, George W.	I
79815	Dart, Eli	I
79815	Jones, Corp Thomas N.	I
79831	Ford, James H.	I
79831	Patterson, George	I
79888	Foster, Adam	I
79890	Mixer, Henry	I
79956	Pelky, Joseph	I
79956	Heighez, Levitt	I
79956	Rigg, James C.	I
80119	Davis, W. P.	I
80152	Quick, John	I
80159	Quick, John	I
80159	Utter, Henry	I
80159	Foster, Adam	I
80177	Kelly, Thos. J.	I
80222	Beals, Wm. M	I
80238	Trees, Davis	I
80325	Griffit, Wm.	I
80611	Wise, Henry A.	I
86745	Grasse, John S.	I
86745	Adams, David	I
86745	Chapel, Philo	I
89229	Mefford, Wm.	I
91470	Davidson, Aleinous G.	C
91762	Smith, Joseph	C
91744	Lunbeck, John	C
92672	Wheelock, Clarendon W.	C

92738	Resor, 1st Sgt Daniel W.	I		C 11850	Johnson, Matthew S.	I
92738	Resor, David	I		C 11889	Clark, 1st Sgt. James	I
92738	Patrick, Samuel C.	I		C 11889	Alexander, Joseph	I
92783	Dyson, Romine	I		C 11908	Wise, Henry A.	I
92783	Trees, Davis	I		C 11969	Marshall, Robert A.	C
92783	Chapel, Philo	I		C 11970	Eastin, John	C
92819	Patterson, George W.	I		C 11979	Warren, William H.	C
92819	Andrews, John	I		C 11988	Baird, Thomas	C
92819	Huffman, Emberry	I		C 12068	Haga, Gabriel	I
92819	Patterson, George	I		C 12103	Crawford, Robert B.	C
92879	Andrews, John	I		C 12148	Hughey, Levitt	I
92879	Barry, John	I		C 12203	Pelkz, Joseph	I
92879	Grasse, John S.	I		C 12292	Potoine, Charles	I
92888	Crawford, James	C		C 12292	Foster, Job C.	I
92914	Stead, Amos	I		C 12299	Perkins, Gabriel F.	I
92914	Martin, Wm. C.	I		C 12333	Chapel, Philo	I
92914	Stead, Amos	I		C 12333	Warren, Wm. J.	I
92943	Ring, Wm. C.	C		C 12341	Eastin, Wm.	C
92968	Payne, Alonzo G.	C		C 12368	Kelly, Thomas J.	I
92994	Ford, James H.	I		C 12371	Potoine, Charles	I
92994	Weaver, George	I		C 12371	Weaver, Thomas	I
93129	Kelly, Richard F.	I		C 12384	Brooke, Thomas E.	I
93129	Cowan, Hugh	I		C 12384	Alexander, Joseph	I
93137	Simms, Hezekiah W.	I		C 12410	Lade, John	C
93137	Barron, Moses J.	I		C 12514	Garrison, Manchester	I
93275	Warren, Corp. Wm.	I		C 12595	Orr, Wm. H	I
93275	Osborne, Ralph H.	I		C 12595	Streltz, Adam	I
93275	Mefford, Wm. H.	I		C 12600	Condon, Edward	C
93275	Carter, David T.	I		C 12607	Florey, Oscar J.B.	C
93397	Riefle, Frederick	C		C 12608	Osborne, Ralph H.	I
93491	Peifer, Charles K.	C		C 12608	Utter, Henry	I
93502	Foster, Job	I		C 12709	Glimpse, Jonathan	C
93502	Johnson, Robert	I		C 12858	Wilkinson, Richard M.	C
93502	Smith, 1st Sgt. Wm. W.	I		C 12901	Schermer, George F.	C
93502	Billett, John B.	I		C 12988	Orr, Jesse F.	I
C 1334	Ramsey, James E.	I		C 12988	Smith, Wm. F.	I
C 7397	Jones, Mathew T.	C		C 12988	Mefford, Wm.	I
C 7959	Warren, Joseph R.	C		C 12988	Mulraney, James	I
C 8325	Watson, Jesse	I		C 13042	Ainsworth, Avory R.	C
C 9338	Smith, William	C		C 13080	Haughey, Andrew M.	C
C 9476	McKay, Wm.	C				
C 9846	McIntyre, Wm. S.	C				
C 9867	Bromley, Josiah	C				
C 11014	Haughey, Henry C.	C				
C 11053	Arndt, John	C				
C 11450	Duffey, James	C				
C 11453	McCulley, Thomas	C				
C 11491	Fossett, Jonathan	C				
C 11562	Smith, Benjamin	C				
C 11585	Stanefirth, John	C				
C 11591	Foot, Burnley	C				
C 11614	Eldridge, Edward	C				
C 11716	Johnson, James	C				
C 11787	Richey, James D.	I				
C 11787	Miler, Sylvester	I				
C 11815	Vining, William	C				
C 11850	Barre, 1st Sgt. John	I				

6TH ILLINOIS CAVALRY (COS. C AND K)

History: The 6th Illinois Cavalry was raised at Camp Butler, Illinois in November 1861. Their primary service consisted of scouts, skirmishes, and raids in west Tennessee and Mississippi. On April 17, 1863, they left LaGrange, Tennessee with two other regiments on a raid whose ultimate objective was Baton Rouge, Louisiana. Their Colonel, Benjamin H. Grierson, was in overall command. Seventeen days later they reached their objective after numerous skirmishes and the destruction of two railroads and large amounts of property. This raid was the subject of a fictionalized John Wayne movie, *Horse Soldiers*. The 6th Illinois was mustered out November 5, 1865.

Arms: The regiment first received Sharps carbines in mid-1862 and carried them along with a few Cosmopolitan and Burnside carbines until they received Spencers on July 13, 1864. They also received a variety of revolvers including Colt, Remington, Starr, and Savage.

Source: The serial numbers and names for Company C can be found in the volume containing the *Descriptive Books* of Cos. A to D. The same information for Co. K is located in that company's *Order Book*.

Carbines

Serial #	Name	Company
53999	Chumley, D. R.	C
72271	Curtis, C. L.	C
74330	Boeckewitz, Wm.	C
75349	Trout, John	K
75803	Yates, Cpl. J. M.	K
75813	Bradley, Robt.	C
75814	Carnahan, Wm.	C
75850	Silkwood, N.	C
75867	Call, John	K
75885	Riley, Cpl. J. D.	K
75899	Belvin, Cpl. R. A.	K
75901	Barker, C.	C
75978	Peterson, J.	C
75978	Lewis, W. C.	C
75984	Lanham, J. J.	K
75999	Poland, P.	C
76047	Hemphill, Cpl. S.A.	K
76050	Rude, Sgt. W. A.	K
76107	Mullin, B.	C
76152	Finn, Michiel	C
76152	Deeds, H. M.	C
76153	Lamb, J. T.	K
76155	Sinclair, John	C
76160	Brady, J. J.	C
76170	Holiday, G. W.	C
76183	Coulan, P.	C
76187	Robinson, Cpl. D.	K
76198	Cannon, J. H.	K
76216	Gibson, Sgt. A.	K
76237	McEvers, H.	C
76262	Hardesty, Sgt. C	K
76363	Hite, S. S.	C
76374	Hardesty, John	K
76424	Wilson, G.	C
76441	Peterson, J.	C
76546	Nagle, Pat	C
76576	Wright, W. J.	K
76634	Wilkinson, G.	C
76666	Poland, P.	C
76685	Lanham, J. G.	K
76697	Parker, H. H.	K
76700	Carpenter, E. W.	C
76738	Jennings, D. N.	K
76750	Mayberry, F.	K
76787	Carpenter, C. L.	C
76787	Buck, J.	C
76826	Ohler, W. J.	C
76826	Lanham, P.	C
76845	Slater, Sgt. J.	K
76876	Wheeler, W. T.	K
76883	Myers, C.	C
76886	Robinson, Jas.	C
76900	Wisecup, B. Smith, J.	K
76906	Lawson, Thos.	C
77002	C. Werner	C
77003	White, Saddler W.	K
77014	Brady, W. C.	C
77029	Whisnant, Wm.	K
77030	Finn, Michiel	C
77055	Yancey, T. G.	C
77070	Hall, J. W.	K
77298	Cleaveland, J. T.	K
77623	Schooley, E. C.	C
77628	Gibson, James	K
77656	Lasalle, T.	C
77657	Snyder, J. J.	C
77657	Barker, T.	K
77658	Cade, J. C.	K
77664	Cook, Cpl. W. D.	K
77672	Davis, S. M.	K
77679	Oliver, R. E.	K
77705	Landers, Z.	C
77708	Glenn, Levi	K
77714	Trout, Henry	K
77720	Mitchell, J. W.	K
77725	Wheeler, W. A.	K
77741	Dunahoo, E	K
77743	Sloun, H. C.	K
77761	Rollman, John	K
77765	Yancey, R. L.	C
85195	Williford, Wm.	D
85256	Allen, H. C.	C
85446	Piles, Henry C.	K
85507	Bradley, Robt.	C
85566	Hrughs, John	K
85608	Bradley, J. O.	C
85622	Pinnell, G. L.	K
85645	Kelly, Jessee A.	K
85666	Jackson, J.	C
85685	Allen, Zacariah	K
85702	Gaines, J. H.	K
85732	Gillian, F.	C
85779	Moore, R. B.	C
85803	Lawrence, W.	K
85819	Allenstine, Bugl. G.	K
85866	Campbell, W. J.	K
85874	Hutchison, Sgt. D.	K

Serial #	Name	Company
85889	Boone, T. R.	C
85898	Douglass, J.	K
85935	Wilson, F. P.	K
85956	Wise, W. H.	K
85969	Wright, Bugl. T. C.	K
85974	Horner, Wm.	K
86010	Watson, N. M.	C
86032	Richey, Farrier W. C.	K
86053	McDonald, J. H.	C
86120	Crawford, G. N.	K
86172	Connard, E. S.	K
86177	Trout, G. H.	K
86204	Nall, R.	K
90384	Perry, Wade H.	K
90412	Metton, L. B.	K
90474	Looker, H. S.	C
90567	Parker, J.	C
90626	Hoagland, J.	C
90630	Rigg, W. P.	C
90674	Nagle, Jas.	C
90700	Adams, C.	C
90723	McMahan, P.	C
90746	Wilkinson, C. W.	C
90818	Gregg, John C.	K
90844	Metton, Wm. L.	K
90850	Smith, R. M.	C
90895	Montgomery, S.	C
90895	Watson, N. M.	C
90917	Chumley, W. J.	C
90927	Cain, G. W.	K
91057	Gibson, James A.	K
91112	Mitchell, R. G.	K
91162	Durfey, M.	C
91343	Larence, Willis	K

7TH ILLINOIS CAVALRY (COS. C AND M)

History: The 7th Illinois Cavalry was organized at Camp Butler, Illinois and mustered in October 13, 1861. Like many cavalry regiments serving in the western theater of the war, their time was largely spent in reconnaissance duty, scouting, and skirmishing. They served largely in Tennessee, Mississippi, Louisiana, and Alabama. They were one of three regiments to participate in the famous raid under Colonel B.H. Grierson from LaGrange, Tennessee to Baton Rouge, Louisiana in April–May 1863. (See 6th Illinois Cavalry.)

Arms: The Sharps carbines listed here date from about the second quarter 1863. They are probably a result of the regiment's desire to fully equip itself with this arm, a goal they never totally reached.

Source: The names and numbers listed can be found in the volume containing the *Order Books of Cos. E to M*.

Carbines

Serial #	Name	Company
90889	Cohen, Louis V.	M
91145	Buhrmester, Christopher	M
90352	Bird, Edgur A.	C
90672	Pair, Joseph	C
91113	Clark, Thomas	C

9TH ILLINOIS CAVALRY (COMPANY K)

History: The 9th Illinois Cavalry was organized at Camp Douglas, Illinois and mustered in November 10, 1861. Its service began in Arkansas where they remained until November 1862 when they crossed the Mississippi on an expedition intended to maneuver the Confederate General Price out of position. Shortly thereafter, they moved to Memphis, Tennessee and served the remainder of the war in the Tennessee, Alabama, Mississippi area participating in numerous expeditions and skirmishes. They were present and took part in the battles of Franklin and Nashville. In one severe fight on November 24, 1864, at Campbellsville, Tennessee, the regiment was hotly engaged, until they were out of ammunition, at which time they fought hand-to-hand using their carbines as clubs. They were mustered out on October 31, 1865.

Arms: This regiment carried a variety of arms including Colt revolving rifles, Burnside carbines, Smith carbines, and Hall carbines as well as Sharps carbines which were issued during the second quarter 1863.

Source: The names and numbers listed here can be found in the bound volume of *Company Order Books for Cos. B to M*.

Carbine

Serial #	Name	Company
37691	Crossley, Charles	K
53020	Kelly, James	K
62996	Wilmat, Bradley A.	K
64732	Padalock, Sgt. Charles B.	K
64746	Leggett, John	K
64746	Cameron, Edward	K
64759	Wilder, John	K
64802	Christian, Samuel S.	K
66057	Stanley, Cpl. James	K
66108	Moloney, Richard	K
66187	Belcher, Wm.	K
66192	Foster, Eratus	K
66244	Cameron, Edward	K
66244	Hanna, Albert M.	K
66250	Toomey, Cpl. Richard	K

66269	O'Keefe, John	K
66341	Woodworth, Sgt. Frank	K
66395	Pullen, Wm. C.	K
66452	Stanley, Sgt. Geo. C.	K
66584	Spinney, Sgt. Joseph O. H.	K
66639	Cohill, Dennis	K
66661	Farnsworth, Wm.	K
66753	Kimbler, Caleb	K
66888	Ward, Nelson	K
67275	Wilkinson, Cpl. Valney S.	K
84296	Martin, Hudson	M
84407	Broad, Ornal D.	M
84463	Dunn, Bernerd	M

10TH ILLINOIS CAVALRY (COMPANY B)

History: The 10th Illinois Cavalry was organized at Camp Butler, Illinois and mustered in November 25, 1861. The regiment was moved to Benton Barracks, Missouri March 13, 1862. From this move and until the war's end, this unit would serve in the Trans-Mississippi area largely in Missouri and Arkansas. The service consisted of scouts and skirmishes with Confederates under Price and Shelby. Unlike most Federal cavalry regiments, the 10th was authorized to use privately owned horses with the stipulation that they carry the "regimental brand." The 10th Illinois was mustered out November 22, 1865.

Arms: The regiment was armed initially with Hall carbines but received Sharps about October 1, 1863. They also carried a variety of revolvers including Remingtons, Colts, Savages, Starrs, and Whitneys.

Source: The Sharps carbines listed can be found on three separate lists in Co. B's *Order Book* which are bound with the *Order Books of Cos. A to M*.

Carbines

Serial #	Name	Company
34183	McQue, John	B
48588	Spellacy, James	B
62332	Davis, Cpl. John	B
68404	Steele, Henry	B
71744	Tuttle, Silas	B
71973	Duff, R. R.	B
72112	Rambarger, Philip	B
72556	Torrence, Wm. H.	B
72605	Clark, Robert B.	B
72794	Smelters, Samul	B
73460	O'Boyle, John	B
73574	Ranebarger, P.	B
73679	Turner, Hbijah	B
73694	Crouch, D. J.	B
73719	Tackel, J. E.	B
73723	Short, Corp. E. G.	B
73730	Fortune, W. E.	B
73732	Leutamayer, Maxamillion	B
73753	Steel, Henry	B
73760	Riley, G. M.	B
73768	Reily, Thomas M.	B
73772	Flowers, Aaron A.	B
73788	Coffield, Enoch	B
73804	Hill, Paul H.	B
73823	West, Andrew G.	B
73829	Sharp, Sanford	B
73829	Boling, Wm.	B
73845	Butter, Samuel	B
73847	Moulan, Burr	B
73854	Taylor, George W.	B
73881	McKee, James S.	B
73898	McMullen, Bk. Smith Samuel	B
73905	Roberts, Farrier Geo.	B
73912	Groenke, Charles	B
73941	McDermott, Edwin S.	B
73975	Cary, George W.	B
74071	O'Neill, John	B
74116	Turner, Abij	B
74116	Green, Geo. W.	B
74137	Creamer, John	B
74140	McMurry, Elihu	B
74158	Roberts, George	B
74164	Philips, Thos.	B
74180	Lowen, John	B
74193	Groaner, Thos.	B
74198	Hill, Andrew S.	B
74208	Butter, QM Sgt. James E.	B
74211	Day, John W.	B
74213	Day, John	B
74214	Westbrooks, Joseph	B
74226	Duff, John	B
74234	Ronnenil, Fletcher	B
74245	Farmer, Sgt. Samuel L.	B
74246	Lowen, John	B
74258	Williams, John	B
74275	Garvey, Martin	B
74294	Smith, Abram	B
74302	Boling, Wm.	B
74307	Short, Wm. M.	B
74309	Ranebarger, Joseph	B
74309	Sharp, Sanford	B
74313	Duff, George	B
74313	Estis, Saddler N. G.	B
74313	Romerei, F.	B
74336	Mayer, Micheal	B
74339	Rager, Sgt. David	B
74344	Wardlow, James	B
74389	Estis, Nathan D.	B
74414	O'Dell, Frank	B
74422	Harris, Cpl. William	B
74456	Keily, Patrick	B

Sharps Carbines & Rifles

74493	Dreman, Cpl. Andy T.	B		82478	West, A. J.	B
74504	Edwards, Comm. Sgt. Archy L.	B		82957	Ennix, Thomas F.	B
74543	Duff, George	B		83824	Park, Geo. W.	B
74552	Watts, Cpl. Issac N.	B		84594	Tuttle, Silas	B
74558	Rambarger, Joseph	B		84594	Morlan, Burr	B
74570	Walker, Samuel C.	B		84594	Westbrooks, John W.	B
74593	Peters, John H.	B		84594	Westbrook, Jno. W.	B
74620	Dillard, Sgt. James	B		84654	Leudermayer, Max.	B
74625	Park, George W.	B		84654	Siner, Warren	B
74634	McReynolds, Geo. F.	B		84665	Turner, Abijah	B
74647	Cofield, Enoch	B		84665	Hutton, Wagoner B. F.	B
74695	Williams, John	B		84758	Silloway, Levi	B
74698	Williams, John	B		84759	Knotts, Jos.	B
75042	Hutton, N. M.	B		84818	Miller, Robert E.	B
75069	Swihart, Jacob	B		84818	Apple, Johnson	B
75192	Carry, Thomas L.	B		84865	Tuttle, Silas	B
75192	Cary, Thos. E.	B		85003	Butler, Samuel	B
75202	Groenke, Charles	B		85084	McKee, J. S.	B
75212	Ennix, Thomas F.	B		85094	Garvey, Martin	B
75285	Hutton, Wagoner B. F.	B		85121	Cary, Thomas L.	B
75307	Tipton, David B.	B		85247	Veach, James W.	B
75312	Taylor, Geo. W.	B		88868	Towner, John	B
75317	Warner, Henry	B		91216	Pierson, John	B
75722	Trickel, Eli	B		92780	Towner, Richard	B
75916	McQue, John	B		33824	McDarmott, Ed. S.	B
76480	Headly, J. G.	B		C 1357	Trickle, Eli	B
76480	Ezell, Geo. E.	B		C 8164	Farrel, R. R.	B
80413	Wardlow, James	B		C 9346	Morgan, John	B
80455	Miller, Robert E.	B		C 9346	Duff, George	B
80524	Duff, John	B		C 9368	Moulan, Burr	B
80540	Duff, Richard	B		C 9388	Smitters, Samuel	B
80690	Palmer, Wm. J.	B		C 9388	Hutton, Wagoner B. F.	B
80742	Hill, Andrew S.	B		C 9388	Ramebarger, Philip	B
80781	Morgan, John	B		C 9471	Pitt, Charles	B
80781	Able, John	B		C 9471	Teel, Jame E.	B
80814	Reynolds, T. F.	B		C 9471	Teel, J. H.	B
80816	Butler, Samuel	B		C 9493	Ennix, Thomas F.	B
80844	Duff, Richard R.	B		C 9493	Hollis, Sgt. John	B
80868	Towner, J. W.	B		C 9493	Ennigs, T. F.	B
81005	Duff, John	B		C 9518	Smith, Simon	B
81053	Westbrook, Joseph	B		C 9524	Carry, George W.	B
81117	Teele, James E.	B		C 9524	Taylor, Cpl. Geo. W.	B
81117	Hearly, Patrick	B		C 9534	Rager, Sgt. David	B
81117	Torrence, Wm. A.	B		C 9556	Smith, Simon	B
81301	McDermott, E. S.	B		C 9556	O'Dell, F. E.	B
81312	McMurry, Elihu	B		C 9743	Phillips, Thomas	B
81485	Morgan, John	B		C 9821	McKee, Bugler J. B.	B
81485	Simon, James J.	B		C 9821	Westbrook, Joseph	B
81576	Teel, J. H.	B		C 9845	Day, John	B
81580	Ezell, George	B		C 9845	Hutton, Sgt N. M.	B
81588	Mayer, Michael	B		C 9845	Morgan, John F.	B
81664	Westbrook, J. W.	B		C 9866	Duff, George	B
81664	Farrel, Richard	B		C 9866	Spellacy, James	B
81749	Peters, John H.	B		C 9866	Harris, Cpl. Wm.	B
81963	Smith, Louis	B		C 9877	Crouch, D. J.	B
81963	Steel, George	B		C 9877	Trickel, Eli	B
82078	Desper, James	B		C 9913	Veatch, James	B

Serial #	Name	Company
C 9939	Green, Geo. W.	B
C 9939	Flowers, Aaron A.	B
C 9947	Romerel, Fletcher	B
C 10037	Drennan, Cpl. S.	B
C 10037	O'Neil, John	B
C 10070	Estes, Sdlr Nathienal G.	B
C 10070	Palmer, William	B
C 10070	Park, Sgt. W. J.	B
C 10090	Scott, Wm.	B
C 10090	Roberts, Farrier George	B
C 10137	Ranebarger, P.	B
C 10148	West, Andrew J.	B
C 10148	Edwards, Sgt. Archy L.	B
C 10157	Groaner, Zac.	B
C 10235	Hill, Cpl. J. W. C.	B
C 10235	Greenwood, C. C.	B
C 10235	Mayer, Michael	B
C 10240	Bowling, Wm.	B
C 10240	McMurry, Elihu	B
C 10356	Tipton, Cpl. D. B.	B
C 10356	Hurley, Patrick	B
C 10357	Pitt, Charles	B
C 10387	McCormac, John	B
C 10387	Desper, James	B
C 10387	Lowen, John	B
C 10392	Farmer, Sgt. S. L.	B
C 10392	Ramebarger, Jos.	B
C 10433	McCue, John	B
C 10435	Watts, Sgt. J. W.	B
C 10435	Druman, Andrew J.	B
C 10435	Ramebarger, Philip	B
C 10436	O'Din, James	B
C 10470	Peters, John H.	B
C 10889	Cofield, Enoch	B
C 13176	Butler, Pvt. Samuel	B
C 14489	Wardlon, J.	B
C 14781	Dunn, John	B
C 15026	McReynolds, Geo.	B
C 15509	Tierney, Micheal	B
C 15509	Rilely, Thomas M.	B
C 15565	McDermott, E. S.	B
C 15568	Simon, James J.	B
C 15574	McKee, James S.	B
C 15574	Sharp, S.	B
C 15579	O'Din, James	B

13TH ILLINOIS CAVALRY (COMPANY F)

History: The 13th Illinois was raised at Camp Douglas, Illinois between October 30, 1861 and February 20, 1862. The regiment spent its entire term of service west of the Mississippi. Their duty consisted of continual scouts and expeditions which resulted in a multitude of skirmishes and obscure battles. They were mustered out August 31, 1865.

Arms: The single Sharps carbine number listed here appears on an arms list dated May 18, 1864. It appears twice, once to a soldier who died December 16, 1864. The regiment was, at this time, primarily armed with Starr carbines.

Source: This number can be found in the *Descriptive Book of Co. F*.

Carbines

Serial #	Name	Company
80001	Johnson, Mordica W.	F
80001	Chiles, Jonathan	F

17TH ILLINOIS CAVALRY (COMPANY A)

History: The 17th Illinois Cavalry was organized at St. Charles, Illinois. The first eight companies were mustered in January 28, 1864. Company A was included in this muster. For nearly the entire service of the regiment, it operated as three separate battalions with Co. A in the 1st Battalion. This battalion served in northern Missouri doing escort and provost duty.

Arms: The Sharps carbines listed here were issued during the third quarter 1864. Due to the late issue of these arms, it is possible they had first belonged to another regiment.

Source: Volume of bound *Descriptive Books Cos. A to K*.

Carbines

Serial #	Name	Company
C 6036	Willer, Cornelius	A
C 7137	Coleman, Andrew	A
C 7660	Miller, Frank	A
C 7660	Harrington, Sgt. Henry	A
C 7886	Hamm, Charles	A
C 7990	Norwell, Sgt Lyman S	A
C 8282	Brown, Wm. A	A
C 8372	Milham, Henry	A
C 8372	Bowers, Bugler Rudolph	A
C 8526	Bell, Edward	A
C 8526	Fletcher, Isaac	A
C 8533	McLaughlin, Michael	A
C 8540	Extien, Charles D	A
C 8572		
C 8647	Smith, Joseph S	A
C 8667	McDermott, Henry	A

Serial #	Name	Company
C 8667	Price, Charles	A
C 8670	Stewart, Robert C	A
C 8679	Treest, Alonzo	A
C 8696	O'Neil, Marcus	A
C 8755	Sharpless, Albert	A
C 8763	Hayes, George N	A
C 8763	Ackhurst, Henry	A
C 8767	Downs, Cpl. James B	A
C 8874	Wilson, David O	A
C 8886	Connor, Edward	A
C 9004	Treest, Charles L	A
C 9034	Harrington, 1st Sgt. Scott W.	A
C 9048	O'Neil, Henry	A
C 9048	Latourette, John H	A
C 9085	Burman, Lisle	A
C 9161	Dorn, Cpl. Albert	A
C 9224	O'Brien, James	A
C 9243	Riley, Patrick	A
C 9246	O'Neil, Henry	A
C 9246	Phillipps, Seth	A
C 9251	Koter, Simon	A
C 9251	Brown, George W	A
C 9260	Simons, Henry	A
C 9260	Brown, Wm. A	A
C 9273	Brown, Cpl. Richard	A
C 9275	Simpson, Peter	A
C 9339	Walsh, Sgt. Charles	A
C 9339	Davis, Sgt. Oscar V	A
C 9358	Kessler, Simon	A
C 9459	Campbell, Robert	A
C 9466	Armstrong, Francis	A
C 9473	Kessler, Michaell	A
C 9541	Lerek, Adam	A
C 9541	Settle, Wm. H	A
C 9541	Treest, Alonzo	A
C 9545	Myers, Joseph	A
C 9545	Yoder, Charles	A
C 9632	Squires, Joseph	A
C 9648	Hayes, George N	A
C 9719	Blair, Sgt. Daniel	A
C 9720	Dalson, Sgt.	A
C 9745	Hopkins, Elliott	A
C 9812	Brown, Wm. A	A
C 9831	Steffens, Bernard	A
C 9838	Armstrong, Francis	A
C 9838	Brown, Truman	A
C 9841	Daly, Wallace	A
C 10049	Brown, Hiram P	A
C 10089	Johnson, James	A
C 10089	O'Neil, Marcus	A
C 10090	Hagadorn, Cpl. John D	A
C 13058	Brown, Truman	A
C 13217	Johnson, James	A
C 13473	Sipple, Augustus	A
C 13575	Underhill, Leonard A	A
C 13747	Taylor, Abram	A
C 13788	Bowers, Bugler Rudolph	A
C 13827	Finn, Wm.	A
C 13879	Smith, M.P.	A
C 13898	Davis, Sgt. Oscar V	A
C 14060	Lewis, John B	A
C 97387	Smith, Wm. P	A

7TH INDIANA CAVALRY (COS. C, E, AND H)

History: The 7th Indiana Cavalry was organized at Indianapolis and mustered in October 1, 1863. Its service consisted largely of scouts and expeditions that included many small battles and skirmishes. They conducted themselves well during the Union retreat from the defeat at Brice's Crossroads, June 10, 1864. They also saw action in Tennessee and Mississippi against guerrillas such as the notorious Dick Davis who was captured by a party of the 7th on October 2, 1864. The regiment was sent to Texas in August 1865 and was mustered out there on February 18, 1866.

Arms: Most of the 7th Indiana were issued Merrill carbines and Colt army revolvers shortly after enlistment. On October 1, 1864, Company E received the Sharps carbines listed, as did portions of Companies C and H. The regiment received Spencer carbines in March 1865.

Source: The Sharps carbine numbers listed can be found in the *Company Order Books* of the companies listed.

Carbines

Serial #	Name	Company
44636	Herrel, John	H
44639	Bryant, Samuel	H
44962	Jean, Samuel F.	B
46206	Armstrong, Jemiah	B
46899	Dixon, Harmon	M
46968	Clark, John	A
47103	Cooper, Ruben	C
48132	Reeves, Lewis	B
51032	Mathews, Benjamin	M
51301	Thomas, Henry C.	M
52677	Hinshaw, John C.	B
52847	Carr, George W.	D
52898	Griffin, Crayton	B
53399	Dayhuff, Eli	D
53545	Clear, David H.	B
53605	Martin, Joseph	M
53613	McDonald, Nathen	M
53642	Gardner, John	H
53642	Anderson, Pvt. Harrison	H
53677	Huishan, John C.	B
53771	English, James A.	A
53780	Pucket, Zacariah	B

53789	Fogley, Geo. W.	D		C 12525	Kitchen, James	H
53803	Brown, Henry	M		C 12535	Nickey, Harrison	B
53823	Haydters, Elijah	B		C 12535	Bigelow, Richard	D
53831	Little, Alexander	B		C 12618	Ackerman, Frank	M
53852	Dupuy, John	E		C 12623	Johnson, Sgt. Nick	D
53852	to 1st Miss. Cav.	E		C 12718	Arnold, John	B
53899	Clear, James	B		C 12720	Stranc, Fred	H
53986	Redenbo, Robert	H		C 12737	Moist, David S.	B
54000	Wagner, Adam C.	D		C 12819	Shirly, Franklin	B
54105	Farl, John	D		C 12870	Schendel, Wm. R.	B
54134	Wood, Elijah T.	B		C 12889	Baldwin, Amos	B
54141	Brandson, Pery	A		C 12964	Whetsel, William	E
54164	Dilsworth, Richard	E		C 12964	Knepper, Joseph	E
54199	Fredrick, George	D		C 12969	Elcott, Nellson	B
63045	Gnllett, Hamillon	B		C 13182	Frasier, Ely	B
65873	Ames, Sanford	E		C 13193	McLeod, Samuel	E
67090	Gorden, Noah H.	A		C 13220	Moore, Francis	E
67290	Cost, Anthony S.	B		C 13257	Patrick, George	D
76588	Woodbery, Daniel	B		C 13260	Gilligo, Micheal	E
76768	to 1st Miss. Cav.	E		C 13260	to 1st Miss. Cav.	E
76882	Bruce, John	D		C 13283	Stevenson, Andrew	D
77082	Ragan, James T.	A		C 13320	Moore, Francis	E
84379	Robinson, Jack	A		C 13331	Conover, George	M
85497	Anderson, F. M.	D		C 13426	Thsop, Benjamin	B
85606	Trulock, Varnal D.	D		C 13451	Gilson, Edward	H
85735	Hodges, James	A		C 13507	Brongher, Sgt. Lewis F.	D
89278	Story, Squire A.	M		C 13513	Johnson, George	D
91132	Ackerman, Frank	M		C 13520	Buchanan, James	M
92165	Booth, Clark B.	A		C 13528	Mullen, John	D
93177	Gardner, William	A		C 13530	Mortorff, Samuel	D
93434	Ludy, Erastus	B		C 13552	Williamson, John D.	B
98309	Ford, George W.	E		C 13557	Morris, Albert	H
98309	Huston, Vinson	B		C 13569	McKinney, James	H
98543	Babb, John W.	E		C 13580	Lhammons, Thomas	E
98969	Kriden, B. J.	B		C 13580	Crow, Abya	E
C 6345	on hand	B		C 13581	Starks, John H.	M
C 6629	Dayhuff, Eli	D		C 13586	Kitsmiller, William	E
C 8542	Wilson, Abraham	M		C 13658	on hand	B
C 10010	Smith No. 1, Geo. W.	B		C 13658	Huffman, A.	B
C 11496	Mossholder, William	A		C 13689	Martin, Mathias	D
C 11686	Smith, Charles	M		C 13703	Donor, Daniel	E
C 11838	Spidle, Clark	H		C 13706	Perkins, John R.	B
C 11878	Bright James	B		C 13708	Carter, Henry	E
C 11940	Chisum, James	H		C 13711	Borgman, Henry	C
C 11941	Maxwille, Sgt. James	H		C 13738	Watts, John	E
C 11966	McQuillion, Cpl. Robert	H		C 13741	Huston, Vinson	B
C 11987	Cavanaugh, Machiel	H		C 13741	Pioner, Jacob	E
C 11987	Duignan, Sgt. Matthew	H		C 13755	Kelly, Sgt. John	H
C 12111	Berry, Hunter	B		C 13761	Cotton, Theodore	M
C 12155	Englehart, Frank	H		C 13796	Ware, John	E
C 12252	Spieknall, Sgt. Geo. W.	D		C 13799	Davis, John	M
C 12260	Graydon, James W.	D		C 13800	Tuttle, Theodore	D
C 12262	to 1st Miss. Cav.	E		C 13803	Heath, Thomas	M
C 12262	Ransbottom, Hickson	E		C 13843	James, Cpl. Geo.	D
C 12281	Underwood, William	E		C 13849	Stoner, Marcus W.	H
C 12336	Rowe, James	H		C 13868	Jackman, James	M
C 12342	Harkens, Henry	E		C 13869	Hass, Cyrus	M

Serial #	Name	Company
C 13869	Grebe, Daniel	M
C 13871	Griffith, Isaac	E
C 13871	Griffetts, Isaac	E
C 13874	Latta, Ehhraim	H
C 13897	Ruby, Joseph	B
C 13906	Selee, Truman	M
C 13915	Falconer, David	M
C 13925	Snowberger, Robert	D
C 13931	on hand	B
C 13936	Watson, Cpl. John Q.	H
C 13983	Nolan, Richard	M
C 13985	Grey, Samuel I.	E
C 13985	Lee, John W.	E
C 13993	Windle, Willaim M. C.	A
C 13997	Coddington, S.	B
C 13998	Gnckert, Richard	D
C 14021	Browning, Reason	H
C 14022	Hunt, Robert G.	B
C 14030	Peterson, Cass M.	B
C 14042	Farris, David	E
C 14051	McNaughton, James	M
C 14059	Osborn, Philip	M
C 14066	Monks, Geo. W.	B
C 14080	Bates, Andrew	H
C 14084	Enerrical, Thomas	E
C 14093	Green, Edward	D
C 14095	Wood, M. P.	E
C 14095	Peters, John K.	E
C 14097	Blackburn, Joseph	E
C 14102	Green, Elias	M
C 14108	Shaw, John	H
C 14110	Lamb, Hiram	B
C 14112	Spaulding, James	A
C 14113	Scott, Samson	B
C 14115	Mitchel, Cpl. Patric	H
C 14117	Clevenger, John G.	E
C 14119	McCabe, James	H
C 14120	Robinson, Sumner	A
C 14126	Frazee, George	E
C 14138	Mckeand, Adam	M
C 14139	Bradburn, Alex.	C
C 14140	Johnson, Henry	M
C 14148	Matheny, John	B
C 14154	Lemon, Cpl. John	D
C 14160	Sherman, Henry	H
C 14169	Hartman, Jacob	B
C 14173	Dashnell, Sgt. John W.	D
C 14181	Sams, Samuel P.	H
C 14278	Squibb, Samuel	C
C 14281	McDavid, Franklin	B
C 14283	Strdhan, Clemant	B
C 14316	Green, Edward	E
C 14323	Jones, John T.	B
C 14336	Detta, Bernard	H
C 14347	Starkey, Thomas	D
C 14348	Porter, Costin	E
C 14362	Bradburn, Alex.	C
C 14375	Clark, Cashius	A
C 14395	Crawford, John	A
C 14400	Bunnel, Justics	B
C 14403	Johnson, Andrew	D
C 14405	More, James	B
C 14416	Benisee, Anthony	E
C 14416	Whetsel, William	E
C 14420	Furgerson, Franklin	A
C 14420	Rains, Allen	A
C 14421	Wallick, Jacob	E
C 14433	Snyder, James	E
C 14433	Cland, James	E
C 14441	Orr, J.	C
C 14441	Harding, Myron	C
C 17579	Currin, Morris	H

1st Iowa Cavalry (Company F)

History: The 1st Iowa Cavalry was organized at Davenport, Iowa and mustered in June 13, 1861. It bears the distinction of being the first volunteer 3-year regiment of cavalry accepted by the United States Government. Like several other volunteer regiments, the men of the 1st Iowa owned their own horses. The regiment saw service in the Trans-Mississippi area, participating in scouts, expeditions, and skirmishes. Their only service east of the Mississippi came in February 1865 when they were ordered to Tennessee. They were mustered out in Austin, Texas, March 16, 1866. While in Texas, they served under General G.A. Custer, who was greatly disliked by these western veterans.

Arms: The regiment was initially armed with Colt navy revolvers and sabres with no carbines. During 1862, they received some Gallager carbines and by early 1863, had received the Sharps listed here.

Source: The numbers listed below may be found in the *Company Descriptive Book of Co. F.*

Carbines

Serial #	Name	Company
45949	McClure, Geo.	F
66569	Poners, Albert	F
66569	Poners, W.	F
67236	Ramsay, Wm.	F
68321	Wilson, Josiah	F
68614	Hart, R. S.	F
71230	Doran, J.	F
71692	Hansel, C. W.	F
71703	Goodwin, E.	F
71731	Mitchell, G. W.	F

71740	Park, R.	F
71740	Woodruff, C.	F
71864	Orun, Alonso	F
72310	Craig, S. R.	F
72352	Catlen, J. S.	F
72371	Branner, T.	F
72371	Smith, Carey	F
72389	George, Wm.	F
72389	Nooinger, J.	F
72465	Savage	F
72485	Cooper, John	F
72561	Boston, Jas.	F
72569	Clark, W.	F
72572	Mathaus, J. S.	F
72875	Klein, M.	F
72875	Priddy, T. W.	F
72875	Tetus, A.	F
72912	Siton, S. M.	F
72928	Mayer, Chas.	F
73023	Hamilton, J.	F
73027	Hamlin, H.	F
73065	Hise, J.	F
73079	McCord, D. M.	F
73079	Rendall, T.	F
73096	Hart, Henry	F
73096	Priddy, T. W.	F
73136	McCoy, Chas.	F
73147	Bolding, W. R.	F
73147	McCord, J. H.	F
73169	Bolton, John	F
73175	Gray, E.	F
73175	Weyley, J. S.	F
73180	Reiley, B. C.	F
73183	Johnson, M. T.	F
73197	Perry, H.	F
73215	Jones, H. P.	F
73215	Nooinger, J.	F
73258	Austin, Dan	F
73258	Corlet, J.	F
73268	Barlow, Chas.	F
73268	Sanders, J. J.	F
73285	Bollinger, B.	F
73304	Park, R.	F
73326	O'Connor, Byran	F
73331	Nourse, C.	F
73371	Boyd, D.	F
73385	Reiley, G. W.	F
73409	Wilson, James C.	F
73412	Bunker, A.	F
73418	Sumner, J. R.	F
73424	Allen, J. S.	F
73424	McCormac, J.	F
73425	Sanders, J. J.	F
73425	Weyley, J. S.	F
73435	Troup, M. G.	F
73912	Bolding, W. R.	F

5TH IOWA CAVALRY (COMPANY M)

History: The 5th Iowa Cavalry was organized by order of General Fremont between September and November 1861. It was formed by a consolidation of several independent cavalry companies and contained men from several different states. Co. M was originally enlisted in Osage County, Missouri by Captain J.K. Kidd and was mustered into U.S. service at Jefferson Barracks, Missouri on September 14, 1861 as the "Osage Independent Mounted Rifles." In March 1862, the battalion containing Company M was ordered to Savannah, Tennessee. The regiment saw extensive service consisting of scouts and raids with numerous engagements in Tennessee, Alabama, and Georgia. In 1865, they participated in Wilson's raid which resulted in the capture of Macon, Georgia. They were mustered out August 11, 1865.

Arms: The regiment was armed with Sharps carbines and Colt army revolvers in early 1863. Co. M had initially carried Hall carbines. By November 1864, they had been issued Spencer carbines.

Source: The Sharps numbers of Co. M can be found in the *Company Order Book*.

Carbines

Serial #	Name	Company
63038	Thompson, Albert G.	M
63622	Kerley, Ben.	M
63622	to QM Murfreesb 7/9/63	M
64800	Perkins, Isaac	M
64865	to QM Murfreesb 7/9/63	M
65895	Tackitt, Lewis	M
65901	Shockley, Oliver	M
65912	Rouhan, Timothy	M
65958	Pryor, Robert F.	M
66159	Miller, John	M
66179	Duncan, Cpl. W. W.	M
66428	Thorp, Daniel	M
66573	Brinn, John	M
66573	to QM Murfreesb 7/9/63	M
66796	Davis, Lewis	M
66953	McKinney, Wm.	M
66953	to QM Murfreesb 7/9/63	M
66996	Moore, Thomas	M
67088	Hargis, J. C. L.	M
67125	Powell, Joh	M
67125	to QM Murfreesb 7/9/63	M
67176	Lane, Cpl. M. V.	M
67195	Snyder, Cpl. Wm.	M
67195	to QM Murfeesb 7/9/63	M
67219	Laughlen, 3rd Sgt. G. D.	M

Serial #	Name	Company
67235	Massii, Peter	M
67235	to QM Murfreesb 7/9/63	M
67271	Tackitt, John	M
67278	Killion, Henry	M
67369	Britt, Wm.	M
67376	Garard, Seaman C.	M
69190	to QM Murfreesb 7/9/63	M
74082	Carwile, Newton	M
76473	Lee, David	M
77871	to QM Murfreesb 7/9/63	M
78041	Cannon, Nathaniel	M
78158	Denoya, Wm. H.	M
78251	Kerley, Ben.	M
78260	Rogers, John R.	M
78279	Hollingsworth, Wm.	M
78279	to QM Murfreesb 7/9/63	M
78282	Hensley, Thos.	M
78285	Wolfe, John	M
78302	Hojswoord, Wm. C.	M
78330	Steinman, Chas. H.	M
78349	McKenney, Geo. W.	M
78366	Walton, Jere	M
78371	Ward, Francis	M
78372	Jordon, 6th Sgt. Hugh	M
78391	Moore, Comm. Sgt. Hez	M
78412	Harty, Roger T.	M
78412	Howard, James	M
78414	McGinn, Patrick	M
78429	Hall, M. R.	M
78432	Harris, Wm. C.	M
78448	Tackitt, Geo. W.	M
78483	Walker, Sam.	M
78556	Moore, Henry	M
78571	Sterling, Wm. H.	M
78571	to QM Murfreesb 7/9/63	M
78583	Millikan, Ben. M.	M
78592	Fowler, Robert	M
78610	Welch, Wm.	M
78636	Duncan, Irven	M
78647	to QM Murfreesb 7/9/63	M
78650	Lambeth, Jassee	M
78683	Sherman, 4th Sgt. Geo.	M
78684	Dubreller, Theopolis	M
78688	Curtit, Emile	M
78688	Hopwood, Wm. C.	M
78688	to QM Murfreesb 7/9/63	M
78689	Anderson, Sterling B.	M
78689	Sterling, Wm. H.	M
78690	Walker, W. E.	M
78720	McAfee, H. A.	M
78728	Curtit, 5th Sgt. Irene	M
78732	Whittenbach, Adam	M
78737	Klnner, Blksmth John	M
78737	to QM Murfreesb 7/9/63	M
78738	Johnson, Thos.	M
78749	Rufie, Jacob	M
78753	Jarvis, Wm.	M
78779	Curtit, Lewis	M
78790	Bunch, Samuel	M
78790	to QM Murfreesb 7/9/63	M
78797	Killion, John	M
78797	Neighbor, John	M
78812	Robertsn, H. R.	M
78839	Dial, James D.	M
78840	Husgen, Henry	M
78840	Millikan, Ben. M.	M
78841	Williams, John A.	M
78857	Bunch, Samuel	M
78857	Lee, David	M
78866	Fowler, Wm.	M
78867	Best, John	M
78867	Massii, Peter	M
78904	Cooley, Cpl. A. O.	M
78916	Rook, Amon	M
78921	Millikan, Wm.	M
78937	Brinn, John	M
79051	Ward, Wm. H.	M
79103	to QM Murfreesb 7/9/63	M

2ND KANSAS CAVALRY (COMPANY E)

History: The 2nd Kansas Cavalry was originally raised as the 12th Kansas Infantry. The designation was changed on March 5, 1862. Throughout the service of the regiment, it was engaged in scouts, expeditions, and escort duty in Kansas, Missouri, and Arkansas. There were numerous small engagements with Confederate forces, including guerrillas, and several battles such as Prairie Grove on December 7, 1862. The regiment was mustered out at Lawrence, Kansas, on August 17, 1865.

Arms: In addition to the Sharps carbines listed, Company E was also armed with Colt army and Remington (Beals) revolvers. Other companies in the regiment received the French Lefaucheux pin-fire revolver.

Source: The Sharps numbers listed for Company E were found in the *Company Descriptive Book*.

Carbines

Serial #	Name	Company
54034	Grey, John	E
68789	Longstraws, Benj.	E
73727	Jones, Theodore	E
73727	Tuxburry, Jesse	E
76665	Racine, John R.	E
76829	Eggleston, Alison H.	E
76856	Armstrong, Jame	E

76856	Ravelestt, Mitchel	E
76903	Bratten, Alex. M.	E
77005	Robinson, Neal C.	E
77042	Murphy, John	E
77047	Lacosto, Joseph	E
77052	Lee, Nathaniel	E
77117	Barrow, Augustus	E
77117	Cass, Thomas M.	E
77142	Cole, Samuel	E
77142	Cummings, John	E
77154	Clark, Sam	E
77189	Glancy, John C.	E
77206	Mayes, Chas.	E
77268	Akin, Cpl. Jos.	E
77276	Startwood, Jacob	E
77284	Domland, John	E
77315	Rimball, Charles A.	E
77321	Dawson, Sgt. Stephen W.	E
77381	Weathery, Wm. H.	E
77394	Burdlow, Mitchel	E
77394	Grey, John	E
77409	Burdlow, Milchel	E
77435	Ravellesto, Peter	E
77461	Bartlett, Cpl. Saml.	E
77471	Wyckoff, Jos.	E
77476	Eubanks, John S.	E
77481	Doran, William	E
77500	Potrine, Israiel	E
77525	Mayes, Henry	E
77530	Winney, Cpl. Claudius P.	E
77539	Lozier, Sgt. Charles W.	E
77547	Charleston, John	E
77590	Powers, James	E
77619	Lewis, Charles	E
77639	Armstrong, Pvt. James	E
78134	McConnell, John	E
78153	Petersen, Charles	E
78205	McFarland, E.S.	E
78220	Walbridge, Sgt. Jerome	E
78223	Baird, John P.	E
78228	Weston, Cpl. Phineas E.	E
78229	Weatherby, M. W.	E

5TH KANSAS CAVALRY (COMPANY I)

History: The 5th Kansas Cavalry was organized during the last half of 1861 and mustered in at Leavenworth City, January 22, 1862. The regiment's entire service was in Kansas and Arkansas with a short time in Mississippi. It conducted a war of constant skirmishes, scouts, and expeditions often with or in pursuit of Confederate irregular forces such as the infamous Quantrell. The regiment was mustered out piecemeal beginning in August 1864. Company I remained in service until June 22, 1865.

Arms: The 5th Kansas was armed with both the Sharps carbine and Colt army revolver.

Source: The Sharps numbers listed below can be found in *The Order Book of Co. I*.

Carbines

Serial #	Name	Company
73953	Hovington, John	I
75769	Sears, David W.	I
81188	Nagle, Simon	I
81360	Howald, Adam	I
81685	Dodson, Daniel	I
81755	Morrison, L.	I
81811	Harris, Jas. G.	I
81848	Tapp, Elias	I
81945	Wilson, Hannibal	I
82341	Sallyers, Sam'l.	I
83472	Fisk, George	I
83755	Robertson, Geo.	I

14TH KANSAS CAVALRY (COMPANY B)

History: The 14th Kansas was raised at Ft. Scott in December 1863. They were assigned to the Army of the Frontier and later to the 7th Army Corps. The regiment spent its entire service in Kansas and Missouri. Here they engaged in numerous scouts and expeditions resulting in a series of skirmishes and small battles. This service resulted in a total killed and mortally wounded equal to many regiments who served in the famous armies and battles east of the Mississippi. The regiment was mustered out June 25, 1865.

Arms: The 14th Kansas was armed primarily with Union and Gallager carbines. The Sharps numbers listed here appear on a list dated March 17, 1864.

Source: The names and numbers given can be found in Co. B's *Order Book*.

Carbines

Serial#	Name	Company
79456	Cox, Clisby	B
95217	Cummings, Wm.	B

2ND KENTUCKY CAVALRY (COMPANY L)

History: The 2nd Kentucky Cavalry (U.S.) began organization September 9, 1861 and was mustered in February 13, 1862. They first served with the Army of the Ohio, but in November 1862 they were assigned to the hard-fighting Army of the Cumberland. The regiment participated in most of the campaigns and major battles in the western theater of the war from Shiloh on, including the entire campaign of Sherman's Army, which resulted in the surrender of Joe Johnston's Confederate Army in North Carolina. The 2nd Kentucky was mustered out in July 1865.

Arms: The 2nd Kentucky received Merrill carbines along with Colt army and Colt navy revolvers in early 1863. The Sharps carbines listed here were issued in 1864.

Source: The Sharps numbers listed were part of the Ordnance account for 1864 included in the *Order Books of Co. L*.

Carbines

Serial #	Name	Co.
48253	Cooper, Wm. M.	L
48539	Gardner, Geo.	L
49503	Groaster, Martin	L
61079	Wise, Wm. W.	L
64034	Ginn, Wm. E.	L
72161	Norris, John H.	L
80218	Forman, Thomas	L

4TH KENTUCKY CAVALRY (COMPANY B)

History: The 4th Kentucky Cavalry was organized at Louisville, Kentucky and mustered in December 24, 1861. During 1862 and early 1863, the regiment was engaged in scouting and reconnoitering in southern Kentucky and Tennessee. During this time they were engaged in numerous skirmishes. In August 1863, the 4th Kentucky advanced with the Army of the Cumberland in the movement which resulted in the Battle of Chickamauga. During the Federal army's withdrawal from that field the regiment, along with two other Kentucky cavalry regiments, covered the retreat and were heavily engaged. In 1864 the 4th Kentucky took part in the cavalry operations of the Atlanta campaign. After the fall of Atlanta, they returned to Nashville and served in that area until becoming part of Wilson's expedition through Alabama and Georgia. The regiment was mustered out August 21, 1865.

Arms: The Sharps carbines listed were probably issued in 1864. The wide dispersal of the numbers seem to indicate they were arms that had originally been issued to other units.

Source: The numbers listed, along with others that were unreadable, can be found in the *Company Descriptive Book of Co. B*.

Carbines

Serial #	Name	Company
36735	Schauer, John	B
37679	Brickman, Christ	B
38937	Lauthart, Chas.	B
51503	Hoertz, J. B.	B
52298	Fenton, David R.	B
52386	Stewart, Thomas	B
52937	Stier, Frank	B
64115	Schneider, G.	B
64410	Black, Fred	B
86442	Bickel, J. H.	B
C 3684	Just, Wm.	B

1ST MARYLAND CAVALRY (US) (COS. G AND I)

History: The 1st Maryland was organized in late 1861 with two companies not joining until May of 1862. The first six companies were from the Baltimore area but others were raised in western Maryland, Pennsylvania, and Washington, D.C. The early service of the regiment was primarily in western Virginia and Maryland. By September 1862 they had joined the Army of the Potomac and until February 1864 they shared the fortunes of that command. This service included Brandy Station and Gettysburg. In February they were transferred to the 8th Corps then quickly to the 10th Corps as a part of the Army of the James. They saw action around Petersburg and were present at Appomattox Courthouse on April 9, 1865. The regiment was mustered out August 8, 1865.

Arms: The regiment was initially armed with Sharps carbines and Colt revolvers. The numbers given here are from two separate lists. The initial list which contains numbers below the "C" series dates from early 1863. These probably are the regiment's initial issue. The "C" prefix numbers are found on lists dated October 12, 1864 and February 11, 1865.

Source: The numbers and names for this regiment can be found in the *Company Descriptive Books* of the companies listed.

Carbines

Serial #	Name	Company
31781	Gibson, Watson	G
34375	Charles, Stewart	G
34533	Schwartz, Charles	G
47802	Schmidt, Augustus	G
48732	Hezler, Michael	G
55311	Gachles, William H.	G
55521	Roth, Sgt. William F.	G
55741	Gorley, Thomas	G
60221	Harvey, Patrick	G
60257	Brand, Jacob	G
61234	Roth, Sgt. William F.	G
61344	Lewis, Cpl. Andrew	G
61344	Horn, Frank	G
61423	Glunt, Cpl. Henry	G
61436	Porter, Cpl. Willlam	G
61457	McCoy, Willlam	G
61457	Neely, Sgt. Alexander	G
61791	Phillips, Joseph	G
62469	Yost, Sgt. Jacob	G
62480	Lewis, Cpl. Andrew	G
67596	Leavitt, Edward	G
67758	Lafferty	G
69299	Irwin, David	G
69310	Heater, John C.	G
69810	Lowstetter, Thomas	G
69932	Brown, Pvt. William	G
70409	Schousler, John	G
70409	Schmidt, Augustus	G
70438	Hemphill, John	G
70532	McKown, Cpl. William H.	G
70578	McCoy, Charles	G
70585	Hezler, Michael	G
70613	Glunt, Cpl. Henry	G
70687	Charles, Stewart	G
70760	Wilson, Sgt. Andrew	G
70786	Sampson, George	G
71004	Megle, Henry	G
71063	Beltzhoovert Sgt. John	G
71064	Baker	G
71093	Rowe, Richard	G
71096	Hibler, Samuel	G
71096	Lafferty	G
71114	Stautmeller, Andrew	G
71119	Walkins, Charles	G
71139	Fundis, Frederick	G
71163	Conely, Patrick	G
71194	Doyle, John	G
71262	Thompson, Luther J.	G
71316	Harvey, Patrick	G
71352	Parkerson, Richard	G
71427	Quill, Timothy	G
75469	McKown, Cpl. William H.	G
C 7048	Williams, William	I
C 8126	Elliott, Robert W.	I
C 8473	Chaney, Ezekiel	I
C 8892	Gettel, Frederick	I
C 8975	Kimball, William A.	I
C 8994	Anderson, David	I
C 9001	Nitzell, William	I
C 9198	Ruthf James M.	I
C 9214	Curtis, John	I
C 9284	Barger, Nelson	I
C 9496	Rutherford, George W.	I
C 9586	Gower, Jacob	I
C 9601	Williams, William	I
C 9601	Frailey, Daniel	I
C 9683	Gower, Jacob	I
C 9692	Finnegan, James W.	I
C 9722	Crawford, Jacob W.	I
C 9902	Leary, William L.	I
C 10016	Huff, John	I
C 10016	Leary, William L.	I
C 10111	Young, Martin	I
C 10161	Carr, John	I
C 10232	Yoder, John	I
C 10255	Gallagher, Thomas	I
C 10283	Manias, John	I
C 10283	Booth, John	I
C 10283	Young, Martin	I
C 10404	Helferstay, George	I
C 10467	Brooks, Samuel	I
C 10933	O'Neal, Thomas	I
C 10933	O'Neal, James T.	I
C 11604	Snyder, Daniel	I
C 11743	Hutzler, John	I
C 11772	Tabler, William	I
C 11772	Devilbiss, Irvin A.	I
C 11841	Manius, John	I
C 11972	Tabler, William M.	I
C 11977	Kerns, Geo. M.	I
C 12159	Sterling, George M.	I
C 25349	Warner, Augustus	I
C 27037	Davis, George	I
C 27107	Gambrill, William	I
C 27467	Marz, August	I
C 29533	Carr, John	I
C 29536	Strawbridge, Aquilla	I
C 29549	Morganhall, Lewis	I
C 29636	Carver, Thomas	I
C 29655	Nowling, Thomas	I
C 29735	Frailey, Daniel	I
C 29810	Leckenburg, William	I
C 30072	Hidden, Benjamin	I
C 30088	Gettel, Frederick	I
C 30155	Long, George	I
C 30384	Rathell, George	I
C 30449	Ramer, John	I
C 30452	Reeger, John	I
C 30463	Fiades, Benjamin	I
C 30484	Little, Henry D.	I
C 30512	Hughes, John	I

Serial #	Name	Company
C 30562	Golle, Julius	I
C 30578	Vogt, Henry	I
C 30580	Dashiell, George M.	I
C 30584	Curtis, John	I
C 30608	Garrett, William	I
C 30633	Brooks, Samuel	I
C 30672	Snyder, Daniel	I
C 30707	Lewis, George	I
C 30733	Gardner, George	I
C 30744	Gabriel, August	I
C 30800	Frankenfield, Reuben	I
C 30846	Nitzell, William	I
C 30861	Corkney, James	I
C 30877	Iiams, Daniel	I
C 30892	Burns, James	I
C 30893	Anderson, David	I
C 30943	Kerns, George M.	I
C 30974	Dyer, Lee	I
C 30975	Mark, John	I

1st Potomac Home Brigade Maryland Cavalry (US) (Company A)

History: This unit consisted of four companies of Independent Maryland Cavalry. These companies were all formed between August and November 1861 at Frederick, Maryland. They were consolidated to a Battalion on August 1, 1862 and designated "Cole's Battalion Potomac Home Brigade Cavalry." Early service was in the northern Shenandoah Valley as part of the Middle Department. In July 1863 they participated in the Gettysburg campaign. All further service was in the Shenandoah Valley and the nearby counties of West Virginia and Maryland. In April 1864 the battalion was raised to regimental strength with companies recruited in Baltimore and Frederick. They were mustered out June 28, 1865.

Arms: Company A was Captain Cole's company. The numbers are found on two separate lists. Those numbers below the "C" series are probably the original issue; however, the list dates from early 1864. The "C" numbers are likely replacement arms. The company also received Gallager carbines.

Source: The numbers and names listed can be found in the *Company Descriptive Books*.

Carbines

Serial #	Name	Company
37624	Kelly, John	A
43319	Kerns, John	A
43603	Albaugh, Basil	A
43603	McKnight, James	A
43631	Kelliam, John	A
43646	Wachter, Gideon R.	A
43863	Sheafer, Charles	A
43989	McDevitt, James H.	A
44003	Hargepp, George B.	A
47876	Speck, David	A
48694	Neighbrout, John	A
48879	Weaver, J.	A
48925	Ulrick, William	A
49127	Leonard, George L.	A
49343	Angleberger, Thomas	A
49512	Angleberger, Thomas T.	A
49876	Hall, John B.	A
52199	Everly, Jeremiah	A
58311	Wheeler, Thomas	A
58377	Belding, Samuel	A
58515	Batehammer, George	A
59555	Grams, Franklin D.	A
59724	Holden, William	A
59745	Atkinson, William	A
59750	Fraley, John	A
60059	Fouch, Temple	A
60094	Grams, Franklinn D.	A
60706	Albaugh, Basil H.	A
60706	Freet, J.	A
60947	Hall, Levi M.	A
60977	Dern, Abraham	A
60986	Wolf, William	A
61830	Devilbyss, Isaac	A
61991	Virks, James M. W.	A
62141	Earley, John W.	A
62164	Kauffman, Martin L.	A
62186	Murphy, H. A.	A
62226	Wheeler, Thomas	A
62308	Smith, George	A
62913	Keiglo, Josiah A.	A
65209	Kauffman, Martin	A
67401	Fraley, John F.	A
67401	Mathews, C.	A
67784	Hall, Levi M.	A
67863	Fogle, Henry	A
67917	Webster, William	A
68121	Washburn, David	A
69747	Miller, John	A
70299	Snyder, George	A
70480	Hanson, Walter	A
70748	Grant, John T.	A
73578	Cubits, John M.	A
75637	Frey, Martin	A
76739	Carmack, Valentine S.	A
79633	Crawford, Benjamin F.	A
82186	Stansbury, Joseph H.	A
82258	Moses, Guy	A
83667	Edwards, John	A
86179	Dixon, Franklin	A

86303	Lancaster, John W.	A
86391	Wachter, Thomas M.	A
86673	Farrow, Samuel W.	A
87245	Crawford, Joshua M.	A
87633	Ridgeway, Richard	A
88048	Disney, Aaron	A
88106	Kellian, John	A
88788	Fry, Martin	A
88843	Washburn, David L.	A
88960	Zeigler, James R.	A
90624	Clark, J. T.	A
91879	Avery, Samuel	A
92390	Zeigler, George F.	A
95800	Early, John	A
96928	Fouch, Temple	A
99210	Harnes, William	A
99322	Fisher, Leonard	A
99371	Mayett, George B.	A
C 827	Amos, Charles E.	A
C 1852	Cook, Ben. F.	A
C 2577	Whip, George C.	A
C 2696	Leonhart, John J.	A
C 2712	Smeltzen, Soloman S.	A
C 3503	Fray, James L.	A
C 3915	Pearson, David	A
C 5142	Yeast, Charles M.	A
C 5300	Hurst, John	A
C 5617	Speck, David	A
C 5996	Dellett, John J.	A
C 7261	Robson, John	A
C 7420	Dicken, William	A
C 7576	Davis, S. G.	A
C 7586	Fogle, Soloman	A
C 8654	Brown, George W.	A
C 8853	Kreuglo, Isaah	A
C 8863	Wolfe, William	A
C 10375	Smith, Martin	A
C 14590	Shilt, Samuel	A
C 14616	Batehamer, John	A
C 15074	Alkinson, William	A
C 15254	Fosler, Charles	A
C 15803	Webster, William T.	A
C 15824	Grams, J. C.	A
C 15846	Wilders, James	A
C 15937	Cromwell, Aurthur H.	A
C 16195	Stottlemeyer, Andrew J.	A
C 18976	McKnight, James T.	A
C 19478	Orrison, Logan	A
C 26492	Kerns, John	A

1ST MASSACHUSETTS CAVALRY (COMPANY D)

History: The 1st Massachusetts Cavalry was organized at Camp Brigham, Reedville, Massachusetts, in December 1861. Its early service was on the islands off the South Carolina coast. In August 1862 they moved by ship to the Washington, D.C., area and shortly thereafter joined the Army of the Potomac. From that time on, the regimental history is that of the Cavalry Corps of that famed eastern army. The 1st Massachusetts shared in nearly every battle from South Mountain in September 1862 to the fall of Petersburg in 1865. The regiment was mustered out at Reedville, Massachusetts, July 24, 1865.

Arms: The 1st Massachusetts was initially armed with the Smith carbine, a weapon the men disliked because of trouble with its cartridge. These weapons were replaced about March 1863 with Sharps carbines. The numbers listed here date from that issue. In addition, the regiment carried Colt, Remington, and Starr army revolvers.

Source: The numbers and names listed can be found in the *Regimental Consolidated Morning Report and Order Book.*

Carbines

Serial #	Name	Company
32098	Cranshaw, James W.	D
43375	Almy, Frank M.	D
44643	Paul, Wm.	D
49450	Marsh, Martin L.	D
49895	Olney, G. F.	D
59185	Ames, David H.	D
59447	Dunbar, Geo. F.	D
62178	Rogers, Cpl. Samuel D.	D
62492	Squier, Roswell	D
63909	Austin, John	D
64323	Waters, P.	D
67776	Kimball, Chas. H.	D
67901	Collins, James E.	D
68812	Littlefield, Albert	D
68939	Hobson, Geo. H.	D
69284	Nicholson, Chas.	D
69731	Hill, Wm. Henry	D
69731	Walls, Chas. C.	D
71876	Kent, Geo. W.	D
74653	Walls, Chas. C.	D
76252	Crombie, H. W.	D
76252	Fay, Chas. A.	D
76252	Whittier, Wm. P.	D
76633	Bellow, Lewis	D
78731	Shepherd, Lewis J.	D

Company G, 1st Massachusetts Cavalry at Edisto Island in May 1862. (USAMHI—Mass. MOLLUS collection)

83449	Bailey, Geo. W.	D
86367	Blasland, Wm.	D
87551	Moore, Wm.	D
88174	Sturdevant, Wm. H.	D
88177	Boole, Geo. T.	D
88285	Hurd, Edwin	D
88291	Pray, Chas. H.	D
89001	Egleston, Wm. R.	D
90003	Lowell, Wm. H.	D
90020	Johnson	D
90973	Bailey, Geo. F.	D
91013	Salsbury, Geo. H.	D
91940	McPhearson, Wm.	D
92498	Clapp, Wm. A.	D
92688	Greely, Warren	D
93442	Bently, Thomas	D
93670	Young, Seth	D
93733	Tucker, Wm. O.	D
93766	Osgood, Joseph H.	D
93838	Boyce, Jerome	D
93851	Bailey, Rufus H.	D
93959	Whitham, Chas.	D
93975	Dennis, Henry W.	D
94069	Morse, Henry M.	D
94122	Fay, Chas. A.	D
94202	Thayer, Henry C.	D
94498	Brown, Curtis M.	D
95229	Bradbury, Cpl. Geo. L.	D
95339	Corning, Warren H.	D
96334	Peale	D
96520	Crombie, H. W.	D
96540	Whittier, Wm. P.	D
96838	Olney, Cpl. Geo. F.	D
97718	Atherton, Chas. D.	D
99022	Austin, John	D

5TH MICHIGAN INFANTRY (COS. I AND K)

History: The 5th Michigan Infantry was organized at Detroit in August 1861. After reaching Washington, D.C., in September, they were assigned to the Army of the Potomac. From that day until the final days of the war, the history of the 5th Michigan was that of the Army itself. As part of the hard fighting 3rd Army Corps, they fought on the Peninsula, at Fredericksburg, and in the bloody Wheatfield at Gettysburg. When the 3rd Corps was disbanded in 1864, the 5th Michigan was assigned to the famous 2nd Corps. It was during the last months of the war that they received Sharps rifles as well as Spencer rifles, an honor often reserved for the most deserving regiments. The 5th Michigan was mustered out at Jeffersonville, Indiana, July 5, 1865.

Arms: The 5th Michigan Infantry carried a variety of arms during its long service. These included Austrian, Enfield, and Springfield rifle muskets as well as Spencer rifles. The Sharps listed here were issued in December 1864 or January 1865. The low serial numbers and the knowledge that those issued to Company K are identified as having sabre bayonets indicate that these arms had previously been issued to another regiment.

Source: The Sharps serial numbers listed here can be found in the *Company Order Books of Cos. I and K*.

Carbines (Rifles w/ sabre bayonets in Company K)

Serial #	Name	Company
30900	Tutle	I
33412	Fitzgerald	I
35100	Peacock, William	K
35435	Lacroido, N.	I
36704	Whittaker, Ezra	K
36752	Harrot, Aaron	K
36822	Budde, William	K
36833	Brach, Cyrus	I
36840	Heelwing	I
36855	Buel, F.	I
36864	Hasse, George	K
36894	Wickman, C.	K
36933	Jones, Samuel	K
36964	Gudschynky, H.	K
37155	Goodrich	I
37324	Miller, August	K
37325	Saseith, A.	I
37325	Tupper, L.	I
37394	Buhler, Christian	K
37417	Overlock	I
37454	Whitaker, A.	I
37458	Tack, John	K
37480	Quinn, Patrick	K
37501	Allen, A.	I
37514	Morton	I
37532	Wolf, C.	I
38136	Stern, Fred	K
38955	Liebenshal, John	K
38971	Brown, Charles	K
38975	Mollison, J.	I
38995	Jacobs, Emmanuel	K
39252	Cameron, A.	I
39276	Low, John	K
39277	Sinkley, D.	I
39335	King, H.	I
39687	Muir, Edgar	I
39904	Jordan, F.	I
39904	Lawrence, G.	I
40092	Wood, J.	I
40104	Bugman, J.	I
40252	Shuer, John	K
40398	Johnson, Gideon	K
40414	Madison, Hugh	K
40478	Lacroix, G.	I
40637	Lawrence, G.	I
40720	Bower, R.	I
40751	Jones, John	I
41282	Starks, Sumner	K
41676	Zeitz, F.	I
42667	Curtis, Henry	I
42845	Higgins, P.	I
42915	Chubb, P.	I
42980	Jordan, F.	I
42980	Regan, J.	I
43328	Herpts, Frederick	K
43338	Carges, Henry	K
43376	Sautter, John	K
43532	Lutz, John	K
43533	Low, Charles	K
43564	Sawyer, D.	I
43765	Demoyer, P.	I
43765	Tupper, L.	I
44443	Hartman, August	K
54590	Sawyer, G.	I

8TH MICHIGAN CAVALRY (COS. K AND L)

History: The 8th Michigan Cavalry was recruited at Mt. Clemens and mustered in May 2, 1863. The regiment's first action involved the pursuit and final capture of John Hunt Morgan during his famous raid across Indiana and Ohio. Following this the 8th served with the cavalry of the 23rd Corps in Tennessee for the remainder of 1863 and early 1864. In June 1864 they left as part of Sherman's Atlanta campaign under the command of General Stoneman. During that general's raid on Macon, Georgia the entire command was surrounded and many were captured. The 8th Michigan elected to cut their way out and made a temporary escape only to lose many men captured before the remnants reached the Union lines. Those remaining, along with recruits, participated in the operations around Nashville. After Hood's repulse the remainder of their service was occupied in scouting and patrol duty including actions against guerrillas. The regiment was mustered out at Nashville, September 22, 1865.

Arms: The 8th Michigan is a story in reverse when it comes to arms. While many Union cavalry regiments began the war with Sharps or Burnside carbines and ended the war with Spencers, the 8th was initially armed with Spencer rifles and ended the war with Sharps carbines and Springfield rifle muskets. The carbines listed here date from a list compiled in late 1864 or early 1865.

Source: The carbines listed can be found in the *Company Descriptive Books* along with the names of those who received them.

Carbines

Serial #	Name	Company
12432	Trimmer, James Y.	K
12742	Patten, Geo.	K
12905	Emmons, B.K.	L
16832	Chase, Henry E.	K
18098	King, Clemens	K
18330	Goodman, Frank	K
22240	Smith, John	L
34717	Wilder, Scott	L
38236	Downey, Frank	K
38425	Dennis, Joseph	L
45385	Walton, James	L
45759	Bentley, James	K
45759	Cowell, Wm.	K
49422	Anderson, Joseph	L
50092	Mott, Edw. R.	K
50092	Beers, Wesley J.	K
50315	Hallick, John W.	L
51252	Fisher, Wm.	K
51904	Parker, Thomas	K
52047	Kimball, Wm. E.	K
52351	_eynols, Wm.	L
52619	Baker, Milon D.	K
53128	Swartz, Henry	K
53209	Wilder, Henry	L
53274	McCarty, Richard	K
53274	Grett, John	K
53331	Honeywell, John	K
53966	Doty, Eugene	L
85248	" "	
56289	Ferrigan, Patrick	K
61250	Clark, Wm.	L
61254	Brunson, Aaron	L
61609	Sitts, James	L
61843	Marsh, Thomas	L
62156	Hart, Frank	L
63149	Klocks, Alexander	L
84532	" "	
63261	Hayle, Samuel E.	L
64040	Shuman, S.	K
64133	Glass, Edw.	K
66017	Morbry, John	L
66573	Donahue, Edw.	K
67203	Berger, Edw.	K
70148	Marsh, Elisha	L
70990	Briggs, John F.	K
71125	Bassett, James	K
71504	Sitts, John	L
71568	Messer, Jacob	K
74916	King, Clemens	K
76505	Sitts, Ezra	L
77133	Quick, Percy	K
81286	Bowers, Geo.	K
82608	Smith, Chas.	L
82616	Lewis, Edwin A.	L
82701	Thompson, James	L
82805	Ycroff, Edw.	L
82855	Davis, Wm.	L
82904	Whitney, Truman	L
82987	Haight, Thimothy B.	K
83238	Knapp, George	K
83375	Clark, Jacob	L
84027	Harvey, Henry	L
84409	Coonradt, Leonard	K
84517	Voorhies, J. G.	K
85248	Jessey, Harmond	L
85257	Warboice, Paul	L
85465	Hune, L. C.	L
85490	Benjman, Marsellas	L
85535	Mathews, Velorus	L
85639	Mellison, Wm.	L
85958	Seabring, Henry	K
85958	Stevens, Frank	K
85976	Nelson, Dennis	K
85976	Toby, Lott	K
86204	Loper, E.	L
88898	White, Rathvan	K
88898	Elder, Charles	K
90321	Hall, Seth	L
90413	Newbray, Luther	K
91219	Farlin, Wm.	K
91269	_____ William	K
92339	Silloway, Joseph	K
98963	Oberly, Godfrey	K
C 9709	McCullough, Thos. J.	K

1st Missouri Cavalry (Cos. I and L)

History: The 1st Missouri Cavalry was organized by order of General John C. Fremont at Jefferson Barracks, Missouri, in September 1861. With the exception of Company F, the regiment served its entire term of service in Missouri and Arkansas. Initially the 1st Missouri was broken into three separate battalions operating independently. Companies I and L were in the 2nd Battalion and took part in several battles, including Pea Ridge and Prairie Grove before being united with the 1st Battalion in 1863. Until they were mustered out September 1, 1865, the consolidated regiment participated in numerous skirmishes, scouts, and expeditions.

Arms: The 1st Missouri Cavalry was originally issued Hall carbines that had been purchased under orders of General Fremont. The Sharps carbines listed here were issued about mid-1863.

Source: The Sharps serial numbers and names were listed in the *Company Order Books of Cos. I and L*.

Carbines

Serial #	Name	Company
73703	Dickey	L
79040	Hawkins	I
79135	Becks, Autrin C.	I
79135	Wilson	I
79135	White, David G.	I
79316	Strong, Geo. W.	I
79316	Williamson	I
80436	Spry	L
80624	Edwards	L
80688	Cole, Wm. P.	I
80737	Nelson, James	I
80839	Withers, Thomas P.	I
80839	Shing	I
80839	Strong, George A.	I
80839	Withers, Thomas P.	I
80850	Gilfert, Robert	I
80850	Billsburg, Cpl. John J.	I
80885	Bogart, Cpl. Chas. C.	I
80885	Seigner, John	I
80892	Ross	L
80932	McElfresh, Emory W.	I
80945	Choate, Riley	I
81038	Riggs, Geo.	I
81067	Leitner, Wm.	I
81198	Nelson, James	I
81217	Smith, Henry	L
81260	Ripper, Wm.	L
81269	Chaffin, Wm.	I
81305	Fefal, Adolph	I
81334	Yeeker, John	I
81339	Debezzinsky, Simon	I
81339	Conradt, Sgt. Chas.	I
81388	Clute, John	I
81405	Smithee, John	I
81409	Hawkins, Thomas	I
81409	Abbott	I
81470	Choate, Pvt. Esquire C.	I
81470	Smithee, John	I
81519	Higbee, David	I
81519	McElfresh, E. V.	I
81526	Connor, Edw.	I
81541	Billsburg, Cpl. John J.	I
81558	Johnson, John	I
81562	Strawn, John P.	I
81578	Gentle, Cpl. Arthor	I
81578	Williams, Jackson J.	I
81578	Moore, H. A.	I
81626	Kelley, Edw.	I
81631	Etter, Wm. G.	I
81649	Wishard, Sgt. John M.	I
81649	Thomas, Cpl. Merit F.	I
81673	Gallaher, John	I
81749	Reeton, Alfred	I
81749	Keeton	I
C 903	Scharpf	L
C 7073	Kierns	L
C 7332	Brandes	L
C 7451	Taylor	L
C 7497	Kingsbury	L
C 7660	Speaks	L
C 7703	Dodds	L
C 7737	Clubb	L
C 7840	Langley	L
C 7976	McAy	L
C 8156	Deavers	L
C 8350	Markey	L
C 8433	Pearse	L
C 8443	Sellers	L
C 8517	Shutz, Jacob	L
C 8538	Baker	L
C 8642	Wilson, G. W.	L

1st New Hampshire Cavalry (Cos. A and M)

History: The 1st New Hampshire Cavalry was organized in January 1864 from a nucleus of four companies of New Hampshire men who had served for two years with the 1st Rhode Island Cavalry. Seven companies left the state for Washington, D.C., in April 1864 and were attached to the Cavalry Corps, Army of the Potomac. They saw considerable action until August when they were sent to join Phil Sheridan's Army of the Shenandoah. From then until the war's end, they were continually on active duty, fighting in numerous battles and skirmishes. Five additional companies left the state in July 1864. These companies served detached in the Washington, D.C., area on guard and patrol duty and operations against Mosby's command until joining the rest of the regiment in the Shenandoah Valley in March 1865. The 1st New Hampshire was mustered out in July 1865.

Arms: The 1st New Hampshire was armed with Sharps carbines upon enlistment. The numbers were determined by the authors to be "C" series.

Source: The names and numbers listed here can be found in the *Company Descriptive Books of Cos. A and M.*

Carbines

Serial #	Name	Company
32778	Williams, John	A
55333	Powers, Joseph T.	M
62707	Harris, Geo. M.	M
68505	Grant, Wm. F.	A
C 456	Smith, Gidion N.	M

C 1660	Gordon, James E.	M
C 1892	Johnson, John A.	M
C 1928	Fifried, Edwin F.	M
C 1944	Matthews, Edwin E.	M
C 2377	Ritchie, Thomas	M
C 2386	Turner, Bugler Chas. H.	M
C 2414	Noyes, Enoch P.	M
C 2531	Fuller, Henry A.	M
C 2612	Munsey, Nathaniel H.	M
C 2655	Gregg, Reuben M.	M
C 2730	Folley, Wm. H.	A
C 2763	Hill, Bradley W.	M
C 2923	Wetherbee, Joseph	M
C 3045	Rankin, Oscar F.	M
C 3313	Lovett, Enoch	M
C 3350	Smith, Cpl. Augustus	M
C 3418	Powers, Wagoner Wm. C.	M
C 3485	Cook, James	M
C 3635	Bryant, Chas. L.	M
C 3850	Moran, Blacksmith David	M
C 3850	Avery, James	M
C 3916	Prentiss, Chas. B.	M
C 4009	Peavey, Wallace	M
C 4035	Bradwich, Wm. T.	M
C 4166	Shapley, Sgt. John H.	M
C 4186	Harrington, Elton	M
C 4332	Warren, Emil	M
C 4451	Camron, Chas.	M
C 4689	Lovering, Wm. H.	M
C 4756	Sheldon, Chas. B.	M
C 6289	Goodwin, Edwin	A
C 7611	Joslyn, Joseph	A
C 7645	Conway, Patrick	M
C 8343	Fifried, Chas. H.	M
C 9548	Bryant, Chas. L.	M
C18771	Mulligan, Bernard	A

2ND NEW JERSEY CAVALRY (COMPANY D)

History: The 2nd New Jersey Cavalry was organized at Trenton, New Jersey, and mustered in August 15, 1863. The regiment was initially sent to Washington, D.C., but was quickly transferred to the western theater arriving in Union City, Tennessee, on December 15, 1863. From this time until the end of the war, the 2nd New Jersey served in Tennessee, Mississippi, and Alabama, guarding railroads and participating in numerous expeditions and skirmishes. From December 20, 1864, to January 15, 1865, they participated in General B.H. Grierson's raid to destroy the Mobile and Ohio Railroad. The regiment moved to Vicksburg, Mississippi, on June 7, 1865 and was mustered out there on November 1, 1865.

Arms: This regiment was armed primarily with Spencer carbines. The Sharps carbines listed below were, however, in the hands of the men named at the end of the war.

Source: The names and numbers listed are in the *Company Order Book of Co. C*.

Carbines

Serial #	Name	Company
84904	Hilderbrand, Frederick	C
84571	Sullivan, Wm.	C

1ST NEW YORK MOUNTED RIFLES (CO. I)

History: The 1st New York Mounted Rifles was organized in and around New York City between July 1861 and August 1862. As companies were mustered, they were sent to Fort Monroe, Virginia. Company I was in the last group to be enlisted and did not leave New York until September 1862. The regiment served its entire term of service in the tidewater areas of Virginia and North Carolina. They participated in numerous reconnaissances and expeditions which resulted in many skirmishes with Confederate forces. During the siege of Petersburg in 1864, they moved to that area and were engaged there and in the operations against Richmond. The regiment was consolidated with the 3rd New York Cavalry in July 1865 and mustered out November 29, 1865.

Arms: During the last months of the war, this regiment was armed with Spencer carbines. Prior to this, they carried Sharps. Those listed for Co. I were probably issued shortly after enlistment.

Source: The names and numbers listed can be found in the *Company Order Book for Co. I*.

Carbines

Serial #	Name	Company
48972	Jones	I
72585	Griswold, Sgt.	I
73101	Duncan	I
76632	Johnson	I
76632	Bates	I
77788	McKenna, Cpl.	I
77925	Wilber, Jos. W.	I
78267	Coon	I
78272	Davis, Cpl	I
78295	Lindsey	I
78295	Holmes	I
78452	Hunt	I
78671	Haytrer	I

Serial #	Name	Company
78722	Pierce	I
78786	Williams (2nd)	I
78788	Ruffman	I
78795	Murray	I
78816	Caow	I
78876	Holmes	I
78934	Carl	I
78993	Laftus	I
79059	Sallisbury	I
79086	Davis, F. W.	I
79086	Jenkins	I
79089	Paff	I
79160	Gibson	I
79172	Clancy	I
79172	Bleitm	I
79198	Shornfelder	I
79211	Laser	I
79240	Paslman	I
79282	Correlius	I
79293	Conley, Cpl.	I
79293	O'Brian	I
79294	Gabeif, Sgt	I
79304	Lindsey, Corp.	I
79311	" "	I
79324	Holden	I
79324	Bradley	I
79346	Gilberth	I
79356	Best, Cpl.	I
79434	Reed	I
79442	Wagner, Cpl.	I
79467	Haflailing	I
79471	Stranahan	I
79474	Hodgson	I
79489	Holden	I
79489	Cunliffe	I
79556	Palmer	I
79558	Davis, Sgt.	I
79560	Palmer, Cpl.	I
79560	Beathie, Sgt.	I
79562	Evertt	I
79572	Briggs, Pvt.	I
79578	Sutheland	I
79581	Wildren, Jas. E.	I
79581	Bayler	I
79599	Lost 10/7/64 Salt Grove Ch., Va.	I
C 10489	Bundmore	I
C 10489	Ashley	I
C 10489	Davis	I
C 11154	Griswold, Sgt.	I
C 11317	Davis, H.	I
C 16911	Jones	I
C 16911	Sutherland	I
C 18054	Farmington	I
C 18358	Williams	I
C 18454	Farmington	I
C 18454	Anderson	I
C 18761	Willoughby	I
C 18796	McKenna	I
C 19240	Smith	I
C 19344	Shamem, Sgt.	I
C 19402	Shamon	I
C 19402	Wilber	I
C 19402	Ben	I
C 19491	Albertson	I
C 19491	Emery	I

1st New York Cavalry (Company H)

History: The 1st New York Cavalry was raised in New York City in July and August 1861. They were transferred to Washington, D.C. and served there until March 1862. The regiment moved with the Army of the Potomac to the Virginia Peninsula and served with that army until September 1862. After the Battle of Antietam, the 1st New York remained in the general vicinity of Harpers Ferry and the Shenandoah Valley, serving with the 8th Army Corps and the Army of West Virginia until the end of Sheridan's 1864 campaign. In 1865, they moved east with the cavalry of the Army of the Potomac and served in the Appomattox campaign. While in the Army of West Virginia, the regiment saw continual marches and skirmishes from Greencastle, Pennsylvania to Woodstock, Virginia. Following the Confederate surrender, the regiment moved to Washington, D.C. and participated in the Grand Review before being mustered out June 27, 1865.

Arms: The 1st New York was armed with a variety of small arms, including Burnsides, Gallagers, and Sharps carbines, along with Colt army and navy revolvers. The Sharps listed here were probably received in early 1863. The regiment received Spencer carbines February 21, 1865.

Source: The names and numbers listed here can be found in the *Company Order Book of Co. H*.

Carbines

Serial #	Name	Company
47698	Fisher, John	H
48804	Spellman, Joseph S.	H
48869	Clarck, R. C.	H
49000	Verander, Wm.	H
49039	McSorley, Hugh	H
49112	Emmons, Chas.	H
49112	Camron, H.	H
49127	McNeil, F.	H
49215	Bennett, John	H
49249	Hasel, Thomas	H
49328	Bogert, John	H
49355	Clemint, Lewis	H

49456	Bullard, Chas.	H
49483	Murry, Martin	H
49483	Murphy, John R.	H
49540	Voohrees, R. C.	H
49563	Anderson, J. H.	H
49630	O'Neil, Eug	H
49797	Rielly, Cornelious	H
86884	Capler, Jacob	H
88884	Clavin, James	H

3rd New York Cavalry (Company A)

History: The 3rd New York Cavalry was raised in central and western New York state from July to September 1861. The regiment moved immediately to Washington, D.C. and from there to the Department of North Carolina. The 3rd New York spent the next two years in the tidewater region of North Carolina and Virginia. During this time, they were constantly occupied by expeditions and raids to inland points of Confederate occupation. This also included several raids on railroads such as the Wilmington and Weldon to disrupt Confederate supply lines. During the 1864 siege of Petersburg, Virginia, the regiment was moved to that area and assigned to Kautz's Cavalry Division of the Army of the James. From then until the end of the war, they saw considerable action and participated in several battles, including Ream's Station and Deep Bottom. After consolidation with the 1st New York Mounted Rifles, they were mustered out November 29, 1865.

Arms: Prior to this research, the arms listed here have been reported to be M1863 Sharps carbines. Careful cross checking of names of soldiers who received these weapons revealed that one soldier, Edwin H. Vedder, was killed in action March 14, 1863. It is certain that since carbine no. 2118 was issued to Vedder, the arms were in the hands of the Company prior to that date. This fact, combined with the previous determination that Sharps did not reach the 100,000 production figure until mid-1863, makes it certain these are not M1863 Sharps. They are without doubt the Sharps and Hankins carbines which had been ordered for the 3rd New York.

Source: The names and numbers listed here can be found in the *Company Descriptive Book*.

Sharps & Hankins Carbines

Serial #	Name	Company
1773	Smith, Hervey H.	A
2000	Hood, Silas M.	A
2028	Wolcot, Asel B.	A
2029	Parsons, Schuyler S.	A
2035	Scoville, Marlc L.	A
2058	Batcomb, Ruben A.	A
2078	Lew, Wm. H.	A
2111	Beecher, Lina	A
2117	Grant, Oscar W.	A
2118	Vedder, Edwin H.	A
2134	Budlong, Walter F.	A
2143	Robinson, Zebulon C.	A
2170	Webb, Wm. S.	A
2174	Collins, Thomas B.	A
2183	McNeily, Samuel	A
2194	Ogden, Wm. L.	A
2210	Jones, Richard M.	A
2215	Bergin, Peter	A
2227	Van Valkenburgh, John P.	A
2230	Bolt, John K.	A
2234	Brown, Johnathan W.	A
2235	Allen, Wm. P.	A
2249	Hopkins, Brice	A
2270	Griffith, Thomas H.	A
2280	Post, John M.	A
2289	Staats, John A.	A
2334	Allen, Chas. I	A
2339	Mudge, Ashel B.	A
2346	Swarwont, Cornelius	A
2355	Warner, Dexter B.	A
2450	Mahoney, John C.	A
2482	Smith, Horace A.	A
2490	Stahler, Enoch	A
2591	Van Schuyver, Chas. G.	A
2666	Pelling, John M.	A
2680	Sanford, Henry A.	A
2729	Wilson, Jerry	A
2745	Cornel, Wm. H.	A
2769	Gifford, Edw. N.	A
2771	Terry, Chas. W.	A
3010	Stan, Irin M.	A
3029	Johnson, Danice S.	A
3037	Patterson, Alexander J.	A
3242	Maxwell, Frederick	A
3337	Emmerson, Chas. W.	A
3437	Jones, Selden L.	A
3438	Buten, Benj. C.	A
3495	Campbell, George	A

6th New York Cavalry (Company H)

History: The 6th New York Cavalry was organized at New York City and mustered in by company between September 12 and December 23, 1861. The regiment saw most of its very active service as part of the Cavalry Corps of the

Sharps & Hankins carbine SN 2591 carried by Charles G. VanSchuyver, Company A, 3rd New York Cavalry.

Army of the Potomac. Two companies (F and H) were detached from March 1862 to October 1863 and served with the 4th Corps in operations on the peninsula below Richmond and in the Washington, D.C. defenses. During 1864, the regiment saw service in all the major battles of the cavalry corps of the famed eastern army. They were transferred to Sheridan's Army of the Shenandoah in August and took part in all the important activity of that command. They returned to the Army of the Potomac in time to take part in the Appomattox Campaign and participated in the Grand Review in Washington May 23, 1865. They were mustered out August 9, 1865.

Arms: The 6th New York carried Sharps carbines until June 10, 1865 when they were issued Spencers. The arms listed here are from a list which appears to date from mid-1863.

Source: The serial numbers and names given below can be found in the *Company Descriptive Book of Co. H*.

Carbines

Serial #	Name	Company
34672	O'Brian, John	H
34836	Picket, Andrew D.	H
44546	McCord, Smith	H
48866	Metz, Michael	H
53356	Gibbons, Jno.	H
55746	Grimshaw, Samuel	H
58141	Latham, Corp. Eldridge P.	H
58334	Prince, Geo. S.	H
58351	Hiner, Edw.	H
58551	Teator, John A.	H
58576	Daley, Andrew	H
58633	Mackison, Jas	H
58708	McAlier, James	H
58708	Preston, Henry H.	H
58911	Evans, John I.	H
59105	Wheeler, Harmon	H
59226	Sweeney, W.	H
59881	Young, Geo. W.	H
59881	Young, Julius B.	H
60994	Johnigan, Benj.	H
70615	McBridge, Edw.	H
88415	See, Adam H.	H
89399	Fry, Sgt. Thomas	H
89866	Wright, Jas.	H
92177	Sweeney, Timothy	H
93494	Miller, Joseph	H
97595	Schahlin, Fresrick	H
97595	Burris, Zachariah	H
99204	Hall, Corp. Wm.	H
99204	Brath, Seb	H
99507	Brigham, Corp. Risley H.	H
99575	Preston, Edgar	H
99759	Cochrane, James H.	H
C 732	Smith, Wm. E.	H

11TH NEW YORK CAVALRY (COS. B AND L)

History: The 11th New York Cavalry was organized at New York City between December 1861 and May 5, 1862 when they were mustered and left for Washington, D.C. During the remainder of 1862 and until March 1864, they were assigned to the Department of Washington and operated between the city and Harpers Ferry. While in this area, they were engaged in several skirmishes with Confederate troops. Upon leaving Washington in 1864, they were assigned to the Department of the Gulf. The remainder of their service was in Louisiana, Mississippi, and Tennessee where they participated in several expeditions and skirmishes. The regiment was mustered out at Memphis, Tennessee on September 30, 1865.

Arms: The 11th New York was armed with Sharps and Hankins carbines. The numbers listed here for Co. B were taken from a list dated June 22, 1865, but most certainly reflect a much earlier issue, as do the Co. L numbers. (See also 3rd New York Cavalry.)

Source: The names and numbers for Co. B can be found in the *Order Book* for that Company. The numbers and names for Company L are located in the *Regimental Order Book*.

Sharps & Hankins Carbines

Serial #	Name	Company
1980	Murren	L
1985	Edwards	L
1991	Rich, J.	B
2019	Fritcher	L
2033	Crama, Jas.	B
2048	Wright	L
2074	Abbott	L
2075	Williams	L
2087	Larmouth, Wm.	B
2116	Waters, Mich.	B
2137	Buch, Jno. E.	B
2140	Orvis, Jas. W.	B
2152	Brown, Jas.	B
2194	Palmer	L
2210	Faulkner, N. P.	B
2223	Fisher, Nathaniel	B
2247	Ballard	L
2247	Madison, J.	L
2277	Lovely, Sitas	B
2303	Seales	L
2307	Miller, Benj.	B
2307	Jacklin, Wm.	B
2314	Duran, Wm. W.	B
2318	Potter, Jas.	B
2323	Jones, F. A.	L
2354	Zarr	L
2370	Stevenson, J.	L
2384	Adset, P.	B
2393	Slocum, Geo. B.	B
2436	Michael	L
2439	Kenny	L
2455	Smith, C.	L
2469	Jaas, Ulrich	B
2486	Magee	L
2547	Ganghan, Jno.	B
2590	Hamilton, Wm. F.	B
2601	Gutbracht, Albert	B
2603	Kinble, Jno	B
2608	Andrews, H. E.	B
2614	Nevins	L
2616	Johnston, Corp. Jno.	B
2646	Calvin, Francis	B
2648	Carhart, Abe B.	B
2654	O'Brien	L
2655	Campbell	B
2697	Gammel, Chas	B
2722	Madison, W.	L
2730	Malone	L
2730	Marshall	L
2745	Manning, Geo.	B
2777	Ringold	L
2782	Becker	L
2803	Kimball, Albert	B
2808	Webster, Stephen	B
2818	Smith, Chas.	B
2870	Howland	L
2940	Hough	L
4355	Long	L

13TH NEW YORK CAVALRY (COS. G AND I)

History: The 13th New York Cavalry was organized at Staten Island, New York between June 1863 and the end of the year. The regiment was assigned to the defenses of Washington, D.C. during its entire term of service. The 13th New York was engaged in continual scouts in northern Virginia which resulted in numerous clashes with Confederate troops, primarily those under the command of John S. Mosby. It was a trooper from the 13th New York who shot and wounded Mosby on the night of December 21, 1864. The regiment was consolidated with the 16th New York in June 1865 and mustered out on September 21, 1865.

Arms: The Sharps carbines listed here for the 13th New York are those initially received by the regiment and carried throughout their service. (See introduction to the serial numbers for story on carbine number 92480.)

Source: The names and serial numbers listed here can be found in the *Company Descriptive Books of Cos. G and I*.

Carbines

Serial #	Name	Company
32784	Dutton	G
62199	Finucan, John	I
65049	Mohis	G
89136	Brenner, Dennis	G
90915	Dunn, Charles	I
90930	Anthony, Peter L.	I
90938	McKeyring, Daniel	I
91307	Barryne, Augustus	I

Noncommissioned officers of the 13th New York Cavalry in 1865. (USAMHI—Mass. MOLLUS collection)

91318	Blanchard, Henry A.	I	92226	McDonald	G
91392	Toepher, Christopher	I	92242	Childs	G
91651	Flynn, James	I	92260	Prendergast, Thomas	I
91690	Kinmouth, Hugh S.	I	92264	Dorman	G
91739	Donohue, James	I	92270	Bryon, Thomas	I
91746	Henderson, Robert	I	92274	Cookson, John M.	I
91798	Lannon, Patrick	I	92307	Carpenter	G
91800	McGrail, John	I	92313	Westen, Joseph	I
91808	Brown, Geo.	I	92352	Barbero, Leon	I
91826	Keeler, Robert	I	92367	Corcoran, Jerimiah	I
91866	Thomas, Ralph	I	92370	Seyfforth, Carl	I
91870	McMickle, James	I	92374	Cuddy, Francis	I
91911	Flood, Bernard	I	92378	English, James	I
91929	Tanner, Milo J.	I	92378	Higgins, Peter	I
91941	O'Brien, John	I	92387	Porter, Joseph	I
91946	Nilen, John	I	92390	Higgins, Peter	I
91985	Flood, Bernard	I	92414	Bradley	G
91996	Hubin, Michael	I	92416	Todd, James	G
92002	Long, Andrew J.	I	92419	Grant	G
92003	Wheeler, Rbt.	G	92422	Starkey, David	I
92029	Gorman, John	I	92434	Brophy, Wm.	I
92032	Wands, John	I	92480	Darrah, Corp.	G
92067	Cunningham, Wm.	I	92481	Lloyd, James	I
92124	Kattnor, John	I	92496	Smith, Hugh	I
92131	Sexsmith, Thomas	I	92514	Noschang, Adam	I
92166	Beeny, Adolphus	I	92518	Heyman	G
92209	Lyons, Patrick	I	92527	Wallace, Morris	I
92220	Manigold, Peter	I			

Serial #	Name	Company
92541	Langhlin	G
92591	Foresythe	G
92604	Fletcher	G
92604	Benson	G
92612	Sprague, Dennis	G
92648	" "	G
92670	Dodd, Peter	G
92706	Micheal	G
92728	Eldridge	G
92752	Wheeler, Phillip	G
92770	Kirt	G
92801	Adams	G
92842	Woodson, Robert J.	I
93141	Prmse	G
93187	Snyder	G
93195	Predergast, Henry	I
93239	Bennett	G

15TH NEW YORK CAVALRY (COMPANY C)

History: The 15th New York Cavalry was recruited in the fall of 1863 at Syracuse, New York. The last companies were mustered in January 24, 1864. The regiment moved to Washington, D.C. and performed scouting duty in northern Virginia and eastern counties of West Virginia until April 1864 when they were assigned to the Army of West Virginia. For the next year the 15th saw extensive duty in the Shenandoah Valley. This service resulted in numerous small actions. In February 1865 they were part of Sheridan's raid from Winchester which took them south for a link-up with the Army of the Potomac. They were part of the Appomattox Campaign and saw action in the various battles which preceded the surrender of Lee's army. They were consolidated with the 6th New York Cavalry June 17 and finally mustered out August 9, 1865.

Arms: The Sharps carbines listed here were issued February 2, 1865 to replace Burnside carbines. With the exception of three numbers, the serial number range of these arms falls within the 'C' series.

Source: The names and numbers listed here can be found in Co. C's *Descriptive Book*.

Carbines

Serial #	Name	Company
79811	Lewis, Henry W.	C
C2238	Morgan, Edw.	C
C4668	Margison, Wm.	C
C19045	Gregg, Leslie	C
C19078	Williams, John H.	C
C19105	Arnold, Wm.	C
C19358	Regan, Edwond	C
C20136	Thompson, Melvin C.	C
C20551	Townsend, Henry	C
C20997	Cummings, Alonzo	C
C21408	Singleton, Edw.	C
C21498	Wilson, Thomas	C
C21621	Grier, James	C
C21657	Lewis, Henry W.	C
C21684	Newell, Geo.	C
C21703	Anderson, Chas. J.	C
C21721	Falkner, George	C
C21725	Oakley, John J.	C
C21736	Shirtliffe, Geo.	C
C21739	Mulligan, Patrick	C
C21776	Warner, John C.	C
C21819	Sayers, Chas. H.	C
C21839	Ostrout, Jonas	C
C21971	Frazer, John I.	C
C22061	Wing, Wm.	C
C22066	Francis, James	C
C22146	Brokaw, James C.	C
C22154	Babock, Hiram	C
C22158	Knowles, Albert	C
C22212	McNulty, Patrick	C
C22217	Vescelius, Alanson S.	C
C22235	Scantling, Michael	C
C22255	Hoagg, Geo. W.	C
C22257	Tuttle, Henry W.	C
C22331	Hodges, Amos	C
C22352	Benson, George	C
C22404	Benedict, Wm. D.	C
C22416	Cheseboro, Giles T.	C
C22435	Worden, Squire	C
C22498	Smiley, Geo.	C
C22522	Randall Almond A.	C
C22536	Bortle, Seymore	C
C22560	Anderson, Edwin	C
C22567	Norman, Abram	C
C22577	Barnes, Jeffry T.	C
C22628	Rose, Oscar F.	C
C22642	Fowler, Wm. C.	C
C22642	Hatten, Wm.	C
C22668	Jarvis, Benj. F.	C
C22702	Beeman, Henry C.	C
C22703	Hennessey, Arthur	C
C22709	Keller, Jacob	C
C22743	Donohue, John	C
C22812	Pratt, Stephen	C
C22818	Hackett, Wm. H.	C
C22894	Barnes, Coridone	C
C22898	Garwood, Wm.	C
C23021	Pullman, Harrison	C
C23024	Siglar, Wm. A.	C

22ND NEW YORK CAVALRY (COS. C AND E)

History: The 22nd New York Cavalry was organized at Rochester, New York and mustered in by companies between December 20, 1863 and February 23, 1864. By May 1864, they had been assigned to the 3rd Division, Cavalry Corps, Army of the Potomac. From this assignment until August, they shared in all the fighting of the Cavalry Corps. In August, the regiment along with the Division was transferred to Phil Sheridan's Army of the Shenandoah. Hard fighting and constant activity would be the rule for the next nine months. The regiment was mustered out August 1, 1865.

Arms: The Sharps carbines listed here were most likely issued in the latter part of 1864, possibly after the move to the Shenandoah. The arms for Co. E appear on a list dated February 11, 1865.

Source: The serial numbers and names listed below may be found in the *Company Order Books of Cos. C and E.*

Carbines

Serial #	Name	Company
59909	Trumble, F.	C
61415	Monroe, C.	C
70700	White, Ocean C.	C
88959	Maherny, Miachle	E
92308	Webb, C.	C
C 1883	Colph, J.	C
C 3588	Colgrove, Albert	E
C 4420	Phillips, Wm. H.	E
C 5525	Salisbury, Chas.	E
C 6349	Wells, Leyman	E
C 6395	Eastman, Neil	E
C 7079	Thompsom, Milton	E
C 7634	Thurston, Theador	E
C 7999	Nelson, C.	C
C 9193	Sawdey, James K.	E
C 10000	Bisbe, Pvt. Leroy H.	E
C 14620	Carlton, J.	C
C 15038	Simmons, M.	C
C 15102	Brown, C.	C
C 15380	Leach, James P.	E
C 15404	Harrington	C
C 15561	Steinbaugh, Hiram	E
C 15878	Stephens, Warren	E
C 15939	Peckham, Henry C.	E
C 16062	Dobbins, G.	C
C 16284	Mowers, D. H.	C
C 16378	Kengon, Francis	E
C 16450	Trumble, Ruben	E
C 16649	Butler, Wm. H.	E
C 16663	Trumble, A.	C
C 18284	Steinburgh, Wm.	E
C 19197	Kengon, Erwin	E
C 19291	Faleoner, A	C
C 19799	Melbyeve, Cpl. Joseph	E
C 19913	Latham, Charles	E
C 20392	Cristall, J.	C
C 20446	Odell, Jothan	E
C 21425	Warren, A.	C
C 22083	Hurlburt, F.	C

3RD INDEPENDENT COMPANY OHIO CAVALRY

History: The 3rd Independent Company was raised in Cincinnati on July 4, 1861. They were immediately transferred to the Kanawha Valley, West Virginia. While there, they participated in the action at Princeton on May 16, 1862 and other operations in the Kanawha and New River region. Along with other troops serving in the area, they were sent east in August 1862 and participated in the Antietam campaign. Following the battle of Antietam, they returned to West Virginia where they remained until the end of the war. During their service, they participated in numerous skirmishes and at least three raids under command of General William W. Averill. The company was mustered out May 22, 1865.

Arms: The exact date of this listing of Sharps carbines has not been determined. It likely was compiled in late 1864 and probably contains the original arms issued as well as replacements received to that time.

Source: The serial numbers and names given can be located in the Company's *Clothing and Order Book.*

Carbines

Serial #	Name
35585	Loeher, Jacob
35817	Konedel, Frederick
36325	Schultz, G. H.
41407	Lutz, August
41434	Ganger, Albert
43973	Sohroeder, Henry
45308	Pistner, Wm.
58440	Knipper, Agust
59787	Beieridafer, 2Cpl., George
59787	Schmidt, David
68880	Milehet
69269	Miller, Jacob
76606	Huber, Jacob

78101	Spies, Anten
78154	Fath, Jacob
78545	Kratz, John
78599	Leibold, Frederick
82487	Fuchs, Jacob
82959	Barnkhard, 1Cpl., Kreb

4TH OHIO CAVALRY (COMPANY C)

History: The 4th Ohio Cavalry was organized at Cincinnati, Lima, St. Marys and Camp Dennison, Ohio beginning in August 1861. They were mustered into U.S. service in November. On January 2, 1862 they saw their first action in Missouri. They were quickly moved back to Kentucky and for the remainder of the year they saw continual action in Tennessee, Alabama, and Kentucky including the Battle of Stones River. For most of 1863 the 4th participated in a continuing series of scouts and expeditions which resulted in numerous skirmishes. Their most notable service was the Battle of Chickamauga. The following year they were part of the battles and maneuvering of Sherman's Atlanta campaign. They returned to Nashville in September and proceeded to Louisville where they remained until January. The regiment then moved to Gravelly Springs, Alabama and remained there until March 22 when they left as part of Wilson's cavalry raid. The 4th Ohio was mustered out July 15, 1865.

Arms: The notation preceding the serial numbers of Co. C's Sharps reads as follows: "Invoice of...carbines and revolvers in possession of each member after the pursuit of Wheeler through Tenn. in the month of Oct. 1863."

Source: The names and numbers listed can be found in Co. C's *Morning Report Book*.

Carbines

Serial#	Name	Company
34100	Reeve, E.	C
45689	Reif,	C
48939	Kreiger, Gustavis	C
49625	Eichman, Casper	C
50253	Bowers, Fielding K.	C
50793	Hammond, James	C
51505	Gillespie, James	C
51569	Kiser, Barney	C
51654	Siewing, Henry	C
51717	Henkey, Adam	C
51946	Bowser, Jacob	C
52121	Wimnerslage, Geo.	C
52200	Baily, John	C
52222	Owens, Wm.	C
52269	Johnson, Edw.	C
52292	Kiser, Barney	C
52324	Strassner, Henry	C
52340	O'Donald, Norman	C
52346	Pacey, James	C
52353	Fulton, James	C
52489	Bolch,	C
52498	Twelling, John	C
52500	Bowser, S.	C
52537	Ackley, Smith	C
52679	Lechtingfelt, Adam	C
52709	Billderbeck, Herschel	C
52766	Baily	C
53128	Malcom, Samual B.	C
61262	Berning, Barney	C
61326	Feldcamp, Geo.	C
62838	Kreiger, John H.	C
62838	Solan,	C
63139	Ochs, Daniel	C
70589	Kirman,	C
70651	Cann, Zadock	C
70959	Cable, Benj. F.	C
71092	Knoul, Jacob	C
71188	Bonnell, John C.	C
71477	Boggess,	C
72105	Murdock, Geo.	C
76565	Calph,	C
C6086	Mountjoy, Wm.	C

5TH OHIO CAVALRY (COMPANY L)

History: The 5th Ohio Cavalry was organized at Camp Dick Corwin, Ohio from September to November 1861. The regiment moved first to Kentucky and in early March moved to Tennessee. They were immediately assigned to the Army of the Tennessee and almost upon reaching the Army, saw action on an expedition to destroy bridges on the Mobile and Ohio Railroad. They were engaged in three skirmishes prior to the battle of Shiloh, where they also saw action. Following this battle, the regiment saw continual service. Raids, expeditions, skirmishes, and battles were common fare. In 1864, the regiment, as part of the 15th Corps, saw extensive activity with Sherman's Army on the Atlanta campaign. The 5th Ohio remained with Sherman on the March to the Sea and the push up through the Carolinas. They were present at the surrender of the Confederate Army under Johnston. The 5th Ohio Cavalry was mustered out on October 30, 1865.

Arms: The 5th Ohio Cavalry was armed with both Burnside and Sharps carbines. The Sharps carbines listed here appear to be those originally issued to the regiment. The list dates from early 1862.

Source: The names and numbers listed below may be found in the *Company Descriptive Book of Co. L.*

Carbines

Serial #	Name	Company
41086	Hughes, Squire	L
43048	Leids, Thomas J.	L
43097	Stullz, Henry F.	L
47985	Trump, George	L
48091	Gerard, Wm. G.	L
48142	Dougherty, Geo.	L
48178	Simpkins, Enoch	L
48281	Montjar, Thomas B.	L
48343	Gray, Aaron S.	L
48361	Behymer, Thomas B.	L
48394	McClain, Sylvester	L

Members of Company F, 5th Ohio Cavalry in 1862. (Ronn Palm collection)

6TH OHIO CAVALRY (COMPANY H)

History: The 6th Ohio Cavalry was organized at Warren, Ohio on October 7, 1861. Their first active service was in the Shenandoah Valley in the early summer of 1862. By August, they were with the Union Army of Virginia. In September, they were assigned to the Army of the Potomac. For the remainder of the war, their history would be that of this famed army. They served in every campaign and battle from Fredericksburg to Appomattox, including several raids under the command of Phil Sheridan.

Arms: The Sharps carbines listed here were most likely obtained by the men who carried them in mid-1863. The remainder of Co. H carried the Burnside carbine. In addition, the company was issued both Colt and Remington army revolvers.

Source: The names and numbers listed here can be found in the *Company Order Book of Co. H.*

Carbines

Serial #	Name	Company
99896	Kearns, Jessie	H
C 1250	Farnum, Darwin	H
C 3297	Holderby, W. R.	H

10TH OHIO CAVALRY (COS. D AND I)

History: The 10th Ohio Cavalry was organized at Camp Taylor, Cleveland, Ohio in October 1862. Upon arrival in Tennessee in February 1862, they were assigned to the hard fighting Army of the Cumberland. They participated in several scouts and skirmishes before going into the campaign which resulted in the Battle of Chickamauga on September 19–20, 1863. Over the following winter the regiment was engaged in scouting and expeditions which resulted in several skirmishes as well as the fight at Cosby Creek, Tennessee on January 14, 1864. Along with its parent army, the 10th Ohio followed Sherman to Atlanta and on to Savannah and the Carolinas. They were present at the surrender of the Confederate Army under Joe Johnston on April 26, 1865. The regiment was mustered out July 24, 1865.

Arms: The 10th Ohio carried Sharps carbines as well as both Colt and Remington army revolvers. The Sharps listed below were issued in early 1863, probably after the regiment arrived in Tennessee.

Sharps Carbines & Rifles

Source: The names and serial numbers listed below may be found in the *Company Descriptive Books of Cos. D and I.*

Carbines

Serial #	Name	Company
43197	Mullen, John	I
43331	Canning, Thos. W.	D
43334	Coakinhour, John	D
43335	Curtis, Albert	I
43539	Baughman, J. H.	D
43543	Casey, George W.	D
43543	Hitchins, Charles	D
43553	Stevens, Chas. L.	I
43563	Butt, Alexander	I
48464	Jones, Andrew J.	D
49434	Wright, Alonzo	D
50197	Bennet, S. B.	I
50532	Waldran, Sgt. Danl. S.	D
51482	Conklin, John C.	I
51483	McDonalely, Peter	I
52315	Smith, Jacob	D
52868	Brown, Hubert	I
52882	Rose, Wm. P.	I
55052	McClarran, Richard J.	D
55169	Betts, Frederick	D
55170	Gray, Benj. J.	I
55486	Murphy, James	D
55490	Russer, Nicholas	D
55697	Jago, Alfred L.	I
56494	Sheppard, Jackson	D
57014	Mahoney, John	I
57019	Farrell, Thomas	I
57305	Wycoff, James	D
57312	Hoover, Hasea E.	I
57316	Smith, Martin	D
57701	McConner, Terry	I
57701	Oakly, J. P.	I
58012	Huyck, Alonzo M.	D
58033	Doolittle, Cassuis	I
58129	Conroy, John	I
59975	Golden, Martin	D
60166	Green, Wm. T.	D
60534	Brainard, Lewis	I
60534	Buitchie, Edwards	I
60933	Bricker, Aaron	D
61275	Breese, Lewis	D
61279	Forman, Ezekiel	I
61286	Burnside, John	I
61286	Hibler, Jacob	I
61614	Eddy, James	I
61627	Griffin, Charles	D
61814	Miller, Homer	D
62451	Pike, Samuel	I
62451	Robertson, Wm. H.	I
63880	Sutton, Jno. E.	I
63880	Williams, George E.	I
66283	Becke, Julius	I
66902	Langwell, Corp. Wm.	D
67130	Benson, W.	I
67130	Harrington, Jedediah C.	I
67130	Jarboe, John M.	I
67130	Sutton, Jno. E.	I
68942	Fry, Thos. C.	D
70014	Gannon, Wilber	D
70823	Hitchins, Ezekill	D
72551	Daul, Peter	I
72551	Pease, Geo. E.	I
72714	Fry, Wm.	D
72715	Hibler, Jacob	I
72715	Lynch, M.	I
72821	Bates, Wm. D.	D
72960	Koehler, Henry	I
73560	Miller, Sgt. John W.	D
73651	Diter, Ferdinard	I
74507	Daniels, Holley	D
74935	Steauble, Jacob B.	I
74945	Ewing, John M.	D
75405	Coyner, Wm. S.	I
75411	Wilcox, John	D
75520	Clingman, John	D
75617	Nash, Wm.	D
75725	McConahy, Hugh	I
75732	McGill, Frederick	I
75922	Kemper, Elijah	D
76411	Davis, Roger S.	D
76927	Fishpan, C. H.	D
76929	Daul, Peter	I
76934	Allen, Hugh L.	I
76990	Hewitt, Henry	D
77532	Wyiarch, J.A.	D
77833	Brown, Benj.	I
77895	McDonalely, Peter	I
77937	Horton, E. C.	I
78011	Mahoney, John	I
78533	Haywood, John	D
78745	Brown, Pomery	I
78854	Stratt, John B.	D
79014	Ally, Frederick	I
79014	Harrington, Jedediah C.	I
79097	Brown, Hubert	I
79936	Brittan, John	D
79937	Morris, Thomas	I
79937	Thompson, Geo. N.	I
80147	Wright, Henry	D
81394	Atkinson, John	D
82263	West, Henry A.	D
83465	Burns, Samuel	I
83467	Shadle, Ferdinnard	D
86059	Weeks, Rhiwald	D
86668	Tippan, James W.	D
87624	Showalter, Alvin	I
87837	Thomas, Wm. J.	I

Serial #	Name	Company
87837	Thompson, Geo. N.	I
88443	Slater, Edward	D
88489	Barber, Bradford	D
88832	Lang, Theodore	I
89002	Miller, Charles J.	D
89454	Slackgood, George	D
89467	Smith, Francis	D
89510	Snider, John H.	I
89655	Lang, Theodore	I
89830	Ross, Robert	D
90339	Rickering, Jacob	D
90531	Biggs, Lester M.	I
90531	Williams, I.	I
90531	Williams, John	I
90608	Biggs, Lester M.	I
90608	Diter, Thomas	I
90936	Ritchey, Abraham	D
91365	Alban, Henry	D
91376	Lyttle, Wm.	D
91486	Neer, Jacob	I
91636	King, Francis	D
91846	Myers, Frederick	D
91963	Sullivan, Patrick	I
92201	Bennet, S. B.	I
92201	Jones, Lewis B.	D
92283	Smith, Fredrick	I
92757	McNamara, Daniel	D
92757	Short, Amasa	D
92815	Condo, Wm. H.	I
92815	Pingree, John	I
93198	Harkness, Lguren A.	I
93198	Smith, Fredrick	I
93297	Teckemeyer, G. H.	I
93409	Coakinhour, Andrew	D
93748	Blair, Seth	D
93854	Oakly, J. P.	I
93854	Range, Joseph W.	I
93921	Lott, John	D
94267	Guisbuhler, Ulrich	D
94640	Ball, Orville	D
94740	Williams, George	D
94948	Williams, George E.	I

2ND PENNSYLVANIA CAVALRY (COS. F AND G)

History: The 2nd Pennsylvania Cavalry was organized at Philadelphia and Harrisburg from September 1861 to April 1862. Their first duty was in the defenses of Washington until July 1862. At this time, they joined the Union Army of Virginia and participated in the campaign of that army as well as the Antietam campaign. Following an engagement at Ashby's Gap, Virginia on September 22, 1862, the regiment returned to the Washington defenses where they remained until June 1863. During this period, they participated in several reconnaissances in the northern Virginia area. The 2nd Pennsylvania bid farewell to garrison and scouting duty when in June 1863 they were assigned as Headquarters Guard to General George G. Meade, Commander of the Army of the Potomac. They held this position and served as provost guard throughout the Gettysburg campaign and until December 1863. Following this, the regiment joined the Cavalry Corps of Meade's Army and from then until the end of the war, the history of the 2nd Pennsylvania is that of this hard fighting command. It is significant that the Gettysburg monument of the 2nd Pennsylvania Cavalry stands near Meade's Headquarters. It is a life size bronze statue of a trooper loading a Sharps carbine.

Arms: The Sharps carbines listed for Co. F are contained on a list which dates from early 1864. These are most likely arms which were issued to the regiment in 1862. In addition, the 2nd Pennsylvania carried Colt army revolvers. Although only two arms are listed here for Co. G, they are significant in that they were issued to officers. At Charles City Crossroads on Aug. 16, 1864, both officers were captured. It can be presumed that if these arms were being carried they spent the remainder of the war in Confederate service.

Source: The names and serial numbers listed below appear in the *Company Order Books of Cos. F and G*.

Carbines

Serial #	Name	Company
48393	Davis, Pvt. John	F
48413	Snover, Lawrence	F
55608	" "	F
58366	Sloan, Lt. B.P.	G
60532	Bush, Cpl. Joseph	F
69811	Gill, Wm. H.	F
73482	Kanady, Geo. A.	F
73482	Marryman, Geo. W.	F
74598	McGovern, Thomas P.	F
74733	Glenn	F
74735	Mallory, Cpl. C.	F
74963	Merryman, John	F
75347	Zimmers, Levi	F
75531	Schwarz, Lt. J.B,	G
75558	Jones, Cpl. Chas.	F
75593	Mallery, Sgt. Harvey	F
75596	Casper, Sgt. Adam	F
75603	Staitiff, Cpl. Ady F.	F
75605	McKee, Alexander	F
75611	Andrews, Sgt. Jesse	F
75611	Singleton, Geo.	F
75675	Armstrong, Pvt. F. H.	F
75675	Miller, Cpl. James	F
75692	Patterson, Wm.	F
75705	Sodders, Roger H.	F

Serial #	Name	Company
75744	Noll, Geo.	F
75744	_ilnitt	F
75759	Piffer, John	F
75773	Potter	F
76343	Henry, M. D.	F
76550	Williams, Cpl. C. R.	F
76598	O_____, Patrick	F
76608	Worden, Chas. H.	F
76611	Sonnsel	F
76630	Crowther, Cpl. Wm.	F
76669	Sones, John N.	F
76778	Snyder, Sgt. Horatio	F

16TH PENNSYLVANIA CAVALRY (COS. C AND L)

History: The 16th Pennsylvania Cavalry was organized at Harrisburg from September to November 1862. The regiment contained men from all parts of the state as well as many from other states. On November 30, the regiment left from Washington, D.C. and in January, they joined the 2nd Division, Cavalry Corps, Army of the Potomac. For the remainder of the winter of 1863, they served on picket duty. The regiment saw its first action at Kelly's Ford on March 17, 1863. They participated in the Gettysburg campaign and during the battle formed the link with the cavalry and the extreme right of the Union infantry. In 1864, the 16th along with the 2nd Division, saw nonstop action from Kilpatrick's raid on Richmond in February to the Hicksford raid in December. The regiment capped its history with a hard fighting role in the Appomattox campaign. They were mustered out August 11, 1865.

Arms: The Sharps carbines listed here were issued to the 16th Pennsylvania during the first quarter 1863 along with Colt army revolvers. There is no doubt that they were the original issue to the regiment and probably remained with them until they were issued Spencers in late 1864.

Source: The names and serial numbers listed below may be found in the *Company Order Books of Cos. C and L.*

Carbines

Serial #	Name	Company
22364	Thornton, Isaac G.	C
39115	Williams, Wm.	C
57549	Smith, Chas. W.	L
57549	Smith, Wilson	L
65673	Goodrich, James P.	L
65973	Raffensperger, Geo.	L
66032	Southwick, Guy	L
66035	Daken, Wm. W.	L
66035	Wells, Juluis C.	C
66467	Logan, Geo.	L
66467	McKenon, John	L
66488	Deverlaux, Th.	L
66763	Dockey, Jos.	L
66859	Price, David	L
67320	Phillipps, Adam	L
67339	Roberts, L. A.	L
67386	Lore, Franklin	C
67389	Wood, Joseph	C
67398	Aurnand, Henry	C
67408	Zarbe, Henry	L
67491	Hudson, Leroy	C
67494	Ormsbee, Horace M.	C
67497	Zarbe, Perservil	L
67499	Dutton, A.	L
67501	Tschopp, Casper	L
67525	Cutter, Charles A.	C
67526	Zarbe, Issac	L
67529	Moore, Orlo	L
67551	Calkins, Stafford C.	C
67647	Russell, John R.	L
67653	Gooney, Michael	C
67667	McKenon, John	L
67667	Reed, Geo.	L
67695	Fonymires, H. J.	L
67699	Rowe, Louis W.	C
67701	Moore, Eugene	C
67706	Withington, Robt.	L
67708	Caughey, Lockwood	C
67709	Muller, Wm. H.	L
67717	Ormsbee, Eli R.	C
67719	Zarbe, Levi	L
67721	Bammer, A. W.	L
67731	Tschopp, Elias B.	L
67732	Hall, Thos.	L
67735	Favinger, H.	L
67751	Thompson, Haney	L
67761	Castatler, C.	L
67768	Day, Franklin	C
67781	Blair, Wm. W.	C
67787	Green, Cooksin	C
67795	Knsinger, Geo.	L
67804	Boyd, Charles P.	C
67809	Richards, Frank	C
67846	Green, John C.	C
67853	Stienwick, John	L
67919	Serrills, John W.	C
67944	Bixler, Henry	C
67993	Kinnamon, Wm.	C
68081	Bacon, Henry L.	C
68102	Yomel, John	L
68155	Michaels, Jerome	C
68155	Mitchell, Hermon I.	C
68168	Hurst, Thomas L.	C
68171	Taylor, Henry	C

68172	Brownell, D. F.	L
68197	Wheeler, J. E.	L
68233	Bloomfield, J.	L
68254	Miller, H. P.	L
68272	St. John	L
68276	Boarchman, Samuel	L
68277	Mitchell, Wallace	C
68280	Sanders, Samuel H.	L
68289	Clark, Hiram	C
68291	Armour, Sidney B.	C
68296	Crawford, Benj. F.	C
68309	Brooks, George	C
68323	Dixon, Wm. J.	L
68326	Kellog, Leander	C
68328	Robinson, Richard	C
68330	Adams, J. F.	L
68337	Lore, Francis	C
68376	McLane, Thomas	C
68415	Bannister, Eli	C
68424	Gilair, Wm.	C
68425	Hamilton, John	L
68439	Ball, Norman	L
68465	McKee, Wm.	C
68482	Kennedy, John	C
68492	Clark, J. B.	L
68503	Platze, Charles	C
68509	Hemperey, Solomon	L
68515	Blair, Robert C.	C
68551	Allsdorf, J.	L
68554	Mayheu, John	C
68560	Warner, Wm.	L
68562	Dighton, T. D.	L
68574	Hinton, David	C
68574	Rothchild, Jos.	L
68576	Johnson, C. F.	L
68580	Fuller, A. J.	L
68587	Burns, J.	L
68590	Ormsbee, Horace M.	C
68617	Heckart, Josiah	L
68628	Morris, Jacob	C
68636	Thatcher, Wm. F.	C
68748	Owen, Henry W.	L
68974	Force, George	L
68986	White, W. W.	L
69001	Holbrook, J. H.	L
69031	Ross, R.	L
69052	Wilkerson, J.	L
69055	Borland, S. R.	L
69067	Hemperly, D.	L
69095	Dammond, H. C.	L
69104	Roach, Tho.	L
69118	Thompson, Haney	L
69487	Merchant, H. J.	L

17th Pennsylvania Cavalry (Company E)

History: The 17th Pennsylvania was organized at Harrisburg beginning September 1862. They left the state for Washington, D.C. on November 25 and soon after were attached to the Army of the Potomac. Until August 1864 their history was that of this famous command. They were present at Brandy Station and Co. E played a key role at Gettysburg when they were placed in support of Calef's Battery A, 2nd U. S. Artillery on July 1. It was during this battle that the regiment first used their carbines, having received them on the march.

In August 1864 the 17th was ordered to join Sheridan's command in the Shenandoah Valley. They participated in all the hard fought engagements of the Army of the Shenandoah. On the morning of October 18, 1864, a detachment of the regiment was ordered to escort General Sheridan. They were with him on his immortalized ride to the Cedar Creek battlefield. The 17th returned to the Army of the Potomac and participated in the Appomattox campaign. They were mustered out June 16, 1865.

Arms: The Sharps carbines listed here were probably not issued until late 1863. Ordnance returns show the regiment was armed with Smith and Merrill carbines at Gettysburg.

Source: The names and numbers listed here were found in the *Descriptive Book of Co. E.*

Carbines

Serial#	Name	Company
22384	Saltzer, Wm. F.	E
47838	Mummah, Jeremiah	E
48831	Eshelman, Isaac	E
49869	Betz, Michel	E
59387	Beickey, Cyrous	E
59444	Siders, Geo. P.	E
60215	McKinney, Moses	E
60402	Kesmetz, Benj.	E
61140	Steiner, Samuel	E
62574	Wertz, Adam	E
62900	Dernmeyer, Lewis	E
64347	Loose, Jacob	E
66008	Mease, Jacob	E
67952	Peiffer, John	E
69594	Noll, Isaac	E
69725	Short, Joseph	E
69847	Garman, Jacob	E
70121	Yengst, Samuel	E
70893	Ault, Henry	E
71357	Seyler, Ephriam E.	E

Serial #	Name	Company
72318	Shaffner, Martin	E
82625	Betz, Henry	E
82802	McQuade, Henry	E
83556	Dierwelter, Daniel	E
83834	Friend, Michael	E
84017	Galebauch, John H.	E
89942	McIntyre, James	E

19TH PENNSYLVANIA CAVALRY (COS. A, C, D, K AND L)

History: The 19th Pennsylvania was raised in Philadelphia between June and October 1863. The regiment was comprised almost entirely of officers and men who had seen prior service. The regiment was sent to Washington, D.C. and from there immediately transferred to Kentucky and assigned to Grierson's Cavalry Division of the 19th Corps. From their arrival, until August 1864, the regiment served in Tennessee and Mississippi. In August they moved west of the Mississippi river and participated in an expedition against Sterling Price. On October 20, the regiment moved by transport to Nashville and in December they were engaged in the Battle of Nashville. For the remainder of the war, the 19th was engaged in numerous small battles in Louisiana, Mississippi, and Alabama. From the end of the war until May 1866 the regiment served in Texas and Louisiana. The 19th was the last Pennsylvania regiment to return home.

Arms: The 19th Pennsylvania was first armed with Starr carbines, but received Sharps carbines in June and July 1864. The arms listed here date from that issue. The regiment also carried Colt and Remington navy revolvers. They were issued Spencer carbines before mustering out.

Source: The arms and names listed can be found in the *Company Order Books* along with issues of clothing and equipment.

Carbines

Serial #	Name	Company
34633	Scluler, Herman	K
42228	Hartzell, Wm. G.	K
47322	Wetherill, Anthony	K
50713	Eusinger, Ferd.	C
52207	Ryan, James	D
52450	Breyer, Jacob	K
53956	Fresler, Elijah	C
72174	Harris, James	C
72177	Taylor, Thomas	C
72177	Eager, Jas. H. D.	C
72216	Feeney, John	C
72264	Hampson	D
72304	Hanley, Samuel	C
72500	Stevens, Clement R.	D
72590	Light, Richard	D
72685	Davis, Kesler	C
72716	Miles, Sam. G.	C
72753	Eirundr, James	D
72787	Knoh, William J.	D
73201	Cummon, Robert	D
73501	Longenecker, James	C
73502	Kelly, John	D
73513	Hancock, Eliseumer	D
73513	Hannah, Henry	D
73536	Nickel, James M.	C
73540	Coughenour, E.	C
73759	Aynes, John	D
74032	Jones, David	D
74052	Lobb, Ben	D
74090	Shusbye, Joseph	D
74118	Slitzberger, Wm.	C
76187	Ely, Charles	K
77055	Jackman, James	K
77904	Byles, Martin	C
78893	Brady, John B.	C
83505	Otto, Anthony	K
83925	Hoffman, Lewls F.	K
84252	Cunningham, J.	C
84312	Crowell, James	K
84320	Dempsey, James	K
84344	McGrath, Wm. J.	K
84722	Subers, Thomas B.	K
84960	Wright, John	K
85314	Maker	A
85733	Thatcher, Jacob N	K
86014	Jones, Isaac	K
91011	Milles, Fred	D
91674	McCartey	D
91829	Depough	D
C 11288	Miles, Sam. G.	C
C 11513	Hunter, Hugh H.	K
C 11525	Kelly, Francis	K
C 11525	Kochersherger, George W.	K
C 11547	Russles, Henry C.	K
C 11560	Breyan, Jacob	K
C 11587	Schuler, Harmen F.	K
C 11593	Hoffman, Lewis F.	K
C 11616	Mulvivan, Robert	K
C 11675	Kampshier, Samuel	L
C 11687	Ohnmacht, Jabel	K
C 11703	Keller, Simon P.	K
C 11782	Arnold, John A.	L
C 11788	Gerlughiman, Elijah	L
C 11811	Walter, Joseph	C
C 11872	McLaughlin, Cornelius	C
C 11872	Longnecker, James	L
C 11891	Taylor, Wm.	L
C 11893	Aunspock, William H.	L
C 11896	Jacoby, John	A
C 11957	Johnson, James	L

C 11993	Welch, Ed. I.	A
C 12005	Thatcher, Jacob N.	K
C 12009	Morgan, Wm. G.	A
C 12072	Burkhart, John	C
C 12075	McLaughlin, Cornelius	L
C 12075	Clemens, Geo.	C
C 12088	Hessian, Dennis	A
C 12106	Zeth, George W.	L
C 12113	Allen, George	C
C 12115	Sheppard, Chas.	A
C 12116	Moore, James	L
C 12152	Rupert, Chas. A.	C
C 12202	Holihan, Richard	A
C 12205	Dodson, Andrew	C
C 12255	Cox, John T.	A
C 12255	Sheppard, Chas.	A
C 12257	Garrett, David N.	C
C 12257	Walter, Samuel	L
C 12274	Brainard, Jos. R.	A
C 12275	Rothrock, Samuel A.	C
C 12275	Allen, George	L
C 12390	Herr, John	C
C 12497	Arnold, John A.	C
C 12515	Witz, Valentine	C
C 12519	Kolb, Stephen	C
C 12522	Knode, Allan G.	L
C 12524	Strickler, Samuel	K
C 12537	Dann, Edward	C
C 12544	Warner, Andrew	A
C 12590	Morrison, James	L
C 12593	Stemmer, Theo.	C
C 12596	Hammel, Henry	A
C 12606	Clewelt, Jos. R.	A
C 12707	Dougherty, Kennedy	A
C 12711	" "	D
C 12733	Stroble, Fred.	A
C 12748	Simpson, Maybry	L
C 12758	Myers, John	C
C 12761	Dessick, William	D
C 12763	Hoar, Sam L.	C
C 12769	Bolinger, James	C
C 12770	McFarland, Jno.	A
C 12821	Wolfkiel, Thomas	L
C 12823	Johnson, James	C
C 12826	McIntyre, Jas.	A
C 12828	Hite, Josiah M.	L
C 12830	Clugstone, Howard	A
C 12833	Miles, Samuel	L
C 12834	Knipple, Andrew	L
C 12834	Brininger, John	C
C 12837	Heiges, John H.	C
C 12857	Walter, Joseph	L
C 12861	Miller, Josiah	L
C 12873	Weitz, Joseph S. L.	L
C 12874	Brady, John B.	L
C 12874	Saltsman, A.W.	C
C 12875	McClain, Wm.	A
C 12879	Fraley, Samuel	C
C 12884	Baker, Samuel	L
C 12898	Coogle, Philip	L
C 12898	Bavars, A. S.	C
C 12902	Kesler, D.	L
C 12907	Moore, James	C
C 12909	Shine, Philip	L
C 12909	Lunard, Simpson	C
C 12985	Clapper, Wm.	C
C 12985	Simpson, Mayberry	C
C 13159	Nill, Wm. F.	C

42ND PENNSYLVANIA INFANTRY

History: The 42nd Pennsylvania Infantry was organized in early May 1861 in Harrisburg as the 1st Rifle Regiment or 13th Regiment Pennsylvania Reserve Corps. This corps had been authorized by the state legislature primarily for the defense of the state. It was not until late June that the regiment was called into United States service. At this time the 13th Reserves was designated the 42nd regiment. The three regimental titles would remain nearly interchangeable when referring to the regiment. It would be still another unofficial designation, however, that would become famous. These men of the 42nd Pennsylvania would win glory as the "Bucktails," a nickname which referred to the piece of deerhide or buck's tail which adorned the forage caps of the men.

The regiment's first action was at Dranesville, Virginia on December 20, 1861. This was followed by duty in the Shenandoah Valley and with the Army of the Potomac on the peninsula below Richmond and the Army of Virginia under Pope. In February the "Bucktails" were again assigned to the Army of the Potomac. From that date on, the history of the 42nd Pennsylvania is that of the famed Union army. At Gettysburg, the regimental monument stands just south of the Wheatfield in the area where the 42nd fought heroically and captured the colors of the 15th Georgia Infantry. The last action seen by the regiment before being mustered out was at Bethesda Church, Virginia on May 30, 1864. On June 11, 1864, the "Bucktails" ended their term of service; however, many men were transferred to the 190th Pennsylvania, a new regiment which was formed in the field from veterans and recruits of the Pennsylvania Reserve Corps. With this organization, they continued to fight to the end of the war.

Arms: The Sharps rifles carried by the 42nd Pennsylvania were originally intended for issue to the 1st and 2nd U.S. Sharpshooters. These rifles had been placed in storage in the Washington Arsenal to replace arms damaged or lost by the sharpshooters or to arm new recruits. A protest in August 1862 by the "Bucktails" over an attempt to issue them inferior arms resulted in them receiving enough Sharps rifles to place between 14-25 in every company. The numbers listed here appeared on a listing which unfortunately contained no names. The list was entitled, "Invoice of Guns, Sharps Rifles, Cal. 52, now in First Rifle Regiment P.R.V.C. January 3, 1862." It is obvious from the well-established date of the receipt of the rifles by the 42nd that the 1862 date should read 1863. An interesting point on the original list was the notation of a small letter "b" behind 12 numbers in Co. A and 11 in Co. B. This letter stood for "bayonet" and except for a notation in Co. H "no bayonets" was the only mention of those weapons' association with these arms.

Source: The "Invoice of Guns" which is listed here was found bound into the *Regimental Descriptive Book of the 190th Pennsylvania*. This is the regiment to which the recruits and veterans of the 42nd Pennsylvania were transferred. It is evident that at least part of the regimental records went along with the men.

Rifles

Serial #	Company	Serial #	Company
44918	D	54720	I
54377	H	54721	E
54379	I	54727	D
54417	A	54735	E
54425	F	54748	D
54433	C	54749	E
54440	C	54750	A
54470	H	54759	E
54503	G	54761	D
54504	K	54783	I
54505	H	54784	D
54512	F	54792	H
54517	E	54798	G
54526	K	54808	K
54555	E	54847	D
54559	K	54856	H
54578	A	54860	A
54604	F	54862	G
54606	H	54863	D
54609	D	54868	K
54613	I	54878	B
54616	B	54884	F
54620	B	54886	F
54621	D	54893	B
54622	E	54900	E
54630	F	54914	B
54644	B	54921	A
54646	H	54944	C
54648	H	54945	F
54651	C	54948	B
54654	K	54957	D
54665	A	54970	E
54682	D	54974	K
54682	I	54979	B
54695	F	54991	D
54997	B	56070	H
54999	H	56079	C
55001	E	56089	C
55002	E	56092	B
55004	K	56119	E
55005	D	56142	C
55014	F	56144	B
55016	D	56160	F
55023	F	56176	C
55040	B	56188	I
55061	B	56193	C
55071	B	56242	G
55080	E	56243	G
55081	C	56246	G
55087	C	56251	H
55095	I	56298	H
55119	B	56332	B
55120	D	56344	C
55123	D	56412	K
55135	I	56430	A
55138	D	56457	E
55143	C	56553	I
55158	F	56599	H
55371	A	56604	H
55378	D	56668	G
55384	F	56767	D
55385	B	56804	G
55386	A	56818	C
55387	B	56822	E
55395	D	56975	I
55398	A	56993	I
55399	D	57012	E
55404	C	57054	G
55406	K	57116	I
55409	H	57123	G
55419	E	57126	G
55428	G	57204	H
55430	B	57207	A
55438	K	57218	A
55447	K	57225	G
55450	C	57275	D
55455	K	57341	A
55459	C	57401	G
55460	E	57441	D
55461	F	57451	C
55466	F	57467	K
55471	K	57484	D
55474	F	57490	C
55832	B	57500	I
55876	F	57512	A
55885	D	57567	H
55886	K	57591	F
55916	F	57641	I
55966	I		
55989	C		
56069	C		

Sharps rifle SN 54783, issued to a soldier in Company I of the 42nd Pennsylvania Infantry.

1st U.S. Dragoons (Company A) (1st U.S. Cavalry)

History: In 1861 the 1st U.S. Dragoons were stationed on the Pacific Coast. Upon the outbreak of the war, the regiment was sent by sea to Washington, D.C. Although the history of the regiment is one of hard fighting with the Cavalry Corps of the Army of the Potomac, the history of the arms listed here is quite different. Based upon the knowledge that the seven arms numbers found in Captain John Adams' report of April 21, 1859, all fall within the serial number range of the 1st California Cavalry, the authors have concluded that the evidence clearly indicates that the 1st Dragoons left their Sharps carbines in California upon their departure. These arms were then issued to the 1st California Cavalry. Careful examination of the 1st California numbers reveals that several of them are the identical weapons seized from John Brown in October 1859. It would stand to reason that once these very serviceable carbines were confiscated by the Federal government, they were quickly issued to regular troops. It is likely they reached the 1st Dragoons sometime in early 1860. Obviously, these would not appear on an 1859 report, but the fact is they were in California and undoubtedly in the hands of the 1st Dragoons. Other 1st California arms match those seized from Free State men in Kansas. These, too, were almost certainly 1st Dragoon carbines.

Arms: The 1st U.S. Dragoons in the period immediately preceding the war were armed with Sharps carbines. Upon arrival in Washington, D.C., they were reissued new Sharps. The arms listed here date from the prewar period.

Source: The letter from Company A, 1st Dragoons, dated April 21, 1859, can be found in Record Group 156, Entry 21, Box 167.

Carbines

Serial #	Company
11527	A
13215	A
13666	A
14368	A
15022	A
16772	A
17646	A

1st Vermont Cavalry (Company D)

History: The 1st Vermont Cavalry was organized at Burlington, Vermont, and mustered in November 19, 1861. The regiment moved to Washington, D.C., in early 1862 and then to the Shenandoah Valley where it saw action at Middletown on May 24 and near Winchester on May 25 and June 18. Following this, the 1st moved east of the mountains and joined the Union Army of Virginia. After the northern Virginia campaign of that short-lived army, the regiment moved to the defenses of Washington where it remained until June 1863. While assigned to the defenses, it participated in several scouts that resulted in skirmishes. In June 1863 it was assigned to the 1st Brigade, 3rd Division, Cavalry Corps, Army of the Potomac. This brigade was commanded by newly promoted General Elon Farnsworth. At Gettysburg on July 3, the 1st Vermont was part of the ill conceived charge ordered by Kilpatrick on the extreme right of the Confederate infantry. This charge resulted in Farnsworth's death and sixty-five casualties in the 1st Vermont. From this time on, the history of the regiment is that of the hard fighting 3rd Division, Cavalry Corps, Army of the Potomac. In August 1864 this division under General Philip H. Sheridan, moved to the Shenandoah Valley where the 1st Vermont once again saw action. They returned to the main army in time for the Appomattox campaign. The regiment was present at the Grand Review in Washington on May 23 and was mustered out on August 9, 1865.

Arms: The Sharps carbines listed here appear on a list which dates from 1865. The regiment was also armed with Colt and Remington army revolvers and Spencer carbines.

Source: The names and serial numbers listed can be found in the *Company Order Book for Co. D*.

Carbines

Serial #	Name	Company
45050	Simmons, Isaac P.	D
89622	Stevens, Zachria	D
C 19595	Fisher, Geo. A.	D
C 20464	Evans, Geo. E.	D
C 22056	Hutton, Abiah	D
C 22072	Hyde, Lewis C.	D
C 22101	Worthen, Geo. B.	D

2ND, 4TH, 5TH, AND 6TH VETERAN VOLUNTEER INFANTRY

History: The history of these remarkable regiments is more one of what might have been than what was. In late 1864 Congress authorized the formation of a "veteran corps." This corps was to be comprised of regiments whose ranks would be filled by veterans whose term of service had ended and who would reenlist to serve in an elite corps to be commanded by General W.S. Hancock. As an inducement, each man who would so serve would be issued a breechloading rifle, either Henry or Sharps, which would be his to keep when discharged. The regiments listed here were all organized in early 1865. With the Confederate surrender in April, the corps, which eventually contained nine regiments of infantry, was left with little but garrison duty to occupy itself. The great might have been is of course what effect such a corps of battle tested veterans, each armed with a breechloading rifle, would have had in actual combat.

Arms: The Sharps rifles listed below are the New Model 1863 Military Rifle. Most of these rifles were produced to arm the Veteran Volunteer Corps. That many survive in exceptionally good condition attests to the very limited use they saw in the service.

Source: The names and serial numbers listed here can be located as follows:
2nd Regiment: *Company Order Books, Cos. B and D*
4th Regiment: *Company Order Books, Cos. H and K*
5th Regiment: *Company Descriptive Book, Co. E*
6th Regiment: *Company Order Books, Cos. C, E, and G*

2nd Veteran Volunteers (U.S.)

Rifles

Serial #	Name	Company
53044	Gillison, Joseph	B
56784	Austin, James E.	B
56919	Hardy, Robert	B
56919	Eager, Chas. J.	B
56988	Scott, Patrick	D
57102	Woods, Francis	B
57103	Spaw, Nicholus	B
57214	Vollmer, John	D
57296	Armstrong, John	B
57393	Andrews, Wm. R.	B
57407	Golden, Cyrus	D
57417	Raney, Francis	D
57419	Sloman, John C.	D
57446	Gambea, James A.	B
57452	McGowen, Martin	B
57461	Leonard, Thomas W.	B
57480	Sampson, Columbus	B
57656	Barlow, Wm.	D
57656	Connally, Edw.	D
57679	Kilcoyn, John	B
57709	Sweeney, Edward	D
57731	Simmons, Isaac S.	B
57831	Coady, Cpl. Wm. J.	B
57844	Callender, Chas. C.	D
57862	Devine, Wm.	B
57887	Cassidy, Thomas J.	B
57901	Perry, James	D
57902	Hall, Cpl. Chas. M.	B
57963	Miller, Lorenzo	B
57981	Timmins, Cpl. Joseph	B
57987	Parsons, Milo C.	D
58037	Davis, Richard	B
58051	Allen, Pvt. Henry J.	B
58056	Slothers, Hampton	D
58069	Woods, Francis	B
58083	Kelley, Wm.	B
58110	Davidson, Cpl. Herbert	B
58114	Dickerson, Joseph C.	B
58115	Scott, Thomas	D
C 24226	Sneidmiller, Henry	B
C 28759	Schneiderwind, Peter	B
C 28759	Shinault, Joshua	B
C 28775	Downey, John	B
C 28777	Folsom, Lewis	D
C 28779	Jones, Wm. V.	D
C 28781	Free, John	B

Serial #	Name	Company
C 28783	Baker, Wm. H.	B
C 28786	Deitrick, Thomas	D
C 28790	Gives, James L.	B
C 28792	Lambert, Frank J.	D
C 28798	Richter, Chas. H.	B
C 28800	Colvin, Albert H.	D
C 28834	Schone, Michael	D
C 28842	Skinner, Edwin	B
C 28847	Andrews, Prince A.	B
C 28849	Williams, Nicholas I.	D
C 28850	McDermott, Chas.	D
C 28857	Monk, Chas. F.	D
C 28875	Muir, George	B
C 28880	Bryant, Francis	D
C 28883	Barnett, Richard	B
C 28889	Heath, John	D
C 28892	Harrington, Mark	B
C 28893	Hill, David	B
C 28896	Thompson, James	B
C 28900	Sprague, Nathan	B
C 28907	Horan, James	D
C 28921	Mulcav, Michael	B
C 28922	Sawyer, Chas.	D
C 28925	Chandler, Robert	D
C 28952	Johnson, Chas. E.	D
C 28952	Cunnion, Michael	D
C 28953	Flick, Mathias	D
C 28954	Albrecht, Ludwig	D
C 28954	Gore, Chas. H.	D
C 29049	Gledhill, John	D
C 29054	Eckhardt, Herman	D
C 29059	Pettis, Benj.	B
C 29060	Neaux, Henry	D
C 29073	Kain, Joseph	D
C 30140	Broken, to be repaired	D
C 30140	Thompson, Wellington	D
C 30141	Houland, Jeremiah	D
C 30148	Heushel, Esher	D
C 30163	Guy, John	D
C 30165	Albrecht, Ludwig	D
C 30167	Ball, Joseph H.	D
C 30173	McCuen, Parker	D
C 30173	Thompson, Wellington	D
C 30181	Broken, to be repaired	D
C 30190	Crilly, Francis	D
C 30194	Kronert, Wm.	D
C 30195	Kinsley, Henry	D
C 30195	Ames, Oakley	D
C 30203	Lamb, Michael	D
C 30208	Mabray, Franklin	B
C 30213	McCruam, Samuel	B
C 30215	Millinet, Wm. F.	D
C 30215	Mason, John	D
C 30225	Andrews, Robert F.	D
C 30228	Berry, James	D
C 30234	McGrath, Danl.	D
C 30240	Perry, John	D
C 30241	Mahoney, John	B
C 30248	Wixsom, Moses I.	D
C 30262	Palmer, Silas N.	D
C 30269	Shulte, John D.	B
C 30283	Broken, to be repaired	D
C 30298	McAfee, John	B
C 30301	Redmond, John Jr.	D
C 30310	Webb, Wm. M.	D
C 30332	Dolan, Thomas	D
C 30336	Dell, Joseph	B
C 30349	Gosell, Martin	B
C 30364	Harris, Wm. H.	D
C 30389	Damon, Daniel	B
C 30519	Thompson, Edward A.	B
C 30523	Galbraith, Wm.	D
C 30525	Wehrle, Emil	D
C 31879	Williams, Chas.	D
C 31886	Schneiderwind, Peter	B
C 31886	Harrington, Mark	B
C 31886	Fleming, Thomas	B
C 31895	Ames, Chas. M.	D
C 31919	Johnson, Joy E.	D
C 31924	Marshal, John	B
C 32030	Bailey, Eli	D
C 32071	Cocoran, John	D
C 32085	Robinson, Josiah W.	B
C 32087	Whipple, Chas. A.	B
C 32087	Dunn, John	D
C 32093	Boersh, John	D
C 32109	Groh, John	D
C 32111	Bremer, Sgt. Charles	B
C 32383	Schaffer, Samuel D.	B
C 33054	Prenderville, John	B
C 33158	Scott, 1st Sgt. Andrew	B
C 33915	Taylor, John M.	B
C 34151	Schaffer, Louis D.	B
C 34151	Jones, Bernard	B
C 34217	Tunncliff, John S.	B
C 34220	Morrarty, John M.	B
C 34263	Chizum, Cpl. James H.	B
C 34280	Maeller, George	B
C 34402	Colwell, John	B
C 34405	Geiger, Jacob	B
C 34784	Davis, Richard	B
C 34932	Gambea, James A.	B

4th Veteran Volunteers (U.S.)

Rifles

Serial #	Name	Company
43989	Rush, Wm.	K
C 30191	Moose, Sgt. Jas. W.	H
C 30281	May, Mus. Chas. E.	H
C 30371	Byeely, Cpl. P. M.	H
C 31538	Perkins, Work	H
C 31539	Ayres, Pvt. Wm. R.	H
C 31587	Humbert, Teams. Philip	H

Sharps Carbines & Rifles

C 31599	Miner, Cpl. Jas. F.	H
C 31633	Munich, John A.	H
C 31639	Broseker, Geo. B.	H
C 31687	Trowbridge, Eliphalet	K
C 31771	Barker, Cpl. Jno. W.	H
C 31829	Vault, Cpl. Const.	H
C 31971	Collins, Chas. J.	H
C 33082	Thompson, Jacob A.	K
C 33085	Orsborn, Owen	K
C 33234	Close, Geo. W.	K
C 33237	Huey, Wm.	H
C 33312	Young, W.	H
C 33501	Dimick, Jerome B.	H
C 33847	Ireland, John F.	H
C 33867	Hoffsher, Cpl. Wm. W.	H
C 33868	Roth, Geo.	K
C 33880	Cutter, Sgt. D. B.	H
C 33900	Murry, Chas. M.	H
C 33919	Frank, Sgt. Walter	K
C 33930	Brinkley, Lafayette	H
C 33959	Keyser, Chas.	H
C 33976	Davis, Wm.	H
C 33987	Lynch, Lewis	H
C 33992	Gillispie, Chas.	H
C 34044	Carroll, Cpl. Albert G.	K
C 34044	Crime, Joseph H.	K
C 34070	Wager, Casper	K
C 34080	Butler, Anthony	H
C 34100	White, Cpl. Levi M.	H
C 34103	Rockhill, Frinnpton	K
C 34129	Jarus, DeForest	H
C 34135	Staples, Frank	H
C 34162	Slattery, Chas.	K
C 34174	Swasic, James C.	K
C 34218	Spilona, John	H
C 34272	Funk, Martin	K
C 34332	Jenness, Geo. B.	K
C 34354	Hartman, Mus. Adam	H
C 34358	Lauderback, Andrew	K
C 34361	Skencu, Francis	K
C 34384	Kimnes, Patrick	H
C 34384	Warner, Chas	K
C 34390	Hawkins, John S.	K
C 34398	Voegtly, Alias	K
C 34399	Shire, Henry	K
C 34413	Vennausdale, Arthur S.	K
C 34454	Simpson, Willard	H
C 34455	Vandyke, Daniel	K
C 34462	McFall, William	K
C 34492	Wheitner, Chas.	K
C 34504	Voegel, Bernhard	K
C 34724	Larkin, Cpl. Geo.	K
C 34752	Grovener, Augustus D.	K
C 34812	Dircks, Paul	H
C 34826	Cunningham, Joseph	K
C 34843	Hill, Sgt. James M.	K
C 34869	Greenfield, Sgt. George	K
C 34880	Dilly, David	K
C 34897	Hurly, Sgt. Nihemiah	K
C 34927	Wilson, John H.	K
C 34932	Stone, Weir	H
C 34935	Loth, Geo	K
C 34936	Kinney, Cpl. Iserel	K
C 34940	Wilson, John	K
C 34947	Jacobs, Geo.	K
C 34955	Miller, Sebastian	K
C 34956	Korkel, Jacob	K
C 35001	Hawkins, Henry A.	H
C 35001	Lee, Samuel	H
C 35019	Vanpelt, John B.	K
C 35036	Greves, Albert	K
C 35038	McKenna, James	H
C 35055	Freshuater, Wm.	K
C 35080	Hennek, Henery	K
C 35093	Farrell, John U.	H
C 35098	Galaspie, Auther	K
C 35105	Segal, 1st Sgt. Bernhart	K
C 35134	Yeckley, Cpl. Aug.	H
C 35144	Giming, Chas. E.	K
C 35151	Sanders, Chas. K.	K
C 35157	Imber, Nicholas	K
C 35169	Evans, Elmore	K
C 35171	Thomas, Sabine R.	K
C 35181	Robertson, Wm.	K
C 35185	Carbaugh, Cpl. Geo.	K
C 35210	Bennett, Cpl. Wm. H.	K
C 35212	Alexander, Pvt. R. F.	K
C 35228	Gale, Cpl. Wm. N.	K
C 35279	Banahorn, James	K
C 35280	Porter, Cpl. Samuel	K
C 35292	Harriess, Harvey	K
C 35303	Souers, Elhman	K
C 35305	Harrifield, Thomas J.	K
C 35314	Harwood, Teams. Joseph F.	K
C 35339	Lattimore, Isaac	K
C 35360	McGarr, James	H
C 35366	Payel, Chas.	H
C 35387	Moore, Wm. S.	K
C 35400	Loux, Whlan B.	H
C 35401	Barber, Edgar W.	K
C 35409	Brestel, Geo. W.	K
C 35452	Wolman, Felix	H
C 35453	Pemberton, Russel	K
C 35468	Honsefall, Mus. Wm.	K
C 35502	Bulls, John	K
C 35515	Kittirell, S. H.	H
C 35554	Loux, Mathaus J.	H
C 35574	Reedger, Wm.	K
C 35578	Bradley, Sgt. F. W.	H
C 35588	Litscher, Christian	H
C 35662	Anderson, Jacob	K
C 35685	Baptist, John	H
C 35688	Docimm, Daniel	K
C 35731	Brooks, Nelson	K

Serial #	Name	Company
C 35796	Malkmers, John	K
C 35809	Gettings, Edw. F.	K
C 38224	Bishir, Wm.	K
C 38330	Brown, James W.	K

5th Veteran Volunteers (U.S.)

Rifles

Serial #	Name	Company
C 28829	Hamilton, Joseph	E
C 28937	Comner, Thomas	E
C 28945	Robinson, Henry W.	E
C 28955	Dickneider, Fredrick	E
C 30132	Inmann, Isaac M.	E
C 30168	Fistle, Wm.	E
C 30169	Boehim, Frefrick	E
C 30186	Foley, Daniel	E
C 30205	Hara, James	E
C 30214	Edmonds, Laurence	E
C 31581	Graff, Fredrick	E
C 31710	Day, Chas. M.	E
C 31723	Hartkopf, Augustas	E
C 31794	Mullalay, Morris	E
C 31810	James, Riker R.	E
C 31811	Huston, Daniel	E
C 31848	Gabhart, Thomas H.	E
C 31850	Housman, Wm.	E
C 31861	O'Brien, John	E
C 31876	Darst, Antone	E
C 31904	Fonnt, Harmon	E
C 31939	Durie, Chas.	E
C 31958	Barry, Stephen	E
C 33101	Woodman, Albert B.	E
C 33161	Bonstle, Christian	E
C 33224	Barman, August	E
C 33833	Chambers, Newman C.	E
C 34069	Whitegrove, Sidney	E
C 34081	Grossman, Herman	E
C 34125	Davis, Laffert Z.	E
C 34149	Longenbeck, Stephen	E
C 34168	Maxwell, Wm. H.	E
C 34177	Pefister, Hannon	E
C 34199	Johnson, Wm.	E
C 34208	McIntyre, David	E
C 34267	Rumpf, Henry A.	E
C 34270	Stonn, Henry	E
C 34276	Schoppe, Wm.	E
C 34279	Grouss, Henrick	E
C 34296	Strott, Alfred	E
C 34304	Workmaster, Simon	E
C 34310	Geisant, Joseph H.	E
C 34322	Mattox, Wm.	E
C 34328	Parrient, Harrison	E
C 34330	Spear, Wm. A.	E
C 34360	Hair, John	E
C 34403	Stephen, Enoch	E
C 34428	Wosternholm, James	E
C 34436	McAlear, Chas.	E
C 34458	Lohmann, Richard	E
C 34476	Hanes, Chas. G.	E
C 34487	White, Thomas	E
C 34495	Chambers, Newman C.	E
C 34500	Conger, Joseph	E
C 34578	Their, Peter	E
C 34727	Belligard, Adolph	E
C 34786	Schlenter, Wm.	E
C 34789	Wymans, Wm. F.	E
C 34798	Henry, Martin L.	E
C 34801	Grary, Michael	E
C 34803	Goulding, Geo. H.	E
C 34808	Teoring, Emil	E
C 34816	Schafer, Henry	E
C 34831	Tompkins, Isaac J.	E
C 34834	Ohlenschlager, Frederick	E
C 34846	Wiley, Ezlra	E
C 34848	Parcels, Geo.	E
C 34855	Crosbie, James	E
C 34861	Cadmus, Geo. L.	E
C 34873	Stage, John H.	E
C 34877	Doyle, John	E
C 34964	Vanderhoof, Jacob C.	E
C 35545	Miller, John	E
C 39325	Goodman, Thomas J.	E

6th Veteran Volunteers (U.S.)

Rifles

Serial #	Name	Company
C30876	Stuever, Frederick	E
C31546	Morgan, Charles	E
C31600	Martin, Chas. G.	E
C31929	Jordan, Samuel S.	E
C31945	Mayhew, Samuel M.	E
C33089	Hardison, John	E
C33089	Haaswaser, Jermiah	E
C33102	Be, Joseph	E
C33232	Davis, John	E
C33362	Holmes, Oscar	C
C33480	Atherson, Wm. H.	E
C33493	Mitchel, Chas.	E
C33528	Eaton, Wm. W.	C
C33538	McCauley, Thos.	C
C33576	Leddy, John	C
C33583	Sels, Wm.	C
C33588	Smith, Albert C.	E
C33650	Kerr, James A.	G
C33688	Hubpart, John	C
C33695	Hagendorf, Emil	E
C33696	Hartman, Aba	E
C34236	Ewing, John	G
C34540	Gender, Peter	E
C34540	Deengey, Wm. W.	E
C34553	Smith, Edw.	G
C34555	Mimmo, Archibald	C

C34565	Hale, Anson	C		C37388	Kuhen, John	E
C34570	Morgan, Edwar	E		C37399	Roush, Jacob	G
C34572	Elmer, Ferdenand	C		C37406	Eichelberger, Singleton	G
C34620	Meyer, Wm.	C		C37427	Struthers, Wm.	G
C34629	Hooker, Chas.	C		C37434	Hennessy, Edward	G
C34630	Grazier, Casper	C		C37442	Hurlbert, Sheldon	E
C34630	Perkins, Wm.	C		C37444	Fay, Chas. M.	G
C34682	Offin, Wm.	E		C37448	Dreer, Henry	E
C34805	Schwartzenhoelzer, Chris	G		C37456	Mabee, Frank	E
C34881	August, Benj.	E		C37469	Smith, Charles T.	G
C34953	Betz, John	G		C37484	Ogden, John	G
C34954	Nichols, Jacobs	G		C37486	Hexames, Charles	G
C35353	Salten, Samuel P.	C		C37496	Weigle, Peter	E
C35353	Pouden, Amadee	C		C37505	Kane, Martin	G
C35496	Herzog, Geo.	C		C37514	Mills, Wm.	G
C35605	Perkins, Wm.	C		C37514	Berry, John	G
C35626	Sayles, Frank	C		C37529	Cogle, Andrew	E
C35651	Lake, Wm. J.	C		C37553	Crangle, Wm.	E
C35654	Williams, John	C		C37555	Clemson, Tilman R.	G
C35665	Johnson, Andrew	C		C37556	Wilson, Jacob	G
C35665	Aufort, Geo.	C		C37567	Jones, John A.	G
C35670	Culley, James A.	C		C37571	Crafts, Eben R.	G
C35693	Mack, Isack J.	E		C37576	Young, Wm.	G
C35694	Sterling, Samuel L.	E		C37581	Kelley, Patrick	G
C35696	Finke, Wm.	E		C37590	Waterhouse, Wm. D.	G
C35756	Nilan, Michael	E		C37604	Fay, Chas. M.	G
C35788	Lumbard, Benj.	C		C37604	Stokes, Robert	G
C35788	Smith, Henry C.	C		C37604	Anderson, John	G
C35789	Himes, Joseph H.	C		C37613	Myres, Patrick	G
C35791	Johnson, Andrew	C		C37613	Gamber, Patrick	G
C35802	Dorelone, Wm.	C		C37619	Ward, Orlando R.	G
C35874	Myers, Jacob	C		C37626	Hottenbeck, Valentine	G
C35923	Dorson, Richard	C		C37642	Martin, Ferdinand	G
C35926	Murrey, Cycrus C.	C		C37672	Martin, Ferdinand	G
C35926	Munn, Theodore	C		C37687	Collins, Daniel H.	G
C35930	Honnor, John P.	C		C37696	Kuhen, John	E
C35949	Sayre, Nimiah	C		C37696	Rrehr, Christopher	E
C35954	House, James	E		C37707	Fay, Chas. M.	G
C37019	Taylor, James	E		C37726	Betz, Adolph	G
C37076	Taylor, James	E		C37726	Shenk, Charles	G
C37087	Danmer, Christopher	E		C37727	Dorr, Auguste	G
C37120	Burkhardt, Edw.	E		C37741	Bearholt, Henry	G
C37159	Cation, wm.	E		C37742	Kerr, James Y.	G
C37231	Hill, thomas	E		C37759	Briggs, Geo.	G
C37245	Kempt, Andrew	E		C37795	Farley, James	G
C37285	Kennedy, John	E		C37849	Morse, John R.	G
C37292	Hatch, Cyrus K.	E		C37884	Grahn, Wm.	G
C37295	Reid, James W.	E		C37897	Christopher, Thomas	C
C37298	Bloomer, Samuel	E		C37948	Mahoney, Michael	E
C37298	Yvange, Henry	E		C37948	Fleming, Geo. F.	E
C37332	Shouse, John	E		C37951	Keihl, Jacob	C
C37332	Crenson, Wm. B.	E		C37959	Martin, Leonard	G
C37336	Greenfield, Thomas H.	E		C37966	Cooke, Wm. P.	G
C37345	Jackson, Cyrus	G		C37972	Gardner, Harry W.	C
C37346	Gamber, Patrick	G		C37985	White, John	E
C37365	Hunt, Thomas C.	E		C38003	Botcher, Rudolph	C
C37373	Mason, Wm.	G		C38017	Johnson, Robert	C

Serial #	Name	Company
C38028	Smith, Wm. P.	G
C38051	Braitliept, John	C
C38064	Schular, Lawrence	C
C38069	Unger, Chas. C.	G
C38080	Cadden, Terrance	C
C38084	Stokes, Robert	G
C38090	Schrader, Adolph	G
C38121	Ingraham, Gilbert C.	G
C38133	Lumbard, Ben.	C
C38172	Reid, James W.	E
C38172	Swaintz, John	E
C38203	Dixon, Wm.	C
C38214	Butler, Patrick	E
C38215	Kerner, Theodore	C
C38222	Seman, John	E
C38227	Morrow, Arthur	G
C38235	Sthrom, George	G
C38241	Crenson, Wm. B.	E
C38247	Zeller, Henry (teamster)	C
C38278	Wood, Franklln	G
C38295	Shmidt, John	E
C38295	Haaswaser, Jermiah	E
C38301	Leasoe, Lewis	E
C38303	Brady, James	C
C38311	Wade, John H.	E
C38333	Karen, John	G
C38350	Weiner, Frank	E
C38365	Longan, Anson	G
C38377	Leddy, John	C
C38396	McDonald, david	E
C38410	Stadel, John	G
C38411	Porter, Sereno	C
C38417	Shafer, Frederick	E
C38427	Hardison, John	E
C38427	Shmidt, John	E
C38457	Clauson, Theadore	C
C38469	Smith, Segiment	G
C38474	Brendal, Adam	C
C38476	Stuever, Frederick	E
C38481	Klingle, Jacob	E
C38501	Robinson, Wm.	E
C38509	Mulgrew, Wm.	G
C38533	Clements, Wm. H.	C
C38548	Graham, Robert M.	E
C38548	Kennedy, John	E
C38562	Fulton, john	E
C38571	Jennings, John	G
C38576	Hoopman, John S.	E
C38589	Parshull, John	E
C38615	Whitnall, Asa M.	C
C38691	Sheffenburger, Jacob	C
C38701	Hannagan, John J.	E
C38727	McCullough, Robert	G
C38742	Graham, Robert M.	E
C38744	Christian, Life	E
C38779	Polterman, Frederick	G
C38787	Moore, Horace	C
C38841	Culley, James A.	C
C38870	VanClief, Slalis	C
C38883	Hatch, Geo.	C
C38890	McGenty, Neil	G
C39001	Reicherd, Charles	C
C39011	Wolf, Gustave	C
C39021	Perkins, Wm.	C
C39021	Pouden, Amadee	C
C39021	Lumbard, Benj.	C
C39035	Church, Ulrich	C
C39048	Scott, Patrick	C
C39179	Mahoney, Michael	E
C39179	Fleming, Geo. F.	E
C39179	Adair, Samuel M.	C
C37x80	Bankhart, Joseph	G

2ND WEST VIRGINIA CAVALRY (COMPANY H)

History: The 2nd West Virginia Cavalry was organized at Parkersburg, West Virginia, from September to November 1861. The regiment moved immediately to central West Virginia and was engaged in scouting and operations against bushwackers. For the next two and a half years the 2nd West Virginia saw continual service in the mountains of the new state. Scouts and expeditions punctuated by skirmishes at Meadow Bluff marked the daily existence of the regiment. In the summer of 1864, the 2nd West Virginia moved into the Shenandoah Valley. For the remainder of the year, it served with the Union forces operating in the Valley. In 1865, the regiment moved even further east and joined the Army of the Potomac in time for the Appomattox campaign. After so long in the shadows, the regiment ended the war by participation in the Grand Review in Washington on May 23, 1865. The men were mustered out on June 30, 1865.

Arms: The 2nd West Virginia Cavalry was primarily armed with Smith carbines and Colt army revolvers. The Sharps carbine numbers listed here were the exception in Company H. The list dates from the first quarter 1863.

Source: The serial numbers and names listed below may be found in the *Company Descriptive Books of Co. H*.

Carbines

Serial #	Name	Company
31496	Hammons, Robert T.	H
41354	Kramer, Martin	H
43649	Hawk, Samuel S.	H
43704	Marshman, Henry H.	H
43819	McMillen, Emerson	H
43841	Tarr, Alonzo	H
43942	Pugh, George	H

Navy Purchases

Navy Rifles, .56 cal., Model 1859

Date Issued	Shipped To	Serial #	Box #
Nov. 6, 1860	W.N.Y.	33000	#15
Nov. 16, 1860	W.N.Y.	33018	#4
Nov. 20, 1860	Phila.N.Y.	33047	#24
Nov. 16, 1860	W.N.Y.	33290	#16
Nov. 5, 1860	W.N.Y.	33290	#7
Nov. 5, 1860	W.N.Y.	33291	#22
Nov. 16, 1860	W.N.Y.	33292	#10
Nov. 5, 1860	W.N.Y.	33293	#4
Nov. 16, 1860	W.N.Y.	33294	#12
Nov. 16, 1860	W.N.Y.	33295	#7
Nov. 5, 1860	W.N.Y.	33297	#24
Nov. 5, 1860	W.N.Y.	33298	#11
Nov. 5, 1860	W.N.Y.	33299	#2
Nov. 20, 1860	Phila.N.Y.	33302	#30
Nov. 16, 1860	W.N.Y.	33303	#6
Nov. 20, 1860	Phila.N.Y.	33304	#26
Nov. 5, 1860	W.N.Y.	33305	#6
Nov. 16, 1860	W.N.Y.	33306	#13
Nov. 16, 1860	W.N.Y.	33307	#19
Nov. 16, 1860	W.N.Y.	33308	#4
Nov. 5, 1860	W.N.Y.	33309	#2
Nov. 5, 1860	W.N.Y.	33310	#5
Nov. 20, 1860	Phila.N.Y.	33311	#27
Nov. 16, 1860	W.N.Y.	33313	#6
Nov. 5, 1860	W.N.Y.	33314	#18
Nov. 16, 1860	W.N.Y.	33314	#5
Nov. 5, 1860	W.N.Y.	33314	#19
Nov. 5, 1860	W.N.Y.	33316	#7
Nov. 16, 1860	W.N.Y.	33317	#12
Nov. 5, 1860	W.N.Y.	33318	#11
Nov. 5, 1860	W.N.Y.	33319	#30
Nov. 5, 1860	W.N.Y.	33320	#9
Nov. 20, 1860	Phila.N.Y.	33321	#23
Nov. 16, 1860	W.N.Y.	33323	#18
Nov. 16, 1860	W.N.Y.	33324	#5
Nov. 5, 1860	W.N.Y.	33325	#12
Nov. 5, 1860	W.N.Y.	33326	#26
Nov. 20, 1860	Phila.N.Y.	33327	#32
Nov. 16, 1860	W.N.Y.	33328	#21
Nov. 16, 1860	W.N.Y.	33330	#8
Nov. 5, 1860	W.N.Y.	33331	#13
Nov. 5, 1860	W.N.Y.	33332	#28
Nov. 16, 1860	W.N.Y.	33333	#12
Nov. 5, 1860	W.N.Y.	33334	#19
Nov. 20, 1860	Phila.N.Y.	33335	#32
Nov. 5, 1860	W.N.Y.	33336	#8
Nov. 16, 1860	W.N.Y.	33337	#14
Nov. 20, 1860	Phila.N.Y.	33338	#29
Nov. 5, 1860	W.N.Y.	33340	#5
Nov. 5, 1860	W.N.Y.	33341	#13
Nov. 16, 1860	W.N.Y.	33343	#21
Nov. 5, 1860	W.N.Y.	33344	#19
Nov. 16, 1860	W.N.Y.	33346	#2
Nov. 5, 1860	W.N.Y.	33347	#15
Nov. 16, 1860	W.N.Y.	33349	#16
Nov. 16, 1860	W.N.Y.	33350	#8
Nov. 16, 1860	W.N.Y.	33351	#9
Nov. 5, 1860	W.N.Y.	33352	#18
Nov. 5, 1860	W.N.Y.	33353	#27
Nov. 5, 1860	W.N.Y.	33354	#10
Nov. 16, 1860	W.N.Y.	33355	#7
Nov. 16, 1860	W.N.Y.	33356	#13
Nov. 5, 1860	W.N.Y.	33357	#15
Nov. 16, 1860	W.N.Y.	33358	#4
Nov. 16, 1860	W.N.Y.	33359	#14
Nov. 20, 1860	Phila.N.Y.	33360	#30
Nov. 5, 1860	W.N.Y.	33361	#21
Nov. 16, 1860	W.N.Y.	33362	#10
Nov. 16, 1860	W.N.Y.	33362	#1
Nov. 5, 1860	W.N.Y.	33363	#20
Nov. 5, 1860	W.N.Y.	33364	#19
Nov. 16, 1860	W.N.Y.	33365	#19
Nov. 5, 1860	W.N.Y.	33365	#12
Nov. 16, 1860	W.N.Y.	33367	#3
Nov. 16, 1860	W.N.Y.	33367	#18
Nov. 16, 1860	W.N.Y.	33368	#4
Nov. 20, 1860	Phila.N.Y.	33368	#28
Nov. 20, 1860	Phila.N.Y.	33370	#30
Nov. 16, 1860	W.N.Y.	33371	#15
Nov. 5, 1860	W.N.Y.	33372	#28
Nov. 16, 1860	W.N.Y.	33374	#16
Nov. 5, 1860	W.N.Y.	33375	#6
Nov. 5, 1860	W.N.Y.	33376	#26
Nov. 16, 1860	W.N.Y.	33377	#12
Nov. 5, 1860	W.N.Y.	33378	#11
Nov. 5, 1860	W.N.Y.	33380	#17
Nov. 5, 1860	W.N.Y.	33382	#23
Nov. 5, 1860	W.N.Y.	33383	#25
Nov. 5, 1860	W.N.Y.	33384	#19
Nov. 16, 1860	W.N.Y.	33385	#7
Nov. 5, 1860	W.N.Y.	33388	#14
Nov. 5, 1860	W.N.Y.	33389	#2
Nov. 5, 1860	W.N.Y.	33390	#5
Nov. 20, 1860	Phila.N.Y.	33392	#22
Nov. 5, 1860	W.N.Y.	33393	#27
Nov. 20, 1860	Phila.N.Y.	33394	#29
Nov. 5, 1860	W.N.Y.	33395	#18
Nov. 5, 1860	W.N.Y.	33396	#26
Nov. 20, 1860	Phila.N.Y.	33397	#24
Nov. 16, 1860	W.N.Y.	33398	#18
Nov. 16, 1860	W.N.Y.	33400	#8
Nov. 5, 1860	W.N.Y.	33402	#28
Nov. 5, 1860	W.N.Y.	33403	#25
Nov. 20, 1860	Phila.N.Y.	33404	#29
Nov. 5, 1860	W.N.Y.	33405	#25
Nov. 16, 1860	W.N.Y.	33406	#2

Date	Location	Serial	#
Nov. 20, 1860	Phila.N.Y.	33408	#28
Nov. 20, 1860	Phila.N.Y.	33409	#24
Nov. 5, 1860	W.N.Y.	33410	#23
Nov. 16, 1860	W.N.Y.	33411	#9
Nov. 16, 1860	W.N.Y.	33412	#11
Nov. 20, 1860	Phila.N.Y.	33413	#30
Nov. 16, 1860	W.N.Y.	33414	#20
Nov. 5, 1860	W.N.Y.	33416	#26
Nov. 20, 1860	Phila.N.Y.	33417	#32
Nov. 5, 1860	W.N.Y.	33418	#11
Nov. 20, 1860	Phila.N.Y.	33419	#26
Nov. 20, 1860	Phila.N.Y.	33420	#33
Nov. 20, 1860	Phila.N.Y.	33421	#25
Nov. 5, 1860	W.N.Y.	33422	#3
Nov. 16, 1860	W.N.Y.	33423	#6
Nov. 16, 1860	W.N.Y.	33424	#5
Nov. 16, 1860	W.N.Y.	33425	#7
Nov. 20, 1860	Phila.N.Y.	33426	#32
Nov. 16, 1860	W.N.Y.	33427	#16
Nov. 5, 1860	W.N.Y.	33428	#11
Nov. 16, 1860	W.N.Y.	33429	#11
Nov. 16, 1860	W.N.Y.	33430	#8
Nov. 5, 1860	W.N.Y.	33431	#22
Nov. 16, 1860	W.N.Y.	33432	#11
Nov. 5, 1860	W.N.Y.	33433	#4
Nov. 5, 1860	W.N.Y.	33434	#19
Nov. 5, 1860	W.N.Y.	33435	#20
Nov. 5, 1860	W.N.Y.	33436	#7
Nov. 16, 1860	W.N.Y.	33437	#21
Nov. 20, 1860	Phila.N.Y.	33438	#29
Nov. 16, 1860	W.N.Y.	33439	#20
Nov. 16, 1860	W.N.Y.	33440	#18
Nov. 16, 1860	W.N.Y.	33441	#17
Nov. 16, 1860	W.N.Y.	33442	#17
Nov. 5, 1860	W.N.Y.	33443	#27
Nov. 5, 1860	W.N.Y.	33444	#10
Nov. 16, 1860	W.N.Y.	33445	#12
Nov. 5, 1860	W.N.Y.	33446	#7
Nov. 5, 1860	W.N.Y.	33447	#1
Nov. 5, 1860	W.N.Y.	33448	#11
Nov. 5, 1860	W.N.Y.	33450	#9
Nov. 16, 1860	W.N.Y.	33451	#1
Nov. 16, 1860	W.N.Y.	33452	#12
Nov. 5, 1860	W.N.Y.	33453	#4
Nov. 5, 1860	W.N.Y.	33454	#24
Nov. 5, 1860	W.N.Y.	33455	#20
Nov. 5, 1860	W.N.Y.	33456	#7
Nov. 16, 1860	W.N.Y.	33457	#12
Nov. 5, 1860	W.N.Y.	33458	#23
Nov. 20, 1860	Phila.N.Y.	33459	#30
Nov. 5, 1860	W.N.Y.	33460	#5
Nov. 20, 1860	Phila.N.Y.	33462	#27
Nov. 5, 1860	W.N.Y.	33463	#27
Nov. 5, 1860	W.N.Y.	33466	#23
Nov. 16, 1860	W.N.Y.	33467	#3
Nov. 5, 1860	W.N.Y.	33468	#18
Nov. 16, 1860	W.N.Y.	33469	#11
Nov. 16, 1860	W.N.Y.	33470	#8
Nov. 16, 1860	W.N.Y.	33471	#9
Nov. 5, 1860	W.N.Y.	33473	#27
Nov. 5, 1860	W.N.Y.	33474	#10
Nov. 16, 1860	W.N.Y.	33475	#7
Nov. 5, 1860	W.N.Y.	33476	#7
Nov. 16, 1860	W.N.Y.	33477	#3
Nov. 5, 1860	W.N.Y.	33478	#21
Nov. 5, 1860	W.N.Y.	33479	#2
Nov. 5, 1860	W.N.Y.	33480	#20
Nov. 16, 1860	W.N.Y.	33481	#21
Nov. 16, 1860	W.N.Y.	33482	#21
Nov. 5, 1860	W.N.Y.	33483	#4
Nov. 5, 1860	W.N.Y.	33484	#10
Nov. 16, 1860	W.N.Y.	33485	#15
Nov. 20, 1860	Phila.N.Y.	33486	#31
Nov. 5, 1860	W.N.Y.	33488	#29
Nov. 16, 1860	W.N.Y.	33489	#20
Nov. 16, 1860	W.N.Y.	33494	#5
Nov. 20, 1860	Phila.N.Y.	33496	#23
Nov. 20, 1860	Phila.N.Y.	33497	#31
Nov. 5, 1860	W.N.Y.	33498	#14
Nov. 16, 1860	W.N.Y.	33499	#18
Nov. 5, 1860	W.N.Y.	33500	#9
Nov. 5, 1860	W.N.Y.	33501	#22
Nov. 5, 1860	W.N.Y.	33502	#3
Nov. 5, 1860	W.N.Y.	33504	#19
Nov. 5, 1860	W.N.Y.	33505	#25
Nov. 16, 1860	W.N.Y.	33506	#19
Nov. 5, 1860	W.N.Y.	33507	#23
Nov. 5, 1860	W.N.Y.	33508	#14
Nov. 5, 1860	W.N.Y.	33509	#30
Nov. 5, 1860	W.N.Y.	33511	#22
Nov. 20, 1860	Phila.N.Y.	33513	#31
Nov. 16, 1860	W.N.Y.	33515	#7
Nov. 5, 1860	W.N.Y.	33517	#15
Nov. 5, 1860	W.N.Y.	33518	#29
Nov. 16, 1860	W.N.Y.	33519	#20
Nov. 5, 1860	W.N.Y.	33520	#17
Nov. 20, 1860	Phila.N.Y.	33521	#23
Nov. 5, 1860	W.N.Y.	33522	#28
Nov. 20, 1860	Phila.N.Y.	33523	#33
Nov. 16, 1860	W.N.Y.	33524	#11
Nov. 20, 1860	Phila.N.Y.	33525	#27
Nov. 20, 1860	Phila.N.Y.	33526	#22
Nov. 5, 1860	W.N.Y.	33528	#29
Nov. 5, 1860	W.N.Y.	33531	#13
Nov. 16, 1860	W.N.Y.	33532	#10
Nov. 5, 1860	W.N.Y.	33533	#27
Nov. 5, 1860	W.N.Y.	33534	#10
Nov. 20, 1860	Phila.N.Y.	33535	#32
Nov. 16, 1860	W.N.Y.	33537	#3
Nov. 16, 1860	W.N.Y.	33538	#16
Nov. 20, 1860	Phila.N.Y.	33539	#30
Nov. 16, 1860	W.N.Y.	33540	#19
Nov. 16, 1860	W.N.Y.	33541	#14
Nov. 20, 1860	Phila.N.Y.	33543	#29

Date	Location	Serial	#		Date	Location	Serial	#
Nov. 16, 1860	W.N.Y.	33544	#5		Nov. 5, 1860	W.N.Y.	33583	#27
Nov. 16, 1860	W.N.Y.	33545	#7		Nov. 5, 1860	W.N.Y.	33584	#19
Nov. 16, 1860	W.N.Y.	33546	#21		Nov. 5, 1860	W.N.Y.	33585	#23
Nov. 20, 1860	Phila.N.Y.	33548	#28		Nov. 16, 1860	W.N.Y.	33586	#2
Nov. 5, 1860	W.N.Y.	33550	#17		Nov. 5, 1860	W.N.Y.	33587	#15
Nov. 5, 1860	W.N.Y.	33551	#13		Nov. 16, 1860	W.N.Y.	33589	#14
Nov. 5, 1860	W.N.Y.	33552	#3		Nov. 5, 1860	W.N.Y.	33590	#9
Nov. 5, 1860	W.N.Y.	33553	#27		Nov. 20, 1860	Phila.N.Y.	33591	#22
Nov. 16, 1860	W.N.Y.	33555	#7		Nov. 5, 1860	W.N.Y.	33592	#28
Nov. 20, 1860	Phila.N.Y.	33556	#25		Nov. 16, 1860	W.N.Y.	33593	#15
Nov. 20, 1860	Phila.N.Y.	33557	#28		Nov. 5, 1860	W.N.Y.	33594	#8
Nov. 16, 1860	W.N.Y.	33560	#17		Nov. 5, 1860	W.N.Y.	33595	#12
Nov. 16, 1860	W.N.Y.	33562	#10		Nov. 5, 1860	W.N.Y.	33596	#26
Nov. 16, 1860	W.N.Y.	33563	#6		Nov. 5, 1860	W.N.Y.	33597	#1
Nov. 5, 1860	W.N.Y.	33565	#6		Nov. 5, 1860	W.N.Y.	33598	#16
Nov. 20, 1860	Phila.N.Y.	33566	#22		Nov. 20, 1860	Phila.N.Y.	33602	#25
Nov. 5, 1860	W.N.Y.	33567	#15		Nov. 5, 1860	W.N.Y.	33603	#25
Nov. 16, 1860	W.N.Y.	33569	#11		Nov. 20, 1860	Phila.N.Y.	33603	#24
Nov. 16, 1860	W.N.Y.	33571	#17		Nov. 20, 1860	Phila.N.Y.	33604	#22
Nov. 16, 1860	W.N.Y.	33572	#10		Nov. 5, 1860	W.N.Y.	33605	#6
Nov. 5, 1860	W.N.Y.	33573	#25		Nov. 16, 1860	W.N.Y.	33606	#2
Nov. 5, 1860	W.N.Y.	33574	#16		Nov. 5, 1860	W.N.Y.	33607	#15
Nov. 5, 1860	W.N.Y.	33575	#6		Nov. 5, 1860	W.N.Y.	33608	#14
Nov. 16, 1860	W.N.Y.	33576	#14		Nov. 16, 1860	W.N.Y.	33609	#16
Nov. 5, 1860	W.N.Y.	33577	#15					
Nov. 20, 1860	Phila.N.Y.	33578	#25					
Nov. 16, 1860	W.N.Y.	33579	#11					

W.N.Y. = Washington Navy Yard
Phila.N.Y.= Philadelphia Navy Yard

U.S.S. Mendata (USAMHI—Mass. MOLLUS collection)

NOTES

A large quantity of information has been obtained from various sources at the National Archives and Records Administration in Washington, D. C. The specific records that have been used are listed below:

Naval Records Collection of the Office of Naval Records & Library, Record Group 45
Entry
464. Subject File Ca. 1775-1900—Appendix F

Records of the Bureau of Ordnance, Record Group 74
Entry
3. Letters Sent to Navy Yards and Stations 1842-84
5. Misc. Letters Sent 1842-83
6. Letters and Telegrams Sent 1861-1911
18. Letters Received From Naval Officers 1842-84
19. Letters Received From Navy Yards and Stations 1842-84
22. Misc. Letters Received 1842-84
101. Reports of Target Practice with Small Arms 1868
145. Correspondence Regarding the Examination of Inventions 1851-80
157. Records of Contracts 1842-62
158. Record of Accounts Approved for Payment 1842-1903
165. Record of Ordnance Contracts for 1861
192. Record of the Permanent Ordnance Board 1869-1871
193. Report of the Board on Breech-Loading Rifles 1869

Records of the Headquarters of the Army, Record Group 108
Entry
75. Abstracts of Reports Received Relating to the Efficiency of Carbines & Rifles (Reports of Arms) 1863-65
77. Consolidated Reports of Monthly Returns from Cavalry Units 1864-1865
91. Abstracts of Property Inspections Reports by Inspectors of Cavalry Units of the Army of the James 1865

Confederate Records, Record Group 109
Entry
M935. Field Inspection Reports (18 rolls)

Records of the Chief of Ordnance, Record Group 156
Entry
3. Letters, Endorsements, and Circulars Sent 1812-89
5. Letters, Endorsements, and Circulars Sent to the Secretary of War 1812-94
6. Letters, Telegrams, and Endorsements Sent to Ordnance Officers and Military Storekeepers 1839-89
20. Register of Letters Received 1827-89
21. Letters Received 1812-94
103. Weekly Statements of Ordnance and Ordnance Stores on hand at Armories, Arsenals and Depots 1864
108. Inventories of Ordnance as of October 24, 1862
110. Quarterly Summary Statements of Ordnance and Ordnance Stores in the hands of Regular Army and Volunteer Cavalry Regiments 1862-64
111. Quarterly Summary Statements of Ordnance and Ordnance Stores in the hands of Regular Army and Volunteer Infantry Regiments 1862-64
112. Quarterly Summary Report
124. Reports of Sales of Ordnance Stores at Depots and Arsenals 1864-1907
125. Journals of Ordnance Stores Sales at Arsenals and Depots 1864-94
152. Statements of Accounts for Contractors 1817-1905
164. Accounts Sent to the Second Auditor 1861-79
201. Reports of Experiments 1862-71
215. Army Officers Reports on Small-Arms 1863-64
232. Ordnance Boards Proceedings 1846-68
1001. Correspondence and Reports Relating to Experiments 1818-70
1012. Reports and Correspondence of Ordnance Boards 1827-70
1354. Springfield Armory, Letters Sent to the Chief of Ordnance 1836-70
1355. Springfield Armory, Press Copies of Letters Sent to the Chief of Ordnance 1871-1900
1362. Springfield Armory, Letters Received 1860-73
1365. Springfield Armory, Letters Received from Officials and Officers of the War Department 1861-98

Inventory of the Record of the Accounting Offices of the Department of the Treasury, Record Group 217
Entry
759. State Claims for reimbursement of Civil War Expense Ca. 1861-1900

For brevity, these records will be cited as follows: National Archives Record Group (NARG) - Entry number, eg. NARG 156-3.

Pre-War Years
1. U.S. Patent Office, U.S. Patent No. 5763 dated Sept. 12, 1848
2. Rywell, Martin. *Sharps Rifle: The Gun that Shaped American Destiny*, p. 32.
3. NARG 156-3
4. NARG 156-152
5. NARG 156-3
6. Frank Seller, *Sharps Firearms*, Hollywood, 1978, p. 30
7. NARG 156-152 and F.J. (Pablo) Balentine, "The Sharps 1851 Boxlock", *The American Society of Arms Collectors Bulletin* No. 58, May 11-15, 1988, pp. 58, 59
8. 1853 Senate Ex. Doc. Vol 3, 33rd Congress, 1st Session, p. 274

9. Louis A. Garavaglia & Charles G. Worman, *Firearms of the American West 1803-1865*, Albuqueruque, 1984, pp. 136,137
10. F.J. Balentine, op. cit., p. 58
11. NARG 156-152
12. NARG 156-5
13. NARG 156-1012
14. Ibid.
15. NARG 156-152
16. Robert M. Utley, *Frontiermen in Blue*, Lincoln, 1967, pp. 115-117
17. NARG 156-3
18. NARG 156-20
19. NARG 156-3
20. NARG 156-152
21. NARG 156-1001
22. NARG 156-21
23. NARG 156-6
24. NARG 156-21
25. Ibid.
26. NARG 156-3
27. NARG 156-21
28. NARG 156-152
29. NARG 156-6
30. NARG 156-1001
31. NARG 156-21
32. NARG 156-3
33. NARG 156-152
34. NARG 156-21
35. NARG 156-6
36. Ibid.
37. 1858 Senate Ex. Doc. Vol. 3, 35th Congress, 2nd Session, p. 1314
38. NARG 156-21
39. Ibid.
40. Ibid.
41. Ibid.
42. NARG 156-1012
43. Ibid.
44. NARG 156-3
45. Ibid.
46. NARG 156-152
47. NARG 156-21
48. Ibid.
49. Ibid.
50. Ibid.
51. Ibid.
52. Ibid.
53. C.E. Fuller, *The Rifle Musket*, New York: 1958
54. Fredrick P. Todd, *American Military Equipage 1851-1872* Vol II State Forces, Chatham Square Press, Inc., 1983, p. 734
55. Ibid., pp. 738,740
56. Ibid., p. 1267 and State of Virginia Record Group 48, Auditors Office, Entry 36

The War Years
1. NARG 156-21
2. NARG 217-State Claims-Connecticut Entry 759
3. Ibid.
4. Ibid.
5. NARG 217-State Claims-Ohio Entry 759
6. NARG 217-State Claims-New York Entry 759
7. *OR*s Series I, Vol. 2, pp. 351, 353-4
8. Ibid., pp. 386-7 and 393
9. NARG 156-21
10. Ibid.
11. Ibid.
12. House Executive Document #99, 40th Congress, 2nd Session, p. 551
13. Ibid., p. 987
14. Ibid., p. 551
15. Wiley Sword, *Sharpshooter: Hiram Berdan, His Famous Sharpshooters and their Sharps Rifles*, Lincoln, 1988, pp. 64-65
16. House Ex. Doc #99, op cit., pp. 551-2
17. NARG 156-21
18. Roy Marcot, *Civil War Chief of Sharpshooters Hiram Berdan Military Commander and Firearms Inventor*, Irvine, 1989, p. 141
19. Wiley Sword, op. cit., pp. 97-98. The author highly recommends for additional information on Berdan Sharpshooters both Roy Marcot and Wiley Sword books on the subject.
20. Captain C. A. Stevens, *Berdan's United States Sharpshooters in the Army of the Potomac 1861-1865*, Dayton, 1972, pp. 202-203
21. NARG 156-108
22. Brian C. Pohanka, "Duryee's Zouaves: The 5th New York Volunteer Infantry," *Civil War Regiments*, Vol I Number Two, pp. 20-26
23. NARG 15-110 December 31, 1862
24. NARG 156-111 December 31, 1862
25. NARG 156-3
26. House Ex. Doc. #99, op. cit., p. 552
27. NARG 156-1001 and *OR*s Series I, Vol 19, Part II, p. 133
28. Abner Hard, M.D., *History of the Eighth Cavalry Regiment Illinois Volunteers*, Dayton, 1984, pp. xxx, xxxii and 256
29. NARG 156-110
30. Ibid.
31. Captain C. A. Stevens, op. cit., p. 343
32. NARG 156-201 letter dated August 27, 1864
33. NARG 156-111 September & December 1863
34. NARG 156-21
35. Ibid.
36. Ibid.
37. NARG 108-75
38. NARG 156-110
39. Ibid.
40. NARG 156-111
41. NARG 109-M935 (18 rolls)
42. NARG 156-3
43. Ibid.
44. *OR*s Series I, Vol. 46, Part I, pp. 524-527; Part II, p. 777 and Part III, p. 1047
45. NARG 156-21
46. *OR*s Series I, Vol. 46, Part I, pp. 535-536
47. NARG 156-21
48. NARG 108-77
49. Ibid.
50. NARG 156-21
51. Ibid.
52. Francis A. Lord, *They Fought For the Union*, Harrisburg, 1960, p. 166
53. NARG 156-21
54. Ibid.

Sharps in the Sea Service
1. NARG 45-464 Subject File Ca. 1775-1900, Appendix F
2. NARG 74-5
3. NARG 74-22

4. NARG 74-145
5. Ibid.
6. Ibid.
7. Ibid.
8. Ibid.
9. Ibid.
10. NARG 74-5
11. NARG 74-22
12. NARG 74-5 and 22
13. NARG 74-5
14. NARG 74-19 Boston Navy Yard
15. NARG 74-5
16. NARG 74-145
17. NARG 74-158
18. NARG 74-19 Boston Navy Yard
19. NARG 74-22
20. NARG 74-19 Philadephia Navy Yard
21. NARG 74-165
22. Ibid.
23. NARG 74-6
24. NARG 74-157
25. NARG 74-22
26. NARG 45-464
27. NARG 74-18
28. NARG 74-5 and 22
29. NARG 156-6 and 1355
30. NARG 156-21
31. Ex. Doc. No. 16-2, 39th Congress, (December 31, 1866)
32. NARG 74-101
33. NARG 74-5
34. NARG 74-193
35. Ibid.
36. NARG 74-192

Sharps & Hankins
1. NARG 156-110
2. Frank Sellers, *Sharps Firearms*, North Hollywood, 1978, p. 103
3. John D. McAulay, *Carbines of the Civil War 1861-1865*, Union City, 1981, p. 95
4. U.S. Patent No. 32,790 of July 9, 1861
5. J. Richard Salzer, "The Sharps & Hankins Carbines," *The Gun Report*, January 1963, p. 8
6. NARG 74-5
7. NARG 74-6
8. NARG 74-5
9. NARG 74-158
10. NARG 74-145
11. NARG 74-5
12. Ibid.
13. Ibid.
14. Ibid.
15. NARG 74-22
16. NARG 74-3
17. NARG 74-5, 6, and 158
18. NARG 74-5
19. NARG 74-5 and 22
20. Ibid.
21. NARG 74-19
22. NARG 74-5
23. Ibid.
24. NARG 74-158
25. NARG 74-5, 6, 19, 22, and 158
26. NARG 74-5
27. NARG 74-5 and 19
28. Ex. Doc. No. 99, 40th Cong, 2nd Session, 1868, p. 544
29. Ibid.
30. NARG 156-103
31. *OR*s Series I, Vol 27, Part I, pp. 1037-38 and Part II, p. 693
32. NARG 156-21 and 108-75
33. Fredrick Pfisterer, *New York in the War of the Rebellion 1861 to 1865*, Albany, 1912, p. 904
34. Ibid., p. 916
35. Thomas W. Smith, *The Story of a Cavalry Regiment Scott's 900*, Chicago, 1897, p. 173
36. NARG 156-110
37. NARG 108-77
38. NARG 156-215
39. Edward A. Hull, "Sharps & Hankins, Carbines for Army Cartridge Trials," *Man At Arms*, May/June 1991, pp. 21-27
40. NARG 156-21
41. Ex Doc #99, op.cit., p. 544
42. Roy M. Marcot, *Spencer Repeating Firearms*, Irvine, 1983, p. 75
43. Ex. Doc. No. 16-2, 39th Congress (December 31, 1866) and NARG 156-21
44. NARG 74-101
45. Ibid.
46. NARG 74-5
47. NARG 156-125
48. NARG 156-124

Corporal John H. Stevens, Co. A, 151st New York Infantry armed with a NM 1859 Sharps rifle with saber bayonet. Richard Carlile collection.

BIBLIOGRAPHY

Albaugh, W.A., III. "Union Armament in the Civil War." *North South Trader*, March/April 1975.

Balentine, F.J. "The Sharps 1851 Boxlock." *The American Society of Arms Collectors Bulletin*, 11-15 May 1988.

Bendict, G.G. *Vermont in the Civil War.* 2 Vols., Burlington, 1888.

Bixley, L.G. "Bucktails: A Short History of Pennsylvania's Intrepid Rifle Regiments." *Military Images*, July/August 1980.

Carlile, R.F. "The Sharps Rifle." *Military Images*, March/April 1987.

---. "Union Cavalry Carbines." *Military Images*, March/April 1986.

Coates, E.J. and D. S. Thomas. *An Introduction to Civil War Small Arms*. Gettysburg: Thomas Publications, 1990.

Davis, W.C. *The Fighting Men of the Civil War*. New York, 1989.

Dyer, F.H. *A Compendium of the War of the Rebellion*. Dayton, 1978.

Edwards, W.B. *Civil War Guns*. Harrisburg, 1962.

_____. *Executive Document*. State of Ohio, 1862.

_____. *Executive Document*. No. 16-2, 39th Congress, December 31, 1866.

_____. *Executive Document*. No. 99, 40th Congress, 2nd Session, 1868.

_____. *Field Manual For the Use of the Officers on Ordnance Duty*. Richmond, 1862.

Flayderman, N. *Flayderman's Guide to Antique American Firearms and Their Values*. Northfield, 1983.

Freeman, D.S. *R.E. Lee*. Vol. 1 of 4. New York, 1962.

Fuller, C.E. *The Breech-Loader in the Service 1816-1917*. New Milford, 1965.

---. *The Rifle Musket*. New York, 1958.

Fuller, C.E. and R.D. Stuart. *Firearms of the Confederacy*. Huntington, 1944.

Garavaglis, L.A. and C.G. Worman. *Firearms of the American West 1803-1865*. Albuquerque, 1984.

Genco, J.G. *Arming Michigan Regiments 1862-1864*. 1982.

Hard, M.D. *History of the Eighth Cavalry Regiment Illinois Volunteers*. Dayton, 1984.

Hopkins, R.E. *Military Sharps Rifles & Carbines*. Vol. I. San Jose, 1967.

Hull, E.A. "Sharps & Hankins, Carbines for Army Cartridge Trials." *Man at Arms*, May/June 1991.

Lewis, Col. B.R. *Notes on Ammunition of the American Civil War*. Washington, 1959.

Lindert, A.W. "Sharps Rifles For the USN." *The Gun Report*, September 1979.

Lord, F.A. *They Fought for the Union*. Harrisburg, 1960.

Marcot, R. *Civil War Chief of Sharpshooters Hiram Berdan, Military Commander and Firearms Inventor*. Irvine, 1989.

---. *Spencer Repeating Firearms*. Irvine, 1983.

McAulay, J. D. *Carbines of the Civil War 1861-1865*. Union City, 1981.

---. *Civil War Breech Loading Rifles*. Lincoln, 1987.

---. *Civil War Carbines*. Vol. II. Lincoln, 1991.

---. "Breech Loading Carbines for Lincoln's Cavalry." *The Gun Report*, April 1980.

---. "Arming the Union Cavlary at Gettysburg." *The Gun Report*, September 1980.

---. "Galvanized Rebels." *Guns and Ammo*, 1986.

Miller, F.T. *The Photographic History of the Civil War*. New York, 1957.

_____. Naval Records Collection of the Office of Naval Records and Library, No. 45; Records of the Bureau of Ordnance, No. 74; Records of the Headquarters of the Army, No. 108; Confederate Records, No. 109; Records of the Office of the Chief of Ordnance, No. 156; Inventory of the Record of the Accounting Offices of the Department of the Treasury, No. 217; National Archives and Records Administration.

Official Records of the Rebellion. (Army) Government Printing Office, 1891.

Official Records of the Rebellion. (Navy) Government Printing Office, 1927.

Pitman, Brig Gen. J. *Breech-Loading Carbines of the United States Civil War Period*. Tacoma, 1987.

Pfisterer, F. *New York in the War of the Rebellion 1861-1865*. Albany, 1912.

Pohanka, B.C. "Duryee's Zouaves: The 5th New York Volunteer Infantry". *Civil War Regiments*. Vol. 1.

Rankin, Col. R.N. *Small Arms of the Sea Service*. New Milford, 1972.

Reid, W. *Ohio in the War*. Cincinnati, 1868.

_____. *Report of the Secretary of War*, Vol. 2. 1872.

_____. *Report of the Secretary of War*, Vol. 3. 1873.

Ripley, Lt. Col. W.Y. *Vermont Riflemen in the War For the Union 1861-1865*. Rutland, 1883.

Reilly, R.M. *United States Military Small Arms 1816-1865*. Baton Rouge, 1970.

Rodenbough, T.F. *The Army of the United States*. New York, 1896.

Roe, A.S. *The Fifth Massachusetts Infantry*. Boston, 1911.

Rywell, M. *Sharps Rifles: The Gun That Shaped American Destiny*. Union City, 1957.

Salzer, J.R. "The Sharps and Hankins Carbines." *The Gun Report*, January 1963.

Sawicki, J.A. *Cavalry Regiments of the U.S. Army.* Dumfries, 1985.

Sellers, F. *Sharps Firearms.* North Hollywood, 1978.

Smith, T.W. *The Story of a Cavalry Regiment: Scott's 900.* Chicago, 1897.

Sword, W. *Sharpshooter: Hiram Berdan, His Famous Sharpshooters and Their Sharps Rifles.* Lincoln, 1988.

---. "The Berdan Sharps Rifles." *Man at Arms*, May/June 1979.

---. "The Berdan Sharps Rifles, An Update." *Man at Arms*, July/August 1980.

Thomas, D.S. *Ready...Aim...Fire! Small Arms Ammunition in the Battle of Gettysburg.* Gettysburg: Thomas Publications, 1981.

Todd, F.P. *American Military Equippage 1851-1872.* New York, 1980.

Turner, W.A. *Even More Confederate Faces.* Orange, 1983.

---. U. S. Department of Commerce. Records of the U. S. Patent Office.

Utley, R.M. *Frontiersmen in Blue, The U.S. Army and the Indians 1848-1865.* Lincoln, 1967.

---. *Frontier Regulars: The U.S. Army and the Indians 1866-1891.* New York, 1973.

Warner, E.J. *Generals in Gray.* Baton Rouge, 1959.

---. *Generals in Blue.* Baton Rouge, 1964.

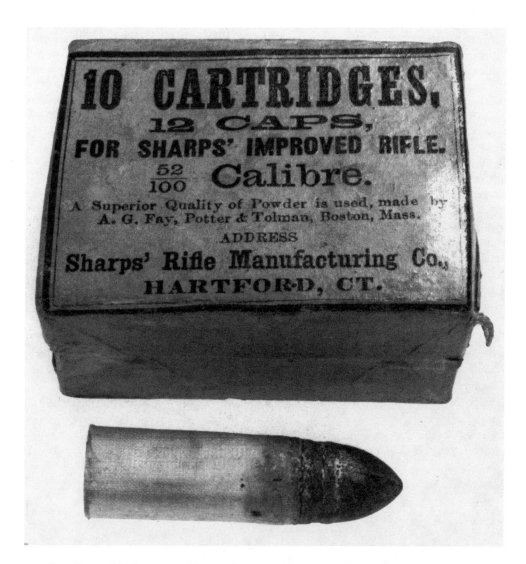

A package of 10 linen cartridges with percussion caps for the Sharps rifle or carbine. These cartridges consisted of a linen powder tube closed at the bottom with paper. This tube was pasted to the bullet.

INDEX TO REGIMENTS

2nd Arkansas Cavalry, 49

1st California Cavalry, 49-52
1st Colorado Cavalry, 52-53

2nd Illinois Cavalry, 53-55
5th Illinois Cavalry, 55-56
6th Illinois Cavalry, 56-58
7th Illinois Cavalry, 58
9th Illinois Cavalry, 58-59
10th Illinois Cavalry, 59-61
13th Illinois Cavalry, 61
17th Illinois Cavalry, 61-62
7th Indiana Cavalry, 62-64
1st Iowa Cavalry, 64-65
5th Iowa Cavalry, 65-66

2nd Kansas Cavalry, 66-67
5th Kansas Cavalry, 67
14th Kansas Cavalry, 67
2nd Kentucky Cavalry, 68
4th Kentucky Cavalry, 68

1st Maryland Cavalry, 68-70
1st Potomac Home Brigade Maryland Cavalry, 70-71
1st Massachusetts Cavalry, 71-72
5th Michigan Infantry, 72-73
8th Michigan Cavalry, 73-74
1st Missouri Cavalry, 74-75

Navy Purchases, 100-102
1st New Hampshire Cavalry, 75-76

2nd New Jersey Cavalry, 76
1st New York Mounted Rifles, 76-77
1st New York Cavalry, 77-78
3rd New York Cavalry, 78
6th New York Cavalry, 78-79
11th New York Cavalry, 79-80
13th New York Cavalry, 80-82
15th New York Cavalry, 82
22nd New York Cavalry, 83

3rd Independent Co. Ohio Cavalry, 83-84
4th Ohio Cavalry, 84
5th Ohio Cavalry, 84-85
6th Ohio Cavalry, 85
10th Ohio Cavalry, 85-87

2nd Pennsylvania Cavalry, 87-88
16th Pennsylvania Cavalry, 88-89
17th Pennsylvania Cavalry, 89-90
19th Pennsylvania Cavalry, 90-91
42nd Pennsylvania Infantry, 91-92

1st U.S. Dragoons, 93

1st Vermont Cavalry, 93-94
2nd Veteran Volunteer Infantry, 94-95
4th Veteran Volunteer Infantry, 95-97
5th Veteran Volunteer Infantry, 97
6th Veteran Volunteer Infantry, 97-99

2nd West Virginia Cavalry, 99